ISLAMOPHOBIA AS A FORM OF RADICALISATION

PERSPECTIVES ON MEDIA, ACADEMIA AND SOCIO-POLITICAL SCAPES FROM EUROPE AND CANADA

EDITED BY
LEEN D'HAENENS & ABDELWAHED MEKKI-BERRADA

D1596961

LEUVEN UNIVERSITY PRESS

Published with the support of KU Leuven Fund for Fair Open Access.

Published in 2023 by Leuven University Press / Presses Universitaires de Louvain / Universitaire Pers Leuven. Minderbroedersstraat 4, B-3000 Leuven (Belgium).

ISBN 978 94 6270 369 8 (Paperback)
ISBN 978 94 6166 509 6 (ePDF)
ISBN 978 94 6166 510 2 (ePUB)
https://doi.org/10.11116/9789461665096
D/2023/1869/13
NUR: 741/812

Layout: Crius Group
Cover design: Daniel Benneworth-Gray
Cover illustration: Raja Atlassi, 2022, *HorizonTales 1*, acrylic on canvas, 50 cm × 50 cm,
Morocco. Green is tolerance, also the colour of Islam; red is the violence of Islamophobia;
a trace of green at the top right of the second red stripe represents, in the midst of the tumult of
social polarisations, tolerance and solidarity that seek to find their place; the large white stripe
at the top represents the blank page that we have to write together, to co-construct an inclusive
world and a better way of living together. www.rajaatlassi.com

GPRC
Guaranteed
Peer Reviewed
Content
www.gprc.be

Table of Contents

PART IV   RESPONDING TO ISLAMOPHOBIA, EXTREMISM AND RADICALISATION

PART I

KEY CONCEPTS

1
ISLAMOPHOBIA AS A FORM OF VIOLENT RADICALISATION[1]

ABDELWAHED MEKKI-BERRADA & LEEN D'HAENENS

Abstract

This book is divided into four parts: Key concepts (part I); Contemporary political discourses on Islamophobia (part II); Media practices (part III); and Responding to Islamophobia, extremism and radicalisation (part IV). In this introductory chapter, we discuss the scope and shattered boundaries of Islamophobia as both a concept and a sociopolitical reality. We then attempt a definition of Islamophobia's theoretical and pragmatic dimensions. This conceptual chapter brings together an anthropologist and a communication scholar to consider whether and to what extent Islamophobia is a form of violent radicalisation. This will serve as a background against which we will present the fifteen chapters of this collective book, which relate inter-disciplinary research, media content analyses, media discourse analysis, ethnographic research, intersectoral advocacy work and action research conducted in Belgium, Canada, France, Germany, Poland, Portugal and Spain.

Keywords: Islamophobia, violent radicalisation, theory, Europe, Canada, media content analysis, discourse analysis, ethnographic research, action research

Radical Islamists searching for legitimacy and seeking to appropriate social, political and ideological spaces undoubtedly tend to fallaciously brandish the notion of Islamophobia the moment any criticism is addressed towards Islam or Muslims. To criticise, however, is a healthy practice derived from the inviolable freedom of expression, which is itself a democratic imperative. As such, the notion of Islamophobia should definitely not be employed as a liberticidal tool. Unquestionably, we see that limiting the multi-dimensionality of the notion of Islamophobia to this liberticidal dimension is also reflective of a cognitive and ideological stance that runs counter to the development of a better form of living-together (*vivre-ensemble*). We are in the presence of two 'radical' tendencies: one that brandishes the Islamophobia notion to silence any criticism of Islam and Muslims as some extremist ideologists do, and another that castigates and seeks to censor this same notion, while also denying the social reality to which it refers as some mediatised scholars (e.g., Kepel, 2016; d'Iribane, 2019) and essayists (e.g., Bruckner, 2017) do.

Much more than a political posture, an attitude or an excessive intransigence, which would make it a *radicalism*, Islamophobia is a gradual process that, since the tragedy of September 11, 2001, and even since the Campaign of Napoleon Bonaparte (Saïd, 2003) and the Crusades (Bibeau, 2017), is cognitively anchored in the minds and the collective unconsciousness, leading to extreme ideas, speeches and acts, which makes Islamophobia a form of *radicalisation*. Furthermore, as per the primary meaning attributed to the notion of radicalisation, to Khosrokavar (2014, p. 7, our translation) radicalisation relates to the 'process by which an individual or group adopts a violent form of action directly linked to an extremist ideology with political, social, or religious attributes', or in the meaning that Schmid (2014) attributes to the notion, namely an individual or collective process typically tied to a socially or politically polarised situation in which the practices of dialogue and compromise between various actors are abandoned by at least one of the parties involved, in favour of a conflicting, sometimes violent escalation. Islamophobia, as a notion and as a lived reality, echoes these definitions, and in this sense represents a form of *radicalisation* that is violent or that leads to violence. As per the multi-dimensionality of Islamophobia, there are, however, many other ways to apprehend its conditions of emergence and durability; in the concluding chapter of this book, we examine certain of the cognitive, ideological and (pseudo-)scholarly mechanisms that function as models for this Islamophobic radicalisation.

This introductory chapter puts forth a plural definition of Islamophobia while also emphasising one of its key aspects, namely *Islamophobia as a form of violent radicalisation or that leads to violence*. Like any other form of radicalisation, Islamophobia is a complex and multi-dimensional social phenomenon (Esposito & Iner, 2019; McGilloway et al., 2015; Verkuyten, 2018). As such, it precludes both simple answers and reductive explanations: a complex problem's answers must themselves be complex. Confronted with the complexity of Islam and Islamophobia, the prevailing tendency is to simplify. In the face of an increasingly anxiety-provoking socio-philosophical Anthropocene, this simplification racialises and essentialises Muslims, while also construing them as both existential threats, and sacrificial victims to be freely employed as a means to atoning for our present-day social and civilisational ills (Freud, 1981/1920; Girard, 2005; Mekki-Berrada, 2014, 2018a). Humiliating and inferiorising discourses and attitudes, often accompanied by declared hatred and violence in regard to Muslims, remain, despite the at times tense but legitimate debates generated by the 'Islamophobia' term, a relevant social reality, both locally and globally. Is Islamophobia as a social reality in part an exaggerated and polarised response to the collective anxiety generated by violent radical Islamism? Is refuting the denial of this reality and once and for all labelling it 'Islamophobia' an urgent matter, if it means we can better comprehend it and thereby better prevent a central aspect of the social polarisations that undermine our democracies and their 'inaccessible' living-together?

The notion of Islamophobia refers, for the purposes of this collective book, to a discursive strategy alluding to mass killings, violent psychological and physical attacks, hateful remarks and acts of exclusion and discrimination targeting Muslim individuals *due to their being Muslim*, and in which Islam tends to be constituted as a 'lasting trauma' (Saïd, 2003, p. 76), both in Canada (Amiraux & Gaudreault-Desbiens, 2016; Helly, 2011, 2015) and elsewhere in the world (Meer, 2014; Razack, 2008; Sayyid, 2014; Vakil, 2010).

Rooted in a relationship of social domination, Islamophobia also encompasses the attempt to ontologically inferiorise, dehumanise and animalise the Muslim Other. *Islamophobia is first and foremost a question of power.* It is, in its Foucauldian sense, a form of 'governmentality of Muslim otherness' (Mekki-Berrada, 2018a, p. 24; 2019) which, far from confining itself to an expression of extreme right-wing violent radicalisation, tends today to be both normalised and globalised (Sayyid, 2018). Lodged in the interstices of everyday-life difficulties, it is increasingly taking on the form of an 'ordinary violence' (Kilani, 2006, 2009; Mekki-Berrada, 2018b; Scheper-Hughes & Bourgois, 2004; Taussig, 2004).

In addition to *virilist Islamophobia*, a notion introduced by Mekki-Berrada (2019), which is at the heart of this technique of government of Muslim women's bodies, Islamophobic attacks, as well as the hate speech that accompanies them, are here viewed as expressions of a form of radicalisation that is violent or that leads to violence: that is, Islamophobic radicalisation (Mekki-Berrada 2019). Violent radicalisation is not the exclusive domain of extremist groups claiming to be Islamic; that it is varied in nature and includes other political, social and religious forms of fundamentalisms is now well known. Islamophobic radicalisation and Islamic-fundamentalist radicalisation mutually feed off each other (Iner, 2019a, 2019b; Kabir, 2019; Pratt, 2019) by adhering to comparable, though not identical, narrative, theoretical, cognitive and practical forms of logic.

Islamophobia: From West to East

Islamophobia is sustained by extreme right-wing ideologies in North America, as well as in Eastern and Western Europe (Pratt, 2019), where confrontational 'trash radio' (Payette, 2017, 2019), print media (Kabir, 2019) and social media platforms contribute to the construction of both Islamophobic and radical-Islamist discourses by polarising public opinion (Esposito, 2019). Islamophobic violent radicalisation is observable in Western democratic countries, such as Canada, New Zealand and Norway, to mention only a few countries. What do Québec City in Canada, Christchurch in New Zealand and Oslo in Norway have in common? At the time of writing (December 2022), they were the sole Western cities in which mosques served as the scene of a mass shooting, together resulting in 57 deaths and dozens of wounded citizens of the Muslim faith, including women and children. These murderous shootings were all the work of young white Western men in their twenties. The genetic nature of their discourse rests on the hatred of otherness and on 'White pride', which renders the Other in general and Muslims in particular existential threats to 'White humanity and civilisation'. Are these killings the expression of social suffering, rather than of a 'pride' so deep that it goes beyond words? Of a desperate youth lacking any anchoring to generative meaning, who are only able to find a voice and make themselves heard through guns and violent Islamophobic radicalisation? While these complex questions exceed the scope of this introduction and require equally complex answers, the fact remains that killings targeting mosques, and therefore Muslims *due to their being Muslim*, are, it must be stressed, Islamophobic crimes, if not terrorist crimes.

Islamophobia is also being fuelled in non-Western states, including in Israel, by ultraconservative, ultranationalist and far-right parties (Bulkin & Nevel, 2014), in India by powerful Hindu fundamentalist political move-ments (Singh, 2009; Siyech & Narain, 2018; Waikar, 2018) in league with the ruling ultranationalist Bharatiya Janata Party, and in China (Luqiu & Yang 2018) where the state is detaining Kazakh and Uyghur Muslim families in gulags and other 're-education camps' reserved for Muslims whose only crime is manifesting Islamic beliefs, refusing to eat pork or naming their sons Mohamed (Buckley, 2018; Buckley & Myers, 2019; Pedroleletti, 2018). Islamophobia is also growing in Philippines and Thailand where it seems to be linked to colonial history and Islamophobic radicalisation that is spreading internationally (Nawab & Osman, 2019). Genocidal Islamophobia is being perpetrated in Myanmar by Buddhist fundamentalists (Yusuf, 2018), the national army (Le Monde, 2019) and armed militias in conjunction with the forced (or consensual?) silence of former leader and Nobel Peace Prize winner

Aung San Suu Kyi, while another Nobel Peace Prize winner, the Dalai Lama, pays lip service to condemning Islamophobia. These two global figures and representatives of non-violence appear nonetheless weary in the face of the Muslim ethnocide and genocide occurring in Myanmar, where nearly 90 per cent of the population is Buddhist. Islamophobia can range from hate speech to violent action, even to the mass and forced displacement of nearly one million (80 per cent) of the Muslims in Myanmar, a country where they have been subjected to mass killings during which more than 10,000 of them (men, women and children) were murdered (UN, 2018), with some being burned alive (Zine, 2018) in what the UN has labelled genocidal acts and crimes against humanity (UN, 2019).

There also exists violent radicalisation perpetrated in the name of Islam, which has ravaged the world since the 1990s and often also involved young adults in their twenties, in this case Muslims. Clearly, in the 21st century, this radicalisation is no longer the sole preserve of young Muslims. It is increasingly the work of far-right Western groups and white supremacists, some of which the Canadian Ministry of Public Safety identifies as forming terrorist entities, notably Blood & Honour and Combat 18, both of whom appear on the same list as Islamic State of Iraq and Syria (ISIS) and Al-Qaeda (Public Safety Canada, 2019). These groups are instigators of hate speech and hate crimes targeting minorities in general, and Muslim minorities in particular. Whether justified in the name of Islamism–fundamentalism–radicalism, white supremacism or individual and collective psychological insecurity, radicalisation that is violent or that leads to violence follows a truth-based discourse that renders the Other into a being requiring assimilation (etymologically: to make similar, identical to oneself) or destruction. Such discourses, often accompanied by heightened identity claims, have resulted in deadly shootings at mosques: in Québec City in 2017, in Christchurch and Oslo in 2019. Synagogues, churches, commercial spaces, schools and summer camps – none have been exempted from the white supremacist, Islamophobic and radical Islamist violence that together characterised the 21st century's first two decades.

Criticising Islamist and Islamophobic Violent Radicalisations

As we emphasise in chapter 15 of this book, several scholars (e.g., Esposito & Iner, 2019; Mekki-Berrada, 2019) find some commonalities and dynamic interactions between Islamophobia and radical Islamism, what Pratt calls 'reactive co-radicalisation' (2019, p. 47). Anyone should be free to criticise both these Islamophobic and Islamist violent radicalisations. Islamophobic discursivity, as highlighted by Mekki-Berrada (2019), views self-criticism within Islam as an inescapable oxymoron. Criticism of violent Islamist and Islamophobic excesses continues to represent a democratic imperative, so long as such criticism does not aim to exacerbate already devastating and murderous social polarisations. Certainly, the most literalist of Muslims, along with their ultraconservative acolytes, who together represent but a minority of their 1.9 billion fellow believers, seek to ban all criticism of Islam in the Muslim world, as well as in the West. In a democracy where freedom of expression is an inalienable and non-negotiable right, banning criticism is simply unthinkable, if not illegal. In Canada, for example, the Canadian Charter of Rights and Freedoms, related to the Constitution Act, considers freedom of expression to be a fundamental freedom, with sections 1 and 2 stating:

> 1. The *Canadian Charter of Rights and Freedoms* guarantees the rights and freedoms set out in it subject only to such reasonable limits prescribed by law as can be demonstrably justified in a free and democratic society.
> 2. Everyone has the following fundamental freedoms: (a) freedom of conscience and religion; (b) freedom of thought, belief, opinion and expression, including freedom of the press and other media of communication; (c) freedom of peaceful assembly; and (d) freedom of association.

The legal restriction on the fundamental freedom of expression guaranteed by the Charter is found in section 319 of the Criminal Code of Canada, which states: 'Everyone who, by communicating statements in any public place, incites hatred against any identifiable group … is guilty of an indictable offence …' Freedom of expression therefore ends, in the eyes of Canadian law, where the safety and freedom of others are threatened. Freedom of expression is a fundamental and inescapable democratic right. We all have the right, and even the duty, to criticise Islam and other religions, as well as racism, anti-Semitism and Islamophobia, extremists and pacifists, right-wing and left-wing parties, violent radicalisation and communal coexistence – even democracy and secularism. However, as sociologist and secularism historian Jean Baubérot (2012, n.p., our translation) rightly points out, 'a clear distinction must be drawn between the right to criticism and hate speech or the call to hatred'. He goes on to say that 'while criticism is a matter pertaining to free debate, hate speech and the call to hatred are a matter pertaining to justice' (Baubérot, 2012). Criticising Judaism or Islam, for example, is a fundamental right. Inciting anti-Semitic or Islamophobic hatred is, however, not a matter of freedom of expression. It is in Canada a crime punishable by the Criminal Code, as Section 319 makes quite clear. The same occurs within the legal framework of the European Union, where incitement to hatred is criminalised and certain forms of discrimination are combatted, based on Article 1 of the Charter of Fundamental Rights of the European Union (European Parliament, 2000) and Article 2 of the Treaty on European Union (2012). The revised Audiovisual Media Services Directive (AVMSD) by the European Parliament and the Council of the European Union (2018) reinforced the protection of television and video-on-demand against incitement to violence or hatred, and public provocation to commit terrorist offences.

In a democracy, citizens are free to criticise Islam and to condemn the excesses that certain radical Islamists might encourage – just as they are free to condemn Islamophobic radicalisation as a polarising social reality toxic to a better living-together. While Islamophobia indeed presently represents a much-debated term, should the word's semantic indecisiveness result in denial of the social and political reality to which it makes reference? We will tentatively answer this question in *From Media and Pseudo-scholarly Islamophobia in Post 9/11 Moral Panic to 'Meta-solidarity'*, which is the last and concluding chapter of this collective book. Moreover, all chapters show different declinations of Islamophobia as a form of radicalised discursivity.

The second chapter of this collective book, written by Erkan Toguslu and Leen d'Haenens, is titled *The Mutual Antagonism between Sharia for Europe and Anti-Islam Far-Right Networks*. The authors discuss significant notions, such as *cumulative extremism* and *reciprocal radicalism* – which help to show how radical Islamism and Islamophobia feed into each other. The authors raise the question: 'Should the relationship between far-right and Islamist extremism be understood as a "simple" dynamic of reaction and counter-reaction based on mutual antagonism, or as a complex web of different styles of interaction?' The authors suggest that the unavoidable and dynamic interactions between the two radicalities lead to the escalation of hate and violence between their representatives in Belgium, such as Sharia4Beligum, and the far-right anti-Muslim movement. It is, however, considerably difficult to define the true nexus between the Islamist and far-right extremisms. Toguslu and d'Haenens aim to meet this challenge by conducting a thorough critical literature review of existing studies that engage with this problem. In doing so, the authors come to realise that while this nexus seems to be binary in some European countries, where radicalised groups are reciprocally fed opposing radicalised movements, it is not the case in other EU countries. They go on to suggest that instead of viewing this nexus in terms of a binary, it 'can be considered a broader process of coevolution involving multiple actors' and multiple factors.

The third chapter, *Building Blocks of Polish Islamophobia: The Case of Polish Youth*, by Katarzyna Górak-Sosnowska and Joanna Sozańska, is a foray into Islamophobia as it is shaped by youth and their allegiance to far-right movements and national patriotism, as well as by their religious knowledge and identity. The authors focus on the life trajectories of youth in Poland, as well as how they are taught about Islam and Muslims in school by looking at both the school curriculum and the personal experiences of Górak-Sosnowska and Sozańska as teachers and instructors. They also look at the role that social media plays in demonising Muslim women, men and youth. It appears that, despite their marginality, as they represent only 0.1 per cent of the Polish population, Muslims are considered an existential threat and, as such, Islamophobic youth adhere to the phantasmatic myth of the imminent 'Islamic invasion' of Europe. With this, it is worth noting that a collective memory exists and may be haunting many Poles, about the murderous tensions and strategic alliances that Poland maintained with and against the Ottoman Empire in the 17th century. While it is worth noting that Polish youth seem to be more attracted to Islamophobic narratives and attitudes than the general Polish population is, Muslims have nevertheless been construed as a 'convenient enemy'. This has been done through the policies put forward by populist–conservative–nationalistic governments to promote an Islamophobic discourse in both the media and among the general population. Although it is not easy to draw a simple and one-dimensional picture of Islamophobia among Polish youth, it nevertheless seems to be based on three building blocks, which are (1) political, where Polish national identity is portrayed as threatened by the *Muslim enemy*; (2) educational, where the school system contributes to the essentialisation of Islam and Muslims and disseminates orientalist and colonial stereotypes; and (3) social media, where hate speech against migrants in general, and Muslims in particular, is widespread. It can therefore be concluded that it is primarily the exposure to Islamophobic narratives within the education system and on social media that youth are more likely to adopt these narratives than the general population. Islamophobia becomes therefore systemic within the education system that educates future Polish decision-makers, and is expressed as a form of extremism and radicalisation inspired radical far-right discursivity.

Chapter four, *The Political and Intellectual Discourse on Islam and Muslims in Flanders,* by Alexander Van Leuven, Stefan Mertens, Leen d'Haenens and Abdelwahed Mekki-Berrada, highlights that while 0.1 per cent of the Polish population is Muslim, as demonstrated in Chapter 3, more than 7 per cent of the Belgian citizens are of Muslim persuasion. However, despite this demographic difference, Muslims are perceived similarly in both countries, whereas they are considered a *national problem* and an *existential threat* to the nation and its native citizens. The authors explore the ways in which intellectuals and politicians inspire the debate on Islamophobia in Flanders (Dutch-speaking part of Belgium). The twenty books analysed by Van Leuven et al. for this chapter were written by Flemish politicians and academics holding either left-wing, centrist or right-wing positions. The analysis demonstrates that these authors represent a variety of opinions that are reflected in the media and that identify concerns such as Muslims in the labour market, Muslims as a potential threat to a seemingly *disappearing* native majority, Muslims as terrorists and about the hijab, which ultimately has become the symbol for all the problems related to immigration of both Muslims and non-Muslims alike. Therefore, the central question asked by the authors of this chapter consists of whether or not this debate is beneficial for Belgian society in general and particularly Flemish society, despite the plurality of voices in a state governed by the rule of law. The authors point at the political and scholarly discourses that contribute to legitimising Islamophobia as a form of radicalisation.

The fifth chapter, *Islamophobia in Germany, still a debate?* by Luis Manuel Hernández Aguilar traces contemporary discussions on Islamophobia in Germany, zooming in on state-led discussions on the issue. It also discusses the Hanau shooting in the context of conspiracy theories about population replacement, and argues for Islamophobia to be considered as one of the empirical faces of racism currently associated with conspiracy theories. While European far-right terrorism is committed to a certain 'racism against "non-white" Germans', the author questions the actual validity of a so-called post-racial Germany and highlights the links between Islamophobia in some political discourses, far-right extremism and Islamophobic radicalisation that led in 2020 to a mass shooting of Muslim citizens in Germany.

Chapter six, *Islamophobia in the Media in the Province of Québec, Canada: A Corpus-assisted Critical Discourse Analysis*, by Vivek Venkatesh, Abdelwahed Mekki-Berrada, Jihène Hichri, Rawda Harb and Ashley Montgomery, leads us to cross the Atlantic Ocean from Europe to Canada. The authors describe how themes related to Islamophobia are relayed by columnists and editorial writers in eight of the most widely read dailies in the Province of Québec, Canada from 2010 to 2020. The authors analysed a corpus of more than three million words from 1,515 chronicles and editorials, and the convergence between how *supposed intellectuals,* actually self-proclaimed essayists, and featured columnists perceive Muslims. Venkatesh et al. conclude with a call to policymakers and other stakeholders to take on an intersectoral approach at developing curricular programmes, to be adopted by the Canadian legal system, that focuses on human rights, preservation and freedom of speech, as well as the need to include clear, precise and strict definitions of hate that translates into Islamophobic radicalisation.

Chapter seven, *The Veil in France: Twenty Years of Media Coverage (1989–2010)* by Camila Arêas and Abdelwahed Mekki-Berrada brings us back from Canada to Europe. The authors analyse public debates concerning the *headscarf affair* (1989–2004) and the *burqa affair* (2009–2010) in France by questioning the mediatisation of the Islamic signs-symbols based on notions of visibility and spatiality. The authors use a semiotic approach to analyse images and discourses from both academic sources, namely scholarly journals in the field of Humanities and Social Sciences, and French national and regional press, to better understand how, and why, French Muslim women have moved back and forth within social visibility and media and political visibility. Arêas and Mekki-Berrada suggest that media coverage constructed a degraded and stigmatised visibility of the veil, legitimising thereby a geographic extension of the ban on the veil from schools to the streets, which led to a legal redefinition of public space. By force of stigmatising the veil in the media, it became easier to move towards legislating a ban. The chapter suggests that the academic and press discourses could easily be used to feed Islamophobic discourses in the social and political spaces.

The eighth chapter, *From Pen to Perception: Does News Reporting Advance Terrorist Agendas?* by Stefan Mertens, David De Coninck and Leen d'Haenens, analyses historically right-leaning and left-leaning Flemish newspapers and how the reader reacts to fear and terrorism. While it is widely understood that there is a strong tendency for a reader to consider only information that confirms their biases... [according to the so-called] 'filter bubble theory', the authors highlight the need for a more nuanced approach when trying to understand the relationship between a newspaper and its readers' perspectives. Similarly, Mertens et al. call for a more nuanced approach to comparing how right-leaning and left-leaning newspapers report about terrorism. The convergence and divergence of the content between the two depend greatly on context, such as whether or not an article is published during a time of crisis or during a time of routine reporting. The authors also show, in such contexts, how Islamist and Islamophobic radicalised discourses feed each other.

The ninth chapter, *Islamophobia in the Portuguese Opinion Press* by Camila Arêas, Alfredo Brant, Ana Flora Machado, Colin Robineau, Helena Cruz Ventura and Abdelwahed Mekki-Berrada, provides the results from a critical semiotic approach to discourse analysis of the majority of available papers that were published by both columnists and editorialists in Portuguese dailies from 2010 to 2020. This analysis is rooted in the debates that surround Islam and Islamophobia and highlights that the question of Islamophobia appears in two forms: in discourses that contain a discriminatory content about Muslims and in discourses discussing the political uses of Islamophobia. While the first form is present in all newspapers analysed in different degrees according to their editorial stance, the second form is mostly visible in the right-wing newspaper *Observador*, which criticises the political function, especially the intimidation (self-censorship) that the notion of Islamophobia fulfils. It would appear that newspapers such as *Observador* maintain and promote aversion, hatred and fear and propose that Muslims are an important threat to the Portuguese nation and identity. Here we see the idea of Islamophobia being condemned as a weapon aimed to censor freedom of speech, while Islamophobia as a social reality is categorically denied, or at most perceived as an epiphenomenon.

The tenth chapter, *Islamophobia and Far-Right Parties in Spain: The 'Vox' Discourse on Twitter* by Alfonso Corral, Cayetano Fernández and Antonio Prieto-Andrés, explores the reach of Spain's far-right party Vox. Vox emerged in the 2010s and is driven by a narrative based on securitisation and the view that Islam and Muslim immigrants are a security threat, more so than a societal one: a threat to traditional Spanish values, and of the increase in public insecurity and crime, which Vox blatantly links to the presence of these groups in Spanish society. An analysis of Vox's Twitter reveals a strong hostility to Islam and Muslims and that any sentiment against the news source's far-right ideology is to be understood as a sign of an Islamic invasion of Spain. An example of this phenomenon can be seen with how the Catalan secessionist movement has become labelled by Vox as an Islamist project aimed at dividing and weakening the identity and catholicity of Spain and Europe. The authors illustrate how radicalised political parties' use of social media could lead to a form of governmentality aimed at controlling both native minorities and Muslim immigrants in Spain.

The eleventh chapter, *Coping with Islamophobia: (Social) Media, a Double-Edged Sword* written by Ans De Nolf, Leen d'Haenens and Abdelwahed Mekki-Berrada, explores how young Muslims in Flanders experience Islamophobia and the different ways they cope with anti-Muslim sentiments. In the media and public spaces, Muslims are generally portrayed as non-humans, invaders, criminals, terrorists, inherently violent and generally incapable of understanding *Western values* and democratic principles. More so, Muslim women are perceived as entirely victimised in that the very thought of a Muslim woman being able to act is an insoluble oxymoron. With this ideological context in mind, the authors analyse the role of both traditional and social media and their Islamophobic implications for Muslim men and women. One of the findings worth noting is the dual role of media. Muslim youth point to traditional media as the primary cause of Islamophobia and social media as a site of comfort and strength. Therefore, within this context, we see social media as one of the seven coping strategies for Flemish Muslim youth experiencing Islamophobia, detailed in this chapter through the subjective experiences recounted in the ethnographic encounters conducted by De Nolf. These adaptive strategies emphasise that young Muslims are active and eager subjects and supporters of an inclusive democracy. The authors underline that Islamophobic radicalisation and alienation could be more easily dealt with when Muslim citizens have the opportunity to mobilise peacefully in *virtual safe spaces*.

The twelfth chapter, *Safe Spaces and Sensitive Issues: Towards an Emic Understanding of Radicalisation*, by Alexander Van Leuven and Ann Trappers, begins with the foundational idea that the concept of radicalisation is usually defined by governmental policy, which is an *etic* perspective. The authors go on to claim that the semantic network in which it forms a core concept serves to hide, both consciously and subconsciously, particular socio-political intentions that hinder any potential intervention strategy against violent radicalisation. They go on to argue for the need to create *safe spaces* where non-judgemental dialogue can be made possible so that young Belgian citizens can provide *emic* definitions of radicalisation as an alternative narrative. Leuven and Trappers explore both the potential and the limits of the idea of *institutional alienation* as a way to replace the concept of radicalisation and as a link between Islamophobia, unresolvable social grievances and radicalism. This should offer a more constructive frame of reference to approach the phenomenon, involving those who might be considered key stakeholders: youth who protest or cease to abide by the democratic rule of law in Belgium. Among the suggestions stemming from their ethnographic encounters with youth from Molenbeek, Van Leuven and Trappers report that when working with young people from a setting like Molenbeek, it is worthwhile to approach them as 'urban' youth, rather than consistently viewing them through the lens of Islam. Too often participants, boys in particular, felt that people would approach them as youth at risk of radicalisation. This kind of *emic* posture is one of the starting strategies for challenging Islamophobic radicalisation and Islamist radicalisation on a long-term basis.

Back once more from Europe to Canada, the thirteenth chapter, *'Wait, What?! Islamophobia Exists in Newfoundland and Labrador?': Theorizing Polite Dismissal of Anti-Islamophobia Public Engagement* by Sobia Shaheen Shaikh and Jennifer A. Selby, engages with the polite dismissal of a university-sponsored public engagement project on Islamophobia in the Canadian province of Newfoundland and Labrador (NL), Canada. Shaikh and Selby explore the dynamics and epistemologies behind the dismissal of Islamophobia by their university and the Newfoundland provincial government. By analysing autoethnographic data and considering university and government attitudes towards advocacy work and an action research project led by the authors, they claim that despite governmental anti-racist discourse and initiatives, Islamophobia and anti-Muslim racism are disregarded by the officials. The authors conclude by arguing that anti-Muslimness is embedded within interlocking relations of oppression, and must be read simultaneously with ongoing and embedded histories of colonial violence against Indigenous, Black and migrant peoples across the globe. This chapter highlights the deep and rhizomatic roots of 'anti-Muslimness' as a form of radicalisation expressed, consciously or not, in academic and political spaces.

The fourteenth chapter, *Muslim Communities and the COVID-19 Pandemic: The Complex Faces of Protection,* written by Salam El-Majzoub, Anabelle Vanier-Clément and Cécile Rousseau, explores the role of spiritual and community resources in the face of adversity during the pandemic in the province of Québec, Canada. El-Majzoub et al. state that this chapter shows how mobilisation during the pandemic was based on pre-existing alliances, but also how the crisis context made it possible to overcome certain divisions and to create or consolidate bridges with the majority and local and national institutions. However, minority groups in Québec, including Muslim minorities, seem to have endured more severe psychological impacts than the majority, despite the close collaborations between Muslim communities and the public health sector. This being said, the dialogic approach between Muslim leaders and Montréal public health services allowed the former to voice their concerns and specific needs, and to co-create culturally adapted solutions with the institutions, showing therefore that bottom-up initiatives can be more impactful when dialogue between actors is horizontal and when the community does not feel instrumentalised to further public health services' agenda. Such a culturally sensitive collaboration demonstrates that during times of crisis, these tensions could be overcome and transformed into a collective effort to co-construct a better shared experience, highlighting the similarities of all citizens regardless of where they come from or what their persuasions are. The question that remains is how we export this ethos of collaborative and bridging efforts into *ordinary,* non-crisis times, especially when it comes to address what is referred to as *ordinary* Islamophobic radicalised discourses, attitudes and behaviors.

We conclude with the fifteenth and final chapter, *From Media and Pseudo-Scholarly Islamophobia in Post 9/11 Moral Panic to 'Meta-Solidarity',* by Mekki-Berrada and d'Haenens, which synthesises what we have learned from the thirteen research initiatives discussed in this book. We will particularly sum up, on the one hand, the authors' views on the dynamic interactions between Islamist and Islamophobic radicalisations and, on the other, the mechanisms through which certain pseudo-scholarly and media discourses contribute to Islamophobic radicalisation. We will also present in this final chapter the authors' evidence-based recommendations to different stakeholders, including policymakers.

In sum, this collective and multi-disciplinary EU–Canada work aims at better understanding Islamophobia as both a form of power, governmentality and radicalisation that is violent or that contributes either directly or indirectly to violence. We look also at the dynamic interactions between political, academic and media discursivities, and the conditions that lead to Islamophobic radicalisation. In addition, we show that Islamophobia is a multi-dimensional and complex issue that could only lead to complex answers that require altogether theoretical, applied, transdisciplinary and intersectoral approaches aimed at suggesting constructive recommendations to contribute to a living-together where subjects are able to manage social tensions, instead of fantasising on a world with no sociopolitical tensions at all.

Notes

1.   This introductory chapter stems from a project mainly funded by the Social Sciences and Humanities Research Council (SSHRC): *Scholarly and mediatic Islamophobia: A transnational study of discourses and their impact* (Original French title *Islamophobie savante et médiatique: Étude transnationale des discours et de leur impact*; SSHRC 2019-2023, #890-2018-0016), for which Abdelwahed Mekki-Berrada is the Principal Investigator.

References

Amiraux, V., & Gaudreault-Desbiens, J. F. (2016). Libertés fondamentales et visibilité des signes religieux en France et au Québec: Entre logiques nationales et non nationales du droit ? [Fundamental freedoms and visibility of religious symbols in France and Quebec: Between national and non-national logics of law?]. *Recherches sociographiques, 57*(2–3), 351–378.

Baubérot, J. (2012). *Islam et laïcité* [Islam and secularism]. YouTube. https://www.youtube.com/watch?v=9N_ehXIyYYk&feature=youtu.be

Bibeau, G. (2017). *Andalucía, l'histoire à rebours* [Andalusia, history in reverse]. Mémoire d'encrier.

Bruckner, P. (2017). *Un racisme imaginaire. Islamophobie et culpabilité* [Imaginary racism. Islamophobia and guilt]. Grasset.

Buckley, C. (2018, September 8). *China is detaining Muslims in vast numbers. The goal: 'transformation'.* The New York Times. https://www.nytimes.com/2018/09/08/world/asia/china-uighur-muslim-detention-camp.html

Buckley, C., & Myers S. L. (2019, August 9). *China said it closed Muslim detention camps. There's reason to doubt that.* The New York Times. https://www.nytimes.com/2019/08/09/world/asia/china-xinjiang-muslim-detention.html

Bulkin, E., & Nevel, D. (2014). *Islamophobia & Israël.* Route Books.

d'Iribarne, P. (2019). *Islamophobie: intoxication idéologique* [Islamophobia: Ideological intoxication]. Albin Michel.

Esposito, J., & Iner, D. (Eds.). (2019). *Islamophobia and radicalization.* Palgrave Macmillan.

Esposito, J. L. (2019). Islamophobia and radicalization: Roots, impact and implications. In J. Esposito & D. Iner (Eds.), *Islamophobia and radicalization* (pp. 15–33). Palgrave Macmillan.

European Parliament. (2000, December 18). *Charter of Fundamental Rights of the European Union.* Official Journal of the European Communities, C364/1.

European Parliament and the Council of the European Union. (2018, November 28). Directive (EU) 2018/1808 of the European Parliament and of the Council of 14 November 2018 amending Directive 2010/13/EU on the coordination of certain provisions laid down by law, regulation or administrative action in Member States concerning the provision of audiovisual media services (Audiovisual Media Services Directive) in view of changing market realities. PE/33/2018/REV/1. *OJ L,* 303, 69–92.

Freud, S. (1981). *Essais de psychanalyse* [Essays in psychoanalysis]. Payot. (Original work published 1920)

Girard, R. (2005). La pierre rejetée par les bâtisseurs [The stone rejected by the builders]. *Théologiques,* 132, 165–179.

Helly, D. (2011). Les multiples visages de l'islamophobie au Canada [The many faces of Islamophobia in Canada]. *Nouveaux Cahiers du socialisme,* 5, 99–106.

Helly, D. (2015). *La peur de l'Islam* [The fear of Islam]. SociologieS. http://sociologies.revues.org/4900

Iner, D. (2019a). Introduction: Relationships between Islamophobia and radicalization. In J. Esposito & D. Iner (Eds.), *Islamophobia and radicalization* (pp. 1–11). Palgrave Macmillan.

Iner, D. (2019b). Interweaving Islamophobia with radicalism: Feeding the radicals with the anti-Halal debate. In J. Esposito & D. Iner (Eds.), *Islamophobia and radicalization* (pp. 73–95). Palgrave Macmillan.

Kabir, N. A. (2019). Can Islamophobia in the media serve Islamic State propaganda? The Australian case, 2014–2015. In J. Esposito & D. Iner (Eds.), *Islamophobia and radicalization* (pp. 97–116). Palgrave Macmillan.

Kepel, G. (2016). *La fracture* [The divide]. Gallimard.

Khosrokhavar, F. (2014). *Radicalisation* [Radicalisation]. Sciences de l'Homme.

Kilani, M. (2006). *Guerre et sacrifice. La violence extrême* [War and sacrifice. Extreme violence]. Presses de l'Université Laval.

Kilani, M. (2009). Violence extrême. L'anthropologie face aux massacres de masse. [Extreme violence. Anthropology in the face of mass killings]. In F. Saillant (Ed.), *Réinventer l'anthropologie ? Les sciences de la culture à l'épreuve de la globalisation* (pp. 109–128). Liber.

Le Monde. (2019, August 25). Au Bangladesh, 200 000 Rohingyas manifestent pour commémorer leurs deux ans d'exil [In Bangladesh, 200,000 Rohingyas demonstrate to commemorate their two-year exile]. *Le Monde.*

Luqiu, R. L., & Yang, F. (2018). Islamophobia in China: News coverage, stereotypes, and Chinese Muslims' perceptions of themselves and Islam. *Asian Journal of Communication,* 28(6), 598–619.

McGilloway, A., Ghosh, P., & Bhui, K. (2015). A systematic review of pathways to and processes associated with radicalization and extremism amongst Muslims in Western societies. *International Review of Psychiatry, 27*, 39–50.

Meer, N. (2014). Islamophobia and postcolonialism: Continuity, Orientalism and Muslim consciousness. *Patterns of Prejudice, 48*(5), 500–515.

Mekki-Berrada, A. (2014). La charte des valeurs québécoises: Co-exister [exister ensemble] dans la catho-laïcité de l'État et la sécurisation de l'immigration [The Quebec Charter of Values: Co-existing in the catholic secularity of the State and the securitization of immigration]. *Diversité canadienne/Canadian Diversity, 10*(2), 5–10.

Mekki-Berrada, A. (2018a). Femmes et subjectivations musulmanes: Prolégomènes [Women and Muslim subjectivations: Preliminaries]. *Anthropologie et sociétés, 42*(1), 9–33.

Mekki-Berrada, A. (2018b). Ayn mika: Traumatic experience, social invisibility, and emotional distress of sub-Saharan women with precarious status in Morocco. *Transcultural Psychiatry, 56*(6), 1170–1190. https://doi.org/10.1177/1363461518757798

Mekki-Berrada, A. (2019). Prolégomènes à une réhabilitation de la notion d'islamophobie [Prolegomena to a rehabilitation of the notion of Islamophobia]. *Religiologiques, 39*, 5–49.

Nawab, M., & Osman, M. (2019). Understanding Islamophobia in Southeast Asia. In I. Zempi & I. Awan (Eds.), *The Routledge international handbook of Islamophobia* (pp. 286–297). Routledge.

UN (2018, September 18). *Myanmar: des enquêteurs de l'ONU dénoncent la brutalité de l'armée contre les Rohingyas* [Myanmar: UN investigators denounce the brutality of the army against the Rohingyas]. UN News. https://news.un.org/fr/story/2018/09/1023842

UN (2019, May 14). *Rohingyas: appel des enquêteurs de l'ONU à couper les finances de l'armée du Myanmar* [Rohingya: UN investigators call for cutting off Myanmar army's finances]. UN News. https://news.un.org/fr/story/2019/05/1043401

Payette, D. (2017, May–June). La crise du modèle d'affaire des médias favorise l'essor de la démagogie [The crisis of the media business model favors the rise of demagogy]. *Relations, 12*. https://cjf.qc.ca/revue-relations/publication/article/la-crise-du-modele-daffaire-des-medias-favorise-lessor-de-la-demagogie/

Payette, D. (2019). *Les brutes et la punaise: Les radios-poubelles, la liberté d'expression et le commerce des injures* [The bullies and the bug. Trash radios, free speech and the insult business]. Lux.

Pedroleletti, B. (2018, December 28). *Kazakhs et Ouïgours dans l'enfer du goulag chinois* [Kazakhs and Uyghurs in the hell of the Chinese gulag]. Le Monde. https://www.lemonde.fr/international/article/2018/12/28/au-xinjiang-dans-l-univers-concentrationnaire-des-camps-chinois_5402864_3210.html?xtor=EPR-33281036-[le_brief]-20181228-[titre_2]

Pratt, G. D. (2019). Reacting to Islam: Islamophobia as a form of extremism. In J. Esposito & D. Iner (Eds.), *Islamophobia and radicalization* (pp. 35–53). Palgrave Macmillan.

Public Safety Canada. (2019). *Listed terrorist entities.* Government of Canada. https://www.publicsafety.gc.ca/cnt/ntnl-scrt/cntr-trrrsm/lstd-ntts/crrnt-lstd-ntts-en.aspx

Razack, S. (2008). *Casting out: The eviction of Muslims from Western law and politics.* University of Toronto Press.

Saïd, E. W. (2003). *L'orientalisme. L'orient créé par l'Occident* [Orientalism: Western conceptions of the Orient]. Seuil.

Sayyid, S. (2014). A measure of Islamophobia. *Islamophobia Studies Journal, 2*(1), 10–25.

Sayyid, S. (2018). Topographies of hate: Islamophobia in cyberia. *Journal of Cyberspace Studies, 2*(1), 55-73.

Scheper-Hughes, N., & Bourgois, P. (Eds.). (2004). *Violence in war and peace: An anthology.* Blackwell.

Schmid, A. O. (2014). *Violent and non-violent extremism: Two sides of the same coin?* ICCT Research Paper.

Singh, K. (2009). *Islamophobia in India: A case study of Gujarat 2002.* University of Tromsø.

Siyech, M., & Narain, A. (2018). Beef-related violence in India: An expression of Islamophobia. *Islamophobia Studies Journal, 4*(2), 181–194.

Taussig, M. (2004). Terror as usual. In N. N. Scheper-Hughes & P. Bourgois (Eds.), *Violence in war and peace. An anthology* (pp. 9-11). Blackwell Publishing.

Treaty on European Union. (2012, October 26). *Consolidated version of the Treaty of European Union.* Official Journal of the European Union, C326/13.

Vakil, A. (2010). Is the Islam in Islamophobia the same as the Islam in anti-Islam; or, when is it Islamophobia time? In S. Sayyid & A. Vakil (Eds.), *Thinking through Islamophobia: Global perspectives* (pp. 23–43). Hurst.

Verkuyten, M. (2018). Religious fundamentalism and radicalization among Muslim minority youth in Europe. *European Psychologist, 23,* 21–31.

Waikar, P. (2018). Reading Islamophobia in Hindutva: An analysis of Narendra Modi's political discourse. *Islamophobia Studies Journal, 4*(2), 161–180.

Yusuf, I. (2018). Three faces of the Rohingya crisis: Religious nationalism, Asian Islamophobia, and delegitimizing citizenship. *Studia Islamika, 25*(3), 503–542.

Zine, Y. (Director). (2018). *I am a Rohynga: A genocide in four acts* [Documentary]. Innerspeak.

2
THE MUTUAL ANTAGONISM BETWEEN SHARIA FOR EUROPE AND ANTI-ISLAM FAR-RIGHT NETWORKS

ERKAN TOGUSLU & LEEN D'HAENENS

Abstract

This chapter analyses research findings on the interaction between anti-Islam/Sharia and Sharia for Europe groups from the perspective of cumulative extremism and radicalisation theory, with a focus on the places and occasions where this antagonism occurs. First, we introduce the concepts of cumulative extremism and reciprocal radicalisation, and explain how they can help us understand processes of escalation between opposite groups. Next, we present a framework for assessing the development of cumulative extremism. Furthermore, we examine the interplay between anti-Islam and Sharia for Europe networks in the 2000s, focusing on the action and reactions between them. Finally, we discuss findings from existing studies and research on these opposite groups, specifically on street activism and public narratives.

Keywords: Islamophobia, far right, Sharia for Europe, English Defence League, Sharia4Holland, Sharia4Belgium, Pegida (Patriotic Europeans Against the Islamicisation of the Occident), Les Identitaires, radicalisation, Stop Islamisation

Defining the nexus between far-right extremism and Islamophobia can be challenging, partly due to the breadth of literature, and missing relevant data on the relation between the two extremist ideologies. This chapter identifies, assesses and synthesises the existing literature on the relation between far-right extremism and Islamophobia in Europe through a systematic literature review of cumulative extremism to understand what these studies say about the nexus between the two. While existing studies on cumulative extremism and radicalisation have methodological shortcomings and are lacking analytical data, common themes can be identified with regard to the relation between cumulative extremism and radicalisation. According to the selected studies, a mutually reinforcing relation exists between various experiences of individuals in far-right extremist organisations on the one hand, and different forms of engagement of Muslims in jihadi groups on the other. The main argument of these studies is that populist radical right movements and parties are responsible for a surge in Islamophobia, and that Islamist extremists are crucial to the rise of the far right in Europe. However, the relationship between far-right and Islamist extremism needs to be investigated further. The current chapter provides a review of existing studies and conclusions with regard to extremist perceptions and interactions. The aim is to answer the following question: Should the relation between far-right and Islamist extremism be understood as a 'simple' dynamic of reaction and counter-reaction based on mutual antagonism, or as a complex web of different styles of interaction?

Recent surveys show an increase in offline and online anti-Muslim attitudes and hate speech in Europe (Field, 2007; Hajjat & Mohammed, 2013; Taras, 2013). In the years following a series of terrorist attacks in the UK, Europe and North America committed by Islamist extremists, anti-Muslim ideologies and attitudes have only grown stronger (Khan & Mythen, 2019). The increase in hate crime against Muslims in Europe after the Charlie Hebdo terrorist attacks has sparked discussions about the relation between Muslim extremism and anti-Muslim hate speech. The far-right National Party was the first party in the UK to 'weaponise' Islamophobia after 2001 (Feldman & Stocker, 2019). For example, in the week following the murder of British soldier Lee Rigby in May 2013, a 373 percent increase in hate crimes against Muslims was reported in the UK.

In France, hate crime increased by 223 percent after the 2015 terrorist attacks on the Charlie Hebdo offices in Paris, from 133 incidents in 2014 to 400 incidents in 2015 (CNCDH, 2016). In the 2019–2020 period, an upsurge of 52 percent in anti-Muslim acts was recorded (CNCDH, 2020). Following the terrorist attacks in Brussels in 2016, Belgium witnessed a record number of verbal and physical attacks against Muslims; however, the number of Islamophobic incidents decreased later on (CIIB, 2021).

Many European countries have observed that the numbers of jihadi and Muslim extremists, including violent radicals, terrorists, propagandists and lone-wolf attackers, remain high (Europol, 2016). These groups and milieus are not hierarchically or centrally organised, but loosely connected to each other, like, for example, the Sharia for Europe groups. They have engaged in non-violent demonstrations, which has in turn encouraged jihadism and terrorist attacks in Europe. These Muslim groups use social connections with other Salafi and jihadi networks to mobilise their supporters for various purposes. They also promote online hate messages using multiple social media platforms. The simultaneous emergence of Sharia and anti-Sharia groups allows us to analyse radicalisation processes in opposite movements. In this chapter, the escalation between these two opposing groups is interpreted from the perspective of different disciplines and theories.

Cumulative Extremism and Reciprocal Radicalisation

Drawing on social movement theories, Roger Eatwell (2006) introduced the notion of cumulative extremism, defined as an escalation of violence between militant Islamists and anti-Islam groups. Eatwell's theory explains how militant Islamist activities generate far-right extremism and mutual antagonism. In this chapter, we scrutinise this thesis and show that it is unsustainable. Following riots between the far-right English Defence League and the Islamist extremist group al-Muhajirun in the UK, Roger Eatwell (2006) coined the term 'cumulative extremism' to describe the process in which one particular form of extremism feeds off other forms. There are multiple, related terms, such as 'reciprocal radicalisation', 'cumulative extremism' and 'co-radicalisation' that refer to how different extremist groups fuel one another's strategies, narratives and actions. While these concepts are widely used in policy papers and counter-extremism debates to explain how people become involved in radical movements (Barnett et al., 2021; Bartlett & Birdwell, 2013; Carter, 2020; Cole & Pantucci, 2014; Knott et al., 2018), they are conceptually and empirically problematic (Busher & Macklin, 2014; Carter, 2020). First, the lack of a clear conceptual definition has led to careless use, and to the emergence of some amalgams that describe opposing movements. There is a strong need for precise conceptual definitions that explain what these terms mean, and what their parameters are. Misinterpretation of the 'cumulative extremism' and 'cumulative radicalisation' terms has led to various ambiguities. Do they refer to a war of rhetoric and narratives, an explicit reciprocal act of violence or performative acts of opposition such as protest marches, hate crime and textual messages, all of which can be part of escalations between groups? Second, the interactions and exchanges between movement and counter-movement need more empirical explanations. How can one group cause an escalation in another group's violent narratives and actions?

Radicalisation processes can happen at different levels with various dynamics and factors. Personal and group grievances (Mccauley & Moskalenko, 2008), social-economic segregation (Piazza, 2011), group polarisation

(Goodwin, 2006) and linkage to extremist ideology (Borum, 2011b); Meleagrou-Hitchens, 2011) are some of the factors that explain extremism and radicalisation processes. Many scholars have outlined the polarisation process between antagonistic groups (Alimi et al., 2015; McCauley & Moskalenko, 2011). Research into the relational dynamics of radicalisation (Alimi et al., 2015) has revealed a complexity of networks and people interacting with one another, and identified various mechanisms and micro-processes. Rivalry between opposite groups is also considered one of the causes of radicalisation. Some analyses of the formation of far-right anti-Islam groups and jihadi networks in Europe (Abbas, 2019; Ebner, 2017; Esposito & Iner, 2018) seem to support Eatwell's (2006) cumulative extremism theory; however, other findings (Lygren & Ravndal, 2021) do not.

Additionally, it is essential to reflect on the nature of the interaction between groups and their embeddedness in a specific social environment. Thus, it is important to understand how radicalisation occurs, and, simultaneously, in what contexts individuals and groups engage in violence. Bailey and Edwards (2017) argue that the holistic picture of radicalisation and its smaller components can explain links between different groups, and counter-reactions of other extremist groups and various sections of society, including non-extremists. Analysing micro-processes can help us understand reactions of smaller segments of society and minority groups to what they perceive as a threat to their interests, values and identity. Describing micro-processes to compare and measure movements and counter-movements by identifying the adoption of tactics, narratives and discourses offers several advantages. Analyses of micro-processes typically focus on traditional mobilisation strategies of social movements and contestation (Della Porta & LaFree, 2012). Looking at extremism through the lens of micro-processes can shed light on the main interconnection between various forms of extremism and the potential escalation of violence, and, specifically, on the everyday interactions and practices through which micro-radicalisation emerges (Bailey & Edwards, 2017; Holbrook, 2015). Studies in this field primarily focus on reciprocal radicalisation in daily interactions, and also present attitudes, activities, motivations and root causes. However, these studies are mainly concerned with the macro-processes of radicalisation for example, with the contents and frequencies of frames used by radicals. Many researchers focus on root causes to explain the dynamics of radicalisation (Borum, 2011a, 2011b; Cross & Snow, 2011; Kundnani, 2015; Neumann, 2013; Schmid, 2013). The analysis of reciprocal radicalisation processes uses similar forms, methods and explanations as existing radicalism studies.

Understanding whether there is a connection between anti-Islam and pro-Sharia groups and how both movements emerge in particular socio-economic contexts requires an analysis of individual and collective processes. These processes can explain why anti-Islam and radical Muslim movements mobilise people and how they create an antagonistic atmosphere. Many studies focusing on far-right and Muslim extremist movements that explain this connection rely on publicly available data, such as propaganda from online social media accounts, flyers, webpages, public events and speeches of members and leaders. However, these studies do not look at interactions between groups. Most of the research is limited to understanding community activities, discourses and narratives of a single group in isolation.

We conducted a review of the literature published in the last 20 years (2000 to 2021) covering events from the mid-2000s – watershed years marked by Islamist and far-right terrorism. While most studies published in this period consider these two types of extremism in isolation, we looked for research into interactions between them, in other terms, into cumulative extremism between anti-Islam and pro-Sharia groups in Europe. Specifically, we searched academic databases for studies into connections between these two forms of extremism. As our query produced few search results, we extended the search to Google Scholar. Most of the literature we found on cumulative radicalisation was very recent.

We used various permutations of the following search terms: 'cumulative extremism', 'radicalisation and anti-Islam networks', 'stop Sharia', 'Sharia for Europe', 'Salafism in Europe', 'Islamophobia', 'far-right in Europe', 'violent extremism in Europe', 'polarisation'. The searches returned a combination of academic journal articles, book reviews, newspaper articles and policy papers. A number of results were excluded due to irrelevancy with regard to interaction and reciprocity. Given the small number of search results from peer-reviewed journals, we expanded the corpus on radicalisation by adding relevant articles on extremism and radicalisation published by known scholars in this field to explain what we found in these studies.

Stop Islamisation versus Sharia for Europe: A Myriad of Networks

The first extremist group mentioned in our corpus is the Stop the Islamisation network, founded in 2005 in Denmark by politician Anders Gravers Pedersen. The network became a transnational network with the launch of Stop the Islamisation of Europe (SIOE). It organised so-called Counter Jihad summits and international conferences to mobilise people from all over Europe. Its goal was to 'create awareness' and stop the 'Islamisation of Europe'. The network included the 'defence leagues' in Australia, Denmark, England,

Finland, Norway, Poland, Scotland and Serbia, the Pro Cologne Movement (later Pro Germany Citizens' Movement), Pax Europa, the Cities against Islamisation initiative (Häusler, 2011), and Casual United (which disbanded in 2014 and became the Pie and Mash Squad; Richards, 2013; Koch, 2020) in the UK. It also included Tommy Robinson's English Defence League, the Identitarian Movement (Zúquete, 2018) in various countries across Europe, Stop the Islamisation of Norway, Pegida (Patriotic Europeans Against the Islamisation of the Occident) and the neo-Nazi organisation Vigrid, which defined Muslims and Islam in Europe as the most urgent problem (Fangen & Nilsen, 2020). These anti-Islam movements are linked to other peer groups in different countries, and to far-right parties. They organise and participate in rallies, demonstrations and petitions against Muslim presence in public spaces (for example, the building of mosques; Allievi, 2009).

A second extremist group mentioned in the corpus is the Salafi jihadi network (Maher, 2016; Nesser, 2018), which comprises individuals, organisa-tions, preachers and militants. It includes al-Muhajirun (Wiktorowicz, 2005), Islam4UK, Sharia4Belgium (Roex & Vermeulen, 2019), Shariah4Holland, Shariah4Austria, Forsane Alizza in France, and Einladung zum Paradies (Invitation to Paradise, EZP) – a network established in 2005 by a group of young preachers in Germany – Millatu Ibrahim in Germany (Baehr, 2014), and Profetens Ummah in Norway.

The militant Islamist al Mouhajirun (Wiktorowicz, 2005) operated in the UK, led by Anjem Choudary. The group was banned, but splinter groups were established later under various names such as Islam4UK, Muslims Against Crusades, Need4Khilafah, al-Ghurabaa and the Saved Sect. Islam4UK propagates Islamist ideology and the establishment of Sharia law in the UK. Its members were implicated in terrorist attacks such as the murder of Lee Rigby, the London Bridge attack and various stabbings. The exact size of the group is not known. Its members were previously active in other Salafi groups (Kenney, 2018; Raymond, 2010). Islam4UK used to organise demonstrations to demand the establishment of sharia rule. They captured the public's attention by carrying symbolic coffins in memory of Muslims 'murdered by coalition forces'. In addition, they frequently held sermons, protests and study groups (Weeks, 2020). Islam4UK, along with groups like Sharia4Belgium and Sharia4Holland, were initially seen as marginal movements. However, with the Syrian war and the increasing number of European Muslims in Syria, perceptions changed, and they came to be seen as a danger to national security.

In Belgium, three young militant Islamists established Sharia4Belgium, which became a well-known organisation. Led by Fouad Belkacem, a prominent spokesperson, Sharia4Belgium gathered militant Islamists (Roex & Vermeulen, 2019). It advocated for the implementation of Sharia in Belgium, and against secular democracy. The group gained media attention in 2010 when Belgian police arrested several of its members for suspected terror attacks. It was active in recruiting jihadis to fight in Chechnya, and, later, Syria. Sharia4Belgium frequently organised street demonstrations, but attendance was typically very low. In 2012 the group collapsed, and its leaders were arrested.

It is interesting that many anti-Islam and pro-Sharia groups have been able to mobilise diverse networks of people from various backgrounds. Successful far-right groups have succeeded in bringing together supporters adhering to different ideologies (Blee, 2007) and opinions about Muslims and migrants. It is often challenging to identify precisely what anti-Sharia groups stand for, and who they support, as many different people, ideologies, stories and discourses are involved. Furthermore, these groups define themselves as an adversary of radical Islam. Thus, they want to attract people from traditional far-right groups, and from broader backgrounds.

Street Demonstrations and Spectacle Activism

In Germany, Salafi preachers used to organise street activities called da'wa, which is also popular in Denmark (Krause et al., 2019). EZP would frequently distribute Quran books (LIES! campaigns), and give speeches in public to provoke the public and authorities. These da'wa activities were carried out by small groups, such as Tawhid Germany, Die Wahre Religion, and EZP (de Koning et al., 2020). In 2012, Millatu Ibrahim followers and activists in Solingen and Bonn clashed with the police. These clashes erupted after the publication of Muhammad cartoons by the right-wing Pro NRW movement. Two police officers were stabbed and wounded. After this violent incident, Millatu Ibrahim was banned. In the wake of these events, the police held targeted raids on the EZP network and many of its preachers. Militant Islamists have represented this event as symbolic resistance to the German state and police, and used photos and videos of the raids to inspire courage, assertiveness and resistance to the non-Islamic regime. These clashes later became the most potent symbol of a 'war against Islam' by the West in jihadi and Salafi narratives in Germany.

Like their German counterparts, Sharia4Belgium followers were active in da'wa street campaigns in various Belgian cities. They would hand out leaflets, give lectures and meet with people to discuss Islam. Videos of their activities were published on the Internet for dissemination and to attract new followers. However, as these street activities frequently created problems for local residents and shopkeepers (Roex & Vermeulen, 2019), police would often intervene and arrest many members. On many occasions, Sharia4Belgium tried to enhance its public recognition and visibility, for example by publishing a video of its leader dressed in a djellaba, an army jacket and a turban, announcing that the group would destroy the Atomium – an iconic monument in Brussels – and through various videos and blog posts declaring that they wanted to establish an Islamic state in Belgium. Sharia4Belgium protested against the film *Innocence of Muslims,* and organised street demonstrations against the ban on the niqab, the full veil (de Koning et al., 2020). These street demonstrations typically ended with arrests and clashes with police.

In the Netherlands, Sharia4Holland drew inspiration from its sister organisations, Islam4UK and Sharia4Belgium. On 5 May 2012, Liberation Day in the Netherlands, Sharia4Holland and Sharia4Belgium jointly organised protests at a prison in the town of Vught where several jihadi prisoners were held. In June 2012, Sharia4Holland members took to the streets to distribute flyers against voting in the Dutch parliamentary elections in September 2012, claiming that 'voting is shirk (idolatry) and therefore a great sin' (cited in de Koning et al., 2020, p. 229). Sharia4Holland also appeared at the demonstration against the anti-Islam film *Innocence of Muslims* at Museumplein in Amsterdam. In 2013, an image of an ISIS flag held up during a football match and barbecue in the city of The Hague was posted on Facebook and Twitter, which fuelled a debate closely followed by journalists. Sharia4Holland was confronted by the police and forced to leave the park where the event took place.

Demonstrations organised by Sharia groups typically gathered few attendees – on average 30–50 people. Some teenagers would join through social media networks. Nevertheless, these Sharia4Europe groups in the UK, Netherlands, Belgium and Denmark drew attention among Muslim youth and non-Muslim groups by creating disturbing events, demonstrations and street activities following a more militant, activist path. These street protests and clashes with the police were in tandem with the rise of anti-Islam groups' discourses and movements. Notwithstanding occasional violent plots and terrorist attacks in various European cities, the Sharia for Europe network disappeared from the public eye in about 2012. However, jihadi cells make Europe a favourable place to recruit terrorists.

In contrast, anti-Islam movements and networks actively reacted against Sharia for Europe groups. Like many Sharia for Europe groups, the aforementioned Stop Islamisation network was split into specific groups that engaged in organising street protests and demonstrations against the burqa, headscarf, mosques and minarets. Increasingly, anti-Islam movements emerged as a form of protest and countermovement not only toward radical Muslims, but toward Muslims in Europe in general. With regard to their activities – street demonstrations and gatherings – there are many parallels between pro-Sharia and anti-Islam groups.

Les Identitaires (formerly Bloc Identitaire) is a French anti-migrant, nativist, anti-Muslim movement that presents itself as a pan-European network. It was created in 2002 in Nice, and became increasingly active in various social debates and by organising street demonstrations (Braouezec, 2016). Les Identitaires primarily targets young people, and promotes anti-migration and anti-Islam ideas. Its founding members have links to Marine Le Pen's far-right party National Rally (Rassemblement National). In 2021, members occupied the rooftop of a mosque in Poitiers, France. The group regularly refers to iconic historical events and symbols to attract more attention (Cutaia, 2013) and recruit young people. They distribute so-called 'identity soup' containing pork in various cities in France and Belgium. They organised a 'pork sausage and booze party' ('apéro saucisson et pinard') in various cities, some of which were banned by local police. In 2012 in Montluçon, a small town in central France, they used a megaphone to protest the opening of a mosque and denounce the 'Islamisation' of the city by changing the name of a street to 'Sharia Street'.

The case of the English Defence League (EDL) in the UK offers a clear example of how Muslim extremism can galvanise anti-Islam movements. The EDL was established in 2009 in the southern English town of Luton to protect non-Muslims from radical Islam. It used to organise demonstrations attracting from 500 to 5,000 activists to protest against the building of Islamic centres, violent Islamists and expressions of solidarity with British West Indians (Goodwin et al., 2016). EDL is popular among young people. Within two years, the EDL had gained many followers. British far-right, anti-Islam activist and former EDL leader Tommy Robinson, for example, attracted more than 85,000 followers on Facebook, and the EDL had many representatives across the country. The murder of British Army soldier Lee Rigby in 2013 in southeast London was followed by an increase in EDL followers. The killing sparked ethnic and religious hate, and fuelled divisions. Following the killing, British National Party leader Nick Griffin posted several tweets indicating Muslims and mass immigration policies as the reason for the attack. The EDL also organised a demonstration in which members clashed with the police. These demonstrations typically took place in areas with large Muslim populations, and provoked the Muslim against Crusades group to burn poppies to incite violence with far-right groups (Bartlett & Birdwell, 2013).

Despite these provocative actions and street clashes, there is little evidence that either group had strong support from the grassroots level. Because of the escalation, there was no increase in members and supporters on online and offline platforms. The increasing number of online supporters did not coincide with an increase in demonstration attendance. On the one hand, the existence of Islamophobia and hate messages from far-right groups can be seen as a justification for the jihadi engagement of Muslim extremists. Still, it is not very clear how the existence and activities of the far right incite and trigger the radicalisation process of Muslims. On the other hand, Muslim extremists' violence cannot be the underlying factor of far-right mobilisation. Many authors discuss the various ways people can become involved with far-right groups and networks, and become active supporters and members (Klandermans & Mayer, 2006; Mudde, 2000; Rydgren, 2018; Wodak, 2015; Wodak et al., 2013). For example, with regard to the EDL, Busher (2016) identifies several identical pathways in different people: the football hooligan scene, patriotic groups, the traditional far right and, lastly, counter-jihad networks. The latter never accounted for more than 5 per cent of the activist community (Busher, 2016).

A War of Two Narratives

One of the more salient arguments of the cumulative extremism theory is that a powerful narrative on one side of the conflict can lead to an escalation of the other side's narratives and discourses (Brzuszkiewicz, 2020; Holbrook, 2015). The dynamics between anti-Islam groups and Muslim extremists in many European countries seem to support this argument. While Sharia groups argue that the 'West is at war with Islam', far-right anti-Islam groups claim that 'Islam is at war with the West'. Such narratives are valuable tools for maintaining the community and revivifying the image of the enemy in various stories and symbols (Frissen & d'Haenens, 2017; Toguslu, 2019). These diametrically opposite extremist ideologies reinforce one another by using the same narratives, themes, characters and images. These images, logos and discourses are shared on various platforms and occasions. On the visual level, the emblem of the EDL and flags used in demonstrations refer to the Crusader-style cross and banners. This heavy use of Crusader imagery fits well with radical Islamist arguments that Westerners are new crusaders invading Muslim lands. This may be a symbolic strategy for Al-Qaeda and ISIS, who define Western allies as crusaders in Muslim lands. This Crusader imagery has become a famous symbol and emblem during demonstrations.

Supporters frequently use images of Crusader knights and swords on their online media channels. In some way, the use of Crusader imagery supports the ISIS arguments that the West is the enemy of Islam (Richards, 2013).

Most counter-jihad and anti-Islam organisations, online as well as offline, share a meta-narrative of Islam: Muslim immigration is a threat to Europe, and Islam dominates Western culture. The thesis of Eurabia and theory of a 'great replacement', a fear of loss of cultural identity and insecurity because of terrorist attacks encourage an atmosphere of moral panic, and xenophobic and racist attitudes and discourses (Goodwin, 2013; Goodwin et al., 2016; Lazaridis et al., 2017). Islamist and anti-Islam narratives reinforce each other using by the same elements, motifs, figures and symbols in their arguments and actions. Some of the themes in these narratives and counter-narratives surface in most anti-Islam and jihadi narratives.

Women's rights and gender have become symbolic issues. Sharia groups have developed a narrative about the 'decadence' of Western societies in which women are exploited and objectified. According to them, only Islam proposes a valuable solution for women to embrace their freedom within religion. The militant Islamist protects Muslim women from Western hedonist culture and civilisation. In opposition to this idea, anti-Sharia movements emphasise that women in the West are non-subordinate and free from domination. A stereotype that far-right anti-Islam groups use is the image of Western women conforming to gender equality. For example, Karina Horsti examines the digital culture of Islamophobic bloggers (Horsti, 2017). In her explorative study, she analyses how the image of the 'raped Swedish woman' was disseminated, with narratives and visual aesthetics entangled with one another. Blogs disseminating this image are seen as networks that produce and distribute the specific idea that Muslim men violently rape unveiled, non-Muslim women.

Thus, the 'brothers and soldiers' should protect the white Scandinavian societies (Horsti, 2017). These bloggers' international call for saving white culture creates a transnational online space of whiteness through fantasies about Scandinavian countries. Horsti also adds that the 'pure white' society discourse intermingles with discourses of civilisation, Nordic exceptionalism, gender equality, a 'pure' national past and national homogeneity. These discourses are also connected to anti-immigration anti-Muslim movements.

Törnberg and Törnberg (2016) and Katrine Fangen (2021) analysed several anti-feminist and Islamophobic discussion topics in online forums and Facebook groups. These discourses focus on criticism of Muslims, such as violence committed by Muslim men against women, the question of the burqa, gender roles and feminist support for migrants and Muslims and their inter-ethnic marriages. In this sense, women's rights are used by far-right groups as an argument for hostility against migrants and Muslims. An interesting aspect of gender equality is emphasised in many far-right groups' narratives. Far-right group members put forward the themes of gender equality, liberty of women to show the superiority of Western civilisation. In opposition to these ideas, the Sharia groups state that women should remain hidden, veiled, not equal to men. They have distinctly different roles under Islamic rule. Both groups actively use women for propaganda purposes against each other. While far-right groups declare that Muslim women are suppressed, the Sharia groups argue that Western women lack morals and ethics. The EDL Angels are a good example propagating that dichotomy. They are female members who are very active in EDL anti-Islam demonstrations in the UK. They convey the message that they are not angels of purity and innocence, but active and sexually assertive, and do not represent conservative femininity (Pilkington, 2017).

Conclusion

While some countries, specifically the UK, have witnessed an escalation of violence between these two opposite movements (British EDL and al-Muhajirun), others, like Belgium, the Netherlands, Denmark and Norway have not experienced a similar escalation of violence. These examples show us different typologies of interactions between groups. The idea that radical Islamism and extreme right groups feed off each other is based on the assumption of reciprocity or cumulative radicalisation. Our literature review revealed that a lot of research in this field is empirically weak. It also aimed to build a knowledge base regarding the critical engaging factors of the two forms of extremism and how these factors stimulate common concerns of threat. Most of the existing studies are exploratory rather than explanatory, with a distinct absence of interlinking levels of explanation. The main problem with these studies is that they explain each form of extremism in isolation, not in connected ways. The evidence supporting the idea that each form of extremism plays a role in developing another remains superficial. The theory of cumulative radicalisation may help us use some comparative tools, notions and narratives to interpret the radicalisation of anti-Islam far-right groups and Islamist radicalisation. Analysing to what extent cumulative extremism occurs and how one movement inspires and impacts counter-movement is another central problem. We recommend that future studies pay attention to the multiple pathways of influence between movements and counter-movements to seek whether the social, political and economic environment shapes interactions between movements or whether opposite movements have a direct or indirect impact on each other by using narratives, symbols and actions.

Consequently, cumulative extremism can be considered a broader process of coevolution involving multiple actors, rather than a binary process. The opposition between far-right anti-Islam movements and radical Islamist groups involves many actors forging coalitions (left-wing, anti-fascist, Black activists, minority groups, anti-migrant activists, feminists), and using various tactics and strategies with different aims, motivations and serving different identities. Furthermore, anti-Islam and Muslim extremist groups and coalitions are heterogeneous and do not reflect a single ideology or identity. They comprise various ideological positions and narratives, and concur with popular perceptions of challenges in society. Thus, the understanding of cumulative extremism should depend not only on the opposing groups in focus and their respective histories, but also on how their narratives are perceived through popular support and media attention.

References

Abbas, T. (2019). Islamophobia and radicalisation: A vicious cycle. *Oxford Scholarship Online*. https://doi.org/10.1093/oso/9780190083410.001.0001

Alimi, E. Y., Demetriou, C., & Bosi, L. (2015). *The dynamics of radicalization: A relational and comparative perspective*. Oxford University Press.

Allievi, S. (2009). *Conflicts over mosques in Europe: Policy issues and trends*. Alliance PublishingTrust (NEF initiative on Religion and Democracy in Europe).

Baehr, D. (2014). Dschihadistischer Salafismus in Deutschland [Jihadist salafism in Germany]. In T. G. Schneiders (Ed.), *Salafismus in Deutschland* [Salafism in Germany] (pp. 231–250). Transcript Verlag.

Bailey, G., & Edwards, P. (2017). Rethinking 'radicalisation': Microradicalisations and reciprocal radicalisation as an intertwined process. *Journal for Deradicalization, 10*, 255–281.

Barnett, J., Maher, S., & Winter, C. (2021). *Literature review: Innovation, creativity and the interplay between Far-Right and Islamist extremism*. International Centre for the Study of Radicalisation. https://www.icsr.info

Bartlett, J., & Birdwell, J. (2013). *Cumulative radicalisation between the Far-Right and Islamist groups in the UK: A review of evidence*. DEMOS. http://www.demos.co.uk/files/Demos

Blee, K. M. (2007). Ethnographies of the far right. *Journal of Contemporary Ethnography, 36*(2), 119–128.

Borum, R. (2011a). Rethinking radicalization. *Journal of Strategic Security, 4*(4), 1–6.

Borum, R. (2011b). Radicalization into violent extremism: A review of social science theories. *Journal of Strategic Security, 4*(4), 7–36.

Braouezec, K. (2016). Identifying common patterns of discourse and strategy among the new extremist movements in Europe: The case of the English Defence League and the Bloc Identitaire. *Journal of Intercultural Studies, 37*(6), 637–648.

Brzuszkiewicz, S. (2020). Jihadism and far-right extremism: Shared attributes with regard to violence spectacularisation. *European View, 19*(1), 71–79.

Busher, J. (2016). *The making of anti-Muslim protest: Grassroots activism in the English Defence League*. Routledge.

Busher, J., & Macklin, G. (2014). Interpreting 'cumulative extremism': Six proposals for enhancing conceptual clarity. *Terrorism and Political Violence, 27*(5), 884–905.

Carter, A. J. (2020). *Cumulative extremism: A comparative historical analysis*. Routledge.

Cole, J., & Pantucci, R. (2014). Community tensions: Evidence-based approaches to understanding the interplay between hate crimes and reciprocal radicalisation. Royal United Services Institute (RUSI). https://static.rusi.org/201407_community_tensions.pdf

Collectif pour l'Inclusion et contre l'Islamophobie en Belgique (CIIB). (2021). *Rapport Chiffres 2020 – État de l'Islamophobie en Belgique*. Brussels.

Commission Nationale Consultative des Droits de l'Homme (CNCDH), (2016). *Rapport sur la lutte contre le racisme, l'antisemitisme et la xénophobie 2015*. (Report on the Fight against Racism, Antisemitism and Xenophobia 2015). https://www.cncdh.fr/fr

Commission Nationale Consultative des Droits de l'Homme (CNCDH). (2020). *Rapport 2020 sur la lutte contre le racisme, l'antisémitisme et la xénophobie 2020*. (Report on the Fight against Racism, Antisemitism and Xenophobia 2020). https://www.cncdh.fr/fr

Cross, R., & Snow, D.A. (2011). Radicalization within the context of social movements: Processes and types, *Journal of Strategic Security, 4*(4), 115–129.

Cutaia, N. (2013). Mouvements islamophobes et Charles Martel: quelle réappropriation ? Cas d'étude sur le Bloc identitaire et l'affaire de la mosquée de Poitiers (Islamophobic movements and Charles Martel: what reappropriation ? Case study on the Bloc identitaire and the Poitiers mosque affair). *Cahiers Mémoire et Politique, 1*, 11–27. https://doi.org/10.25518/2295-0311.69

De Koning, M., Becker, C., & Roex, I. (2020). *'Islands in a sea of disbelief': Islamic militant activism in Belgium, the Netherlands and Germany*. Palgrave Macmillan.

Della Porta, D., & LaFree, G. (2012) 'Guest editorial: Processes of radicalization and de-radicalization', *International Journal of Conflict and Violence, 6*(1), 4–10.

Eatwell, R. (2006). Community cohesion and cumulative extremism in contemporary Britain. *The Political Quarterly, 77*(2), 204–216.

Ebner, J. (2017). *The rage: The vicious circle of Islamist and far-right extremism*. I.B. Tauris.

Esposito, J. L., & Iner, D. (Eds.) (2018). *Islamophobia and radicalization: Breeding intolerance and violence*. Springer International Publishing AG.

Europol. (2016). *European Union Terrorism Situation and Trend Report 2016*. https://doi.org/10.2813/525171

Fangen, K. (2021). Gendered images of us and them in anti-Islamic Facebook groups. *Politics, Religion & Ideology, 21*(4), 451–468.

Fangen, K., & Nilsen, M. R. (2020). Variations within the Norwegian far right: From neo-Nazism to anti-Islamism. *Journal of Political Ideologies, 26*(3), 278-297. https://doi.org/10.1080/13569317.2020.1796347

Feldman, M., & Stocker, P. (2019). Far-right Islamophobia. From ideology to 'mainstreamed' hate crimes. In I. Zempi & I. Awan (Eds.), *The Routledge international handbook of Islamophobia* (pp. 352–362). Routledge.

Field, C. D. (2007). Islamophobia in contemporary Britain: The evidence of the opinion polls, 1988–2006. *Islam and Christian–Muslim Relations, 18*(4), 447–477. https://doi.org/10.1080/09596410701577282

Frissen, T., & d'Haenens, L. (2017). Legitimizing the Caliphate and its politics: Moral disengagement rhetoric in Dabiq. In S. F. Krishna-Hensel (Ed.), *Authoritarian and Populist Influences in
the New Media* (pp. 138–164). Routledge.

Goodwin, J. (2006). A theory of categorical terrorism. *Social Forces, 84*(4), 2027–2046.

Goodwin, M. (2013). *The roots of extremism: The English Defence League and the counter-
Jihad challenge.* https://www.chathamhouse.org/sites/default/files/public/Research/
Europe/0313bp_goodwin.pdf

Goodwin, M. J., Cutts, D., & Janta-Lipinski, L. (2016). Economic losers, protestors, Islamophobes
or xenophobes? Predicting public support for a counter-Jihad movement. *Political Studies,
64*(1), 4–26. https://doi.org/10.1111/1467-9248.12159

Hajjat, A., & Mohammed, M. (2013). *Islamophobie: Comment les élites françaises fabriquent le
« problème musulman »* (Islamophobia: How French elites manufacture the 'Muslim problem').
La Découverte.

Häusler, A. (2011). *Die 'PRO-Bewegung' und der antimuslimische Kulturrassismus von Rechtsaußen*
(The 'PRO movement' and anti-Muslim cultural racism from the far right). www.fes-gegen-
rechtsextremismus.de

Holbrook, D. (2015). Far Right and Islamist extremist discourses: Shifting patterns of enmity. In
M. Taylor, D. Holbrook, & P. M. Curie (Eds.), *Extreme right wing political violence and terrorism*
(pp. 215–238). Bloomsbury Academic. https://doi.org/10.5040/9781501300967.CH-011

Horsti, K. (2017). Digital Islamophobia: The Swedish woman as a figure of pure and dangerous
whiteness. *New Media & Society, 19*(9), 1440–1457.

Kenney, M. (2018). *The Islamic State in Britain.* Cambridge University Press.

Khan, F., & Mythen, F. (2019). Micro-level management of Islamophobia. Negotiation, deflec-
tion and resistance. In I. Zempi & I. Awan (Eds.), *The Routledge international handbook of
Islamophobia* (pp. 313–321). Routledge.

Klandermans, B., & Mayer, N. (Eds.). (2006). *Extreme right activists in Europe: Through the
magnifying glass.* Routledge.

Knott, K., Lee, B., & Copeland, S. (2018). *Reciprocal radicalisation.* Crest Research. https://
crestresearch.ac.uk/resources/reciprocal-radicalisation/

Koch, A. (2020, August 25). The transnationalization of White Supremacist discourse: The
Hundred-Handers and the It's Okay To Be White campaign. *Centre for Analysis of the Radical
Right.* https://www.radicalrightanalysis.com/2020/08/25/the-transnationalization-of-
white-supremacist-discourse-the-hundred-handers-and-the-its-okay-to-be-white-campaign/

Krause, D., El-Jaichi, S., Karacan, B. T., & Sheikh, M. K. (2019, December 19). Islamic State in
Europe: The network and doctrine of Millatu Ibrahim. *DIIS.* https://www.diis.dk/en/research/
islamic-state-in-europe-the-network-and-doctrine-of-millatu-ibrahim

Kundnani, A. (2012). Radicalisation: The journey of a concept. *Race & Class, 54*(2), 3–25.

Lazaridis, G., Polymeropoulou, M., & Tsagkroni, V. (2017). Networks and alliances against
the Islamisation of Europe: The case of the Counter-Jihad Movement. In G. Lazaridis & G.
Campani (Eds.), *Understanding the populist shift: Othering in a Europe in crisis* (pp. 70–103).
Routledge. https://doi.org/10.4324/9781315656779-12

Lygren, S., & Ravndal, J. A. (2021). Why reciprocal intergroup radicalisation happened between
Islamists and anti-Islamists in Britain but not in Norway. *Terrorism and Political Violence.* https://
doi.org/10.1080/09546553.2021.1933957/SUPPL_FILE/FTPV_A_1933957_SM5108.
DOCX

Maher, S. (2016). *Salafi-Jihadism: The history of an idea.* Hurst Publishers.

McCauley, C., & Moskalenko, S. (2008). Terrorism and political violence mechanisms of political radicalization: Pathways toward terrorism. *Terrorism and Political Violence, 20*(3), 415–433. https://doi.org/10.1080/09546550802073367

McCauley, C. R., & Moskalenko, S. (2011). *Friction: How radicalization happens to them and us.* Oxford University Press.

Meleagrou-Hitchens, A. (2011). *As American as Apple Pie: How Anwar al-Awlaki became the face of Western Jihad.* International Centre for the Study of Radicalisation (ICSR). https://www.icsr.info

Mudde, C. (2000). *The ideology of the extreme right.* Manchester University Press.

Nesser, P. (2018). *Islamist terrorism in Europe: A history.* Oxford University Press.

Neumann, P. R. (2013). The trouble with radicalization. *International Affairs, 89*(4), 873–893.

Piazza, J. A. (2011). Poverty, minority economic discrimination, and domestic terrorism. *Journal of Peace Research, 48*(3), 339–353.

Pilkington, H. (2017). 'EDL angels stand beside their men ... not behind them': The politics of gender and sexuality in an anti-Islam(ist) movement. *Gender and Education, 29*(2), 238–257.

Raymond, C. Z. (2010). *Al Muhajiroun and Islam4UK: The group behind the ban. Developments in radicalisation and political Violence.* International Centre for the Study of Radicalisation (ICSR). www.icsr.info

Richards, J. (2013). Reactive community mobilization in Europe: The case of the English Defence League. *Behavioral Sciences of Terrorism and Political Aggression, 5*(3), 177–193. https://doi.org/10.1080/19434472.2011.575624

Roex, I., & Vermeulen, F. (2019). Radicalization in Belgium and the Netherlands: Critical perspectives on violence and security. In N. Fadil, F. Ragazzi, & M. de Koning (Eds.), *Radicalization in Belgium and the Netherlands: Critical perspectives on violence and security* (pp. 131–145). I. B. Tauris.

Rydgren, J. (Ed.). (2018). *The Oxford handbook of the radical right.* Oxford University Press. https://doi.org/10.1093/oxfordhb/9780190274559.001.0001

Schmid, A. P. (2013). *Radicalisation, de-radicalisation, counter-radicalisation: A conceptual discussion and literature review.* International Centre for Counter-Terrorism Research Paper.

Taras, R. (2013). 'Islamophobia never stands still': Race, religion, and culture. *Ethnic and Racial Studies, 36*(3), 417–433.

Toguslu, E. (2019). Caliphate, hijrah and martyrdom as performative narrative in ISIS dabiq magazine. *Politics, Religion and Ideology, 20*(1), 94–120.

Törnberg, A., & Törnberg, P. (2016). Combining CDA and topic modeling: Analyzing discursive connections between Islamophobia and anti-feminism on an online forum. *Discourse & Society, 27*(4), 401–422.

Weeks, D. (2020). *Al Muhajiroun: A case-study in contemporary Islamic activism.* Palgrave Macmillan.

Wiktorowicz, Q. (2005). *Radical Islam rising: Muslim extremism in the West.* Roman & Littlefield.

Wodak, R. (2015). *The politics of fear: What right-wing populist discourses mean.* Sage Publishing.

Wodak, R., KhosraviNik, M., & Mral, B. (Eds.). (2013). *Right-wing populism in Europe.* Bloomsbury Publishing.

Zúquete, J. P. (2018). *The Identitarians: The movement against globalism and Islam in Europe.* Notre Dame Press.

PART II

CONTEMPORARY POLITICAL DISCOURSES ON ISLAMOPHOBIA

3

BUILDING BLOCKS OF POLISH ISLAMOPHOBIA: THE CASE OF POLISH YOUTH

KATARZYNA GÓRAK-SOSNOWSKA & JOANNA SOZAŃSKA

Abstract

In this chapter we analyse the building blocks of Polish Islamophobia, and how Islamophobia plays out in the case of Polish youth. We start by drafting a profile of young Poles and the factors that shape their identity, including political views (strongly polarised, with a significant share of young people voting for a far-right nationalist party), patriotism (including so-called 'banal patriotism'), religious identities and attitudes towards the European Union (EU). We then analyse the building blocks of Islamophobia, i.e., how and by which factors anti-Muslim attitudes are shaped. We focus on (a) teaching practices in Polish schools including the role of religious education and its representations of Islam, (b) types of information about Islam and Muslims that pupils might acquire and (c) the role of social media in demonising the Muslim Other. This study is informed by published studies, including public opinion research with Polish youth, school curricula and the authors' own experiences as teachers and trainers of inter-cultural education in Polish schools.

Keywords: Islamophobia, youth, Poland, monocultural school, right-wing, social media

Context of the Study

Within the EU context, Islamophobia in Poland stands out for three reasons. First, it drives on an empty tank, as Muslims represent only 0.1 per cent of the Polish population, and are hardly visible in the public sphere. Second, despite their marginal numbers, Muslims are a prominent 'issue' on the political agenda. Fear and anger appeals related to Muslims have brought certain political parties significant political gains. Third, it seems that Polish Islamophobia is related to perceptions of the EU and of Poland's position within the EU. On the one hand, Poland borrows Islamophobic narratives to feel included in the core of the EU; on the other, it expands this narrative with a theme of rescuing the rest of the continent from a so-called 'Islamic invasion' (Balicki, 2021).

When it comes to Polish youth, the picture gets more complicated. While, in general, younger people are less Islamophobic than older people, it seems that young people in Poland are particularly prone to anti-Muslim attitudes. Young Poles are more inclined to believe that Islam causes danger (59 per cent of people aged 18–24 support this claim, compared to 37 per cent of people aged over 65; CBOS, 2015), they have higher levels of anti-Islamic prejudice and are more prone to accepting Islamophobic hate speech (Stefaniak, 2015).

In this chapter we aim to explain this phenomenon by analysing the building blocks of Islamophobia in Poland, and how Islamophobia plays out in the case of Polish youth in society, education and discourse. We start by drafting a profile of young Poles and the factors that shape their identity. We then analyse the building blocks of Islamophobia, i.e., how and by which factors anti-Muslim attitudes are shaped. We focus on three factors: the ways in which Polish national identity is constructed and consumed, the role of school and religious education and the influence of social media.

It is critical to note that it is impossible to present the complexity of contemporary Polish youth in a single picture. The younger population of Poland is undergoing various changes. Rather than trying to present generalised conclusions and interpretations of what Polish youth is and is not, we focus on what might trigger Islamophobia among young Poles.

Polish Youth: Apolitical, Radical or Maybe Just Complex?

Almost two decades ago, Krystyna Szafraniec (2005) observed that Polish youth has found itself between the deficiencies of a post-Socialist society and the lures of liberal capitalism, a situation that resulted in a peculiar collage of elements from different eras and social orders. On the one hand, this situation provided young people with a vast pool of options to choose from; on the other, it brought significant risks, and made young people vulnerable to challenges. Szafraniec claims that, in a way, these challenges and vulnerabilities can be compared to those of the so-called 'lost generation' in the West. At the same time, Polish youth has been politically inactive, a characteristic that has been attributed either to young people's priorities, which were more about 'everyday' matters like building a career, or to their discontent with politics and what it can offer (Kornacka, 2012).

The current picture is even more complex. Polish youth – generations 'Y' and 'Z' – are still apolitical, while simultaneously holding more right-wing views. The proportion of young people who reported having absolutely no interest in politics was about 25 per cent in 2018 as well as in 2003 (Badora et al., 2019). Similarly, the proportion of youth reporting leftist or rightist political views (10–12 per cent for the left, 14–15 per cent for the right) has been fairly constant from 2003 to 2018. At the same time, the proportion of young people unable to decide whether they like any political party at all is at its highest ever (38 per cent in 2018, compared to 17 per cent in 2003), and less than 25 per cent of young Poles report liking any of the existing political parties (Badora et al., 2019).

Simultaneously, many young Poles turn to right-wing parties that are often beyond the traditional right of the political scene. Among politically interested youth, right-wing conservative views are currently prevalent. In addition, the number of supporters of radical movements has increased. Millennials now make up the core of supporters of radical movements. A possible reason for that increase is the new generations' participation in the political scene. Another possible explanation lies in global processes, such as the rise of right-wing and populist parties and movements worldwide (Messyasz, 2015).

Right-wing and populist parties started to consolidate support among young Poles during the 2014 European Parliament election campaign. Interestingly, the campaigns of the right-wing and populist parties, including Janusz Korwin-Mikke's New Right-Wing Congress, and the National Movement, was based on anti-EU rhetoric. The New Right-Wing Congress has built its campaign around the negation of the EU institutions. It was supported by a Eurosceptic electorate that included many young Poles (aged 18–25). Jakubowski (2016) attributes the increased support for Eurosceptic movements among young Poles to the economic and political crisis of the EU, as well as to the social crisis related to increased migration from the Middle East and North Africa.

The attraction of young Poles to right-wing politics is visible in the election results: parties on the right of the political spectrum have received significantly higher shares of votes among young people compared to the general popula-tion. According to a 2019 opinion poll for the Konrad Adenauer Stiftung (KAS), conducted just before the parliamentary elections, the right-wing nationalist party Confederation Liberty and Independence (Konfederacja) was supported by 20.4 per cent of young Poles, and was the third most popular party, just 4.7 percent points behind the ruling Law and Justice party (KAS,

2019). However, among the general population, more than 43 per cent supported Law and Justice, while only 6.8 per cent supported Konfederacja. This confirms Głowacki's (2017) insight that, although young Poles in general are not more radical in their political views than the overall population, it is due to the indifference of the majority. Ilona Kość (2017) indicated that the lack of interest and political involvement among Polish youth is related to the lack of shaping civil society attitudes among them, e.g., young Poles learn about democracy in school. At the same time, a significant share of the young Poles identifies with ultra-right political parties and their nationalistic, Eurosceptic and nativist views.

Nativism and the Idea of Polishness

In 2016, one year after the conservative Law and Justice Party came into power again, the WiseEuropa think tank published a study on the troubled relation of Poland with the EU (Balcer et al., 2016). The authors predicted the end of consensus between Poland and the EU, based on strong integration, stability of Poland in the EU (except for the mere support of Polish membership in the EU, which is declarative and does not mean a lot). Apparently, they were correct. They had related the end of consensus to the polarisation of Polish society between openness (supporting post-materialistic values) and closedness (idealising the own nation, material values and traditionalism).

One of the backbones of the 'closed' position is nativism, i.e., a desire to preserve one's own culture through affirmation and stressing its uniqueness. Polish ethnic and religious homogeneity makes it particularly prone to defining national identity in a 'closed' manner, by stressing ethnic and religious boundaries between 'us' and 'them'.

Furthermore, a new trend has emerged that combines a gradual shift towards conservatism with consumerism. As Nowicka-Franczak (2016) argues, this consumer patriotism manifests itself as

> not broadening one's knowledge of history and cultivating civic attitudes but rather making national symbolism an attractive product and lifestyle marker. And wearing cool t-shirts with participants of the Warsaw Uprising often leads to supporting those parties and movements which wear the word 'nation' on their sleeve.

As a matter of fact, 35 per cent of Polish youth wear patriotic clothes at least sometimes (Badora et al., 2019). To some young Poles, wearing clothes with national symbols means identifying with the social group (to which they belong or aspire to belong) and emphasising their political views. However, the lines between patriotism and nationalism are blurred.

Poland's shift to the 'closed' attitude towards the EU has been visible in a semi-peripheral rebellion against EU values and policies. After Poland joined the EU in 2004, Poles used to be the biggest supporters of EU politics. While they still report high levels of support for the EU, the content of this support brings in a wider picture. Asked about what the main assets of the EU are, Poles have most frequently pointed to the standard of living enjoyed by EU citizens (35 per cent, compared to the EU average of 20 per cent). The economic, industrial and trading power of the EU ranked second (27 per cent, compared to 28 per cent). The values considered the most important by EU citizens – respect for democracy, human rights and the rule of law – ranked fourth for Poles (21 per cent, compared to 31 per cent; EC, 2019). It seems therefore that Poles cherish the EU mostly for the economic benefits it brings, rather than for common European values.

Interestingly, young Poles are more Eurosceptic than their Western European counterparts. According to an IPSOS survey from 2016, 27 per cent of the youngest respondents (aged 18–29) would like Poland to leave the EU, compared to a national average of 16 per cent (Pacewicz, 2016). By 2018 only 36 per cent of the youngest respondents were in favour of integration, while 42 per cent opted for limiting cooperation to economic affairs only, and 18 per cent wanted to leave the EU altogether (Pacewicz, 2018). Furthermore, the youngest adults were the ones who were most against accepting refugees,[1] even though the range of narratives used to justify their negative attitudes was very complex and diverse. In fact, as Hall and Mikulska-Jolles (2016) point out, negative attitudes towards refugees do not exist on their own. Instead, they reflect different cognitive identity structures, including gender, national, ethnic and religious identity, and power relations. 'Europe' and 'Muslims' have become the representatives of the 'Other'.

It would be naive to say this is a comprehensive picture of Polish youth today, as many young Poles enjoy the benefits that the EU membership brings. At the same time, there is a significant segment of young people who are favourable to the right wing of the political scene, and far less so when it comes to the idea of the EU, or accepting refugees, although these two seem to be interlinked. During a series of open lectures we conducted about Muslims in Europe and terrorism motivated by radical Islamism, some attendees would state that the EU is overrated, that Poland would do better on its own or that they would prefer to die fighting for their values (thus embracing the possibility of war). This illustrates a striking shift away from older generations' longing to become a part of the EU, and appreciating being a part of it. This shift has been observed by Nowicka-Franczak (2016) while studying the relative absence of young people in the demonstrations in support of independent judiciary or civil rights that started to take place soon after the Law and Justice Party began to change the political system of the country.

Nativism, which is one of the building blocks of the Polish attitude of 'closedness', provides a fertile ground for Islamophobic narratives for three reasons. First, Poland has been religiously (Catholic) and ethnically (native Polish) monolithic for a long time. It is hard to fit into such a concept if one is a Muslim or a refugee. Second, rebellion against the EU is related to opposition against Islam/Muslims and refugees (categories often used interchangeably). The EU is criticised for its multi-culturalism – seen as moral decay – and for its ineffectiveness in dealing with refugees. Poland is positioned as smarter and more powerful (because it has not accepted Muslim migrants or refugees), yet in danger of possible Islamisation. This imagined danger is a tool to mobilise cultural capital against the Muslim Other (Bobako, 2017). As a matter of fact, Poland has not been directly affected by the refugee crisis that started in 2015, not only because of its political stance, but also because it is economically and socially less attractive than the older EU member states.

Teaching about Other Cultures in a Monocultural School

In 2018 one of the authors visited Polish schools with a series of open lectures and seminars about contemporary Islam and Muslims. While at these schools, she had numerous opportunities to talk to teachers and to experience cultural school activities first-hand. In some schools 'days of nations' or 'international days' were organised – events during which a class group would present a particular country through dress, arts or cuisine to other classes. In some cases, countries' cultures were presented in an essentialised manner; in others, they were presented in sophisticated, creative and funny ways. However, it was particularly striking that several classes chose to represent Polish culture. According to the teachers, this has been a relatively recent phenomenon. Only a couple of years earlier all classes had naturally been choosing assignments about other nations – the more exotic, the better. Today, multiple classes will often compete for 'Polish culture', or several Polish culture presentations will be organised at a single school (along with several non-Polish culture presentations). While there is nothing wrong with presenting one's own culture, the shift is striking as these kinds of events were traditionally meant to be a tool for learning about other cultures.

Polish schools have witnessed significant changes in inter-cultural education in general. Markowska-Manista (2019, p. 83) stresses that

> the Polish system of education operated without the confrontation with multiculturalism (unlike Western European countries). Additionally, due to a limited presence of foreigners in Poland, schools and other educational institutions rarely faced problems connected with [sic] the implementation of intercultural education, the construction of intercultural relations, solving culture-based conflicts and cooperation on the contact point of cultures from outside the Central and Eastern European cultural circle.

After Poland became a member of the EU, inter-cultural education was introduced on a wider scale, and was made prevalent in the curriculum. While still delivered in the absence of 'cultural Others' (Badowska, 2015), and therefore sometimes in essentialist terms, it was a way to make pupils familiar with cultural differences. In other words, this was education related more to learning about other cultures and tolerating them, rather than learning to live together (Kitlińska-Król, 2013). Although non-existent, cultural diversity was to some extent celebrated and perceived as an important marker of the Polish EU membership (as the old EU member states were multi-cultural). Classes and activities aimed at inter-cultural education were conducted by non-governmental organisations (NGOs) and offered by higher education institutions as majors. Additionally, thanks to the EU programmes, international students have had a possibility to engage in inter-cultural contacts (within their optional inter-cultural classes) with students in Polish schools.

The fascination with other cultures has faded away for several reasons. One was practical: knowledge about other cultures did not necessarily translate into skills that would advance one's career. Poland has remained a monocultural country, and most of the 'cultural Others' have been coming from neighbouring countries rather than from far away. Another reason is the political shift that manifests itself in defining Poland in narrow nationalistic terms. This trend is visible in the new curricula at the Polish schools. In sum, there is neither the will nor the way to provide inter-cultural education.

Polish pupils can learn about other cultures mostly in Polish literature and language, geography and civics classes. This does not leave much space to learn about Islam or Muslims. The body of knowledge is very fragmented, and Islam is often essentialised through formulation (e.g., the geography curriculum includes a topic on the 'causes and consequences of terrorism, relations between Western and Islamic civilisation', which seems to provide an explanation for global terrorism). The case of history classes is even more troublesome, as these seem to serve the purpose of teaching nationalism, while many history teachers seem to take these nationalist representations for granted (Jaskułowski & Surmiak, 2017). Furthermore, teachers believe that they should reinforce the nationalist discourse in pupils, and do not distinguish between history as a science and as a nationalising tool (Jaskułowski et al., 2018).

The case of religious education is even more obvious. Despite its name, it focuses on teaching one set of religious beliefs (the one that the pupils adhere to) rather than knowledge about different religious traditions. The number of religion classes in the whole curriculum exceeds the time provided for learning biology or geography, and pupils learn only about their own religious beliefs. This means they are religiously illiterate: ignorant about other religious traditions (Moore, 2007). This context does not leave much room for teaching about other religions, including Islam. What is more, it seems that many priests hold negative or even extreme attitudes towards Islam, such as sympathising with banning this religion (Pędziwiatr, 2018).

In fact, the Polish education system provides a favourable context for increased Islamophobia among young people. First, it has never managed to effectively teach about other cultures. One could argue this is due to the marginal presence of 'cultural Others' in Poland (especially of visible or 'distant cultural Others'). Why would one teach about someone who is not even there? However, this approach deprives pupils of inter-cultural competences, which are among the core competencies of global citizenship (Deardorff, 2006). While inter-cultural competences include culture-specific knowledge, openness and respect for other cultures, they also allow for cultural self-awareness.

Second, pupils get a rather one-sided, nationalistic image of their own culture as it is delivered during history classes. What is more, the idea of Polishness is coined around an ethno-nationalistic perspective and set of values, without much space left for Others. The third building block is interlinked with the second one, as the nationalist discourse is often embedded in a religious framework, and this relation is incredibly durable (Hildebrandt-Wypych, 2017). Again, the way in which religious education is devised and (often) delivered in Poland, does not leave much space for learning about other religions. To summarise, Polish schools rarely provide their students with inter-cultural understanding, or skills related to living together and respecting diversity. The two causes of that situation are insufficient competences of teachers and, more importantly, the systemic approach to education by the Polish authorities.

Spreading Islamophobia through Social Media

Cyberbullying and 'cultures of offence' have become one of the greatest challenges related to the use of the Internet. The problem of hate speech in virtual spaces predominantly affects young people: about 40 per cent of young Poles (14–17 years old) encounter hate speech on the Internet. This often results in anxiety and depression (Włodarczyk, 2014). Unlike adults, young Poles encounter hate speech predominantly online (95.6 per cent, compared to just 54.3 per cent of adults; Wieniawski et al., 2017). However, the Internet is not only the most popular source of hate speech for young people, but also their most important source of information.

Muslims are one of the most popular targets of online hate speech; only refugees and sexual minorities are targeted more often (Wieniawski et al., 2017). In fact, 80 per cent of young Poles have encountered hate speech directed at Muslims on the Internet, compared to about 30 per cent on TV, on the street or during a discussion (Wieniawski et al., 2017). Furthermore, Muslims are also presented online in the most bizarre ways. As such, they are not only essentialised, but also dehumanised. Strong negative stereotypes and media narratives (Leszczuk-Fiedziukiewicz, 2019), combined with marginal opportunities for contact with Muslims, makes many Poles prone to believing this kind of misinformation, or sharing it without further reflection (Górak-Sosnowska, 2016).

The Internet has become a pool of anti-Muslim narratives and hate speech since the political shift of 2015 and the European refugee crisis. Even though there was less hate against Muslims and refugees in the election campaign of 2019 compared to that of 2015, it was still present and affecting young generations (Mikulska-Jolles, 2020). Since 2015, the Polish government has allowed hate speech directed against particular social groups (women's movements, the lesbian, gay, bisexual, transgender/transsexual plus (LGBT+) community, migrants, Muslims). As a result, Polish society in general, and young people in particular, have become less sensitive to hate speech: hate speech directed at certain minorities is no longer considered hate speech. In the case of Muslims, the shift has been most striking, with a 25 per cent drop in the number of people who believe that hate speech addressed at Muslims is indeed hate speech (Wieniawski et al., 2017). Interestingly, young males are the least prone to defining hate speech as it is. Only 27 per cent of them believe that hate speech towards Muslims is offensive, compared to 41 per cent of adult males and 45–48 per cent of females (Wieniawski et al., 2017).

The Internet seems to be a significant building block of Islamophobic attitudes among young Poles. It is the space where Islamophobic content is produced, narrated and manipulated. Furthermore, it is the biggest resource of Islamophobic content available to young people. At the same time, it is often the most important source of news and knowledge. According to Wieniawski et al. (2017), there is a correlation between exposure to hate speech and prejudice in the case of the most stigmatised minority groups. However, among young Poles the strongest correlation occurs in the case of Muslims. In other words, young Poles who encounter hate speech against Muslims are more reluctant to collaborate with Muslims, or accept a Muslim as a friend or neighbour.

Conclusion

In this chapter we have tried to identify the factors behind the higher levels of Islamophobia among young Poles compared to the general population of Poland. Regardless of age, negative attitudes towards Islam and Muslims are widespread in Poland, despite the marginal presence of Muslims, or any realistic assessment of immigration flows from Muslim majority countries. In this respect Poland is similar to the other Visegrad countries (Czech Republic, Hungary and Slovakia), which are also culturally homogeneous – either Slavic or Finno-Ugric. Furthermore, as most of these countries have no history or experience of colonising,[2] postcolonial reflection is not that present in the public debate. What is present is the post-Soviet legacy – which might be considered an experience of being colonised – that has shaped all four Visegrad states both economically and socially.

In the case of Poland and Hungary, an additional element that has tremendously impacted perceptions of Muslims is the political shift to the right, and the dominance of populist, conservative and nationalistic governments that have not only influenced national media but also produced and maintained anti-Muslim discourses (Górak-Sosnowska & Molodikova, 2018). While Hungary has been affected by refugees travelling across Europe, Poland has not. These negative discourses are therefore not supported by any real events. They are nothing but a tool to advance a political agenda. Islam and Muslims have become a convenient enemy, as Poles have very limited contact with either, and little opportunity to counter-check negative narratives. This situation is exacerbated by their rather superficial and essentialised knowledge of Islam and Muslims.

The case of the Polish youth is even more complex due to generational changes that make the picture less coherent. Despite that, it is possible to identify several building blocks of Islamophobia that make Polish youth more prone to anti-Muslim narratives and attitudes than the general Polish population.

The first block is political, and is related to the ways in which Polish national identity is constructed and narrated as antagonistic to the Muslim enemy. In this regard Polish youth sometimes consume patriotism without any deeper reflection. At the same time – not having experienced everyday reality before Poland's accession to the EU – they are much more sceptical of the Polish EU membership, which is (mis)used by local populist political parties. The general Polish population is less prone to consuming patriotism in a similar manner as Polish youth, and to sharing its Europscepticism, as older generations have direct experiences with living inside as well as outside of the EU.

The second building block of Islamophobia are schools and the education system. While the general Polish population has only partial knowledge about other cultures, Islam in particular, Polish schools do not alleviate the problem, as they tend to provide very limited, often biased or essentialised education about Islam or Muslims. Furthermore, the school curriculum is currently shifting from teaching history to teaching nationalism. In the same manner, religious instruction teaches religious practice instead of teaching about different religions.

The third building block are social media, where young people can encounter substantial amounts of anti-Islamic content both in terms of news (including fake news) and hate speech. At the same time, social media are among the most important information sources of for young people, in Poland and elsewhere. In fact, the Internet is where Polish youth most frequently encounter Islamophobic hate speech. Furthermore, it seems that many young Poles, especially males, are inclined to accept Islamophobic hate speech.

These three building blocks propose an explanation for the higher levels of Islamophobia among young Poles, but only a partial one. As young Poles' political preferences show, the picture is complex and far from coherent. With the majority of young Poles holding apolitical attitudes and being removed from any political movement, and a significant minority holding right-wing views, our building blocks can begin to explain the occurrences of certain activities or behaviours, rather than paint a comprehensive picture of contemporary Polish youth. Furthermore, because it is impossible to draw one single profile of Polish youth, it is necessary to consider the generational gap that, by default, makes older Poles unable to fully comprehend what young Poles really think.

Notes

1.   This attitude is shared by young people in the other Visegrad countries (Czech Republic, Hungary and Slovakia). When asked about accepting refugees, vast majorities of young Germans and Austrians were in favour (73 per cent and 61 per cent), unlike young people from the Visegrad countries (24 per cent to 29 per cent in favour; Łada & Schöler, 2017).
2.   While some scholars consider these expansions as a kind of colonialism, it is not one in the classical sense, nor is it perceived as such by the mainstream public (despite Polish colonial aspirations; Puchalski 2022).

References

Badora, B., Głowacki, A., & Hermann, M. (2019). Młodzież o polityce i demokracji [Youth on politics and democracy]. In M. Grabowska & M. Gwiazda (Eds.), *Młodzież 2018* (pp. 99-137). CBOS.

Badowska, M. (2015). Różnorodność kulturowa uczniów wyzwaniem dla współczesnej szkoły [Students' cultural diversity as a challenge for the school of today]. *Kultura-Społeczeństwo-Edukacja, 7*(1), 179–192. https://doi.org/10.14746/kse.2015.1.12

Balcer, A., Buras, P., Gromadzki, G., & Smolar E. (2016). *Polacy wobec UE: koniec konsensusu* [Poles towards the EU: The end of consensus]. Fundacja im. Stefana Batorego.

Balicki, J. (2021). *Obrona „Chrześcijańskiej Europy" przed „Inwazją Islamu"?: Populistyczny dyskurs polityczno-religijny w Polsce w kontekście kryzysu migracyjnego w UE* [Defending 'Christian Europe' against the 'Islamic Invasion'?: Populist political-religious discourse in Poland in the context of the EU migration crisis]. Wydawnictwo Naukowe UKSW.

Bobako, M. (2017). *Islamofobia jako technologia władzy. Studium z antropologii politycznej* [Islamophobia as a technology of power. A study on political anthropology]. Universitas. https://doi.org/10.15804/so2018112

CBOS (2015). *Postawy wobec islamu i muzułmanów* [Attitudes towards Islam and Muslims]. (Report No. 37/2015). Fundacja Centrum Badania Opinii Społecznej.

Deardorff, D. (2006). The identification and assessment of intercultural competence as a student outcome of internationalization at institutions of higher education in the United States. *Journal of Studies in International Education, 10,* 241–266.

European Commission (EC). (2019). *Special Eurobarometer 486: Europeans in 2019.* Directorate-General for Communication. https://data.europa.eu/data/datasets/s2225_91_2_486_eng?locale=en

Głowacki, A. (2017). *Czy młodzi Polacy są prawicowi? Komunikat z badań nr 102/2017* [Are young Poles right-wing? Research Paper No. 102/2017]. CBOS.

Górak-Sosnowska, K. (2016). Islamophobia without Muslims? The case of Poland. *Journal of Muslims in Europe, 5,* 190–204.

Górak-Sosnowska, K., & Molodikova, I. (2018). 'Polish, Hungarian, cousins be'. Comparative discourse on Muslims and refugee crisis in Europe. *Rocznik Instytutu Europy Środkowo-Wschodniej* [Yearbook of the Institute of Central and Eastern Europe], *16*(5), 141–158.

Hall, D. & Mikulska-Jolles, A. (2016). *Uprzedzenia, strach, czy niewiedza? Młodzi Polacy o powodach niechęci do przyjmowania uchodźców* [Prejudice, fear or ignorance? Young Poles on the reasons for reluctance to accept refugees]. Stowarzyszenie Interwencji Prawnej.

Hildebrandt-Wypych, D. (2017). Religious nation or national religion: Poland's heroes and the (re)construction of national identity in history textbooks. In J. Zajda, T. Tsyrlina-Spady, & M. Lovorn (Eds.), *Globalisation and historiography of national leaders* (p. 105). Springer.

Jakubowski, P. (2016). Kampania wyborcza do Parlamentu Europejskiego w 2014 roku w Polsce – analiza strategii i taktyk wyborczych [Election campaign to the European Parliament in 2014 in Poland – analysis of electoral strategies and tactics]. *Prawo i polityka, 7*, 7–29.

Jaskułowski, K., Majewski, P., & Surmiak, A. (2018). Teaching the nation: History and nationalism in Polish school history education. *British Journal of Sociology of Education, 39*(1), 77–91.

Jaskułowski, K., & Surmiak, A. (2017). Teaching history, teaching nationalism: A qualitative study of history teachers in a Polish post-industrial town. *Critical Studies in Education, 58*(1), 36–51.

Kitlińska-Król, M. (2013). Nauczyciele i edukacja międzykulturowa [Teachers and intercultural education]. *Chowanna, 2*, 275–288.

Konrad Adenauer Stiftung (KAS). (2019). *Polityczny portret młodych Polaków w 2019 roku. Raport z badania* [The political portrait of young Poles in 2019. Survey report]. Konrad Adenauer Stiftung.

Kornacka, M. (2012). (Nie)uczestnictwo młodzieży w życiu politycznym Polski po 1989 roku. Wpływ medialnych kampanii społecznych na aktywność wyborczą młodych Polaków [(Non-) participation of youth in the Polish political sphere after 1989. The influence of social media campaigns on the electoral activity of young Poles]. In A. Turska-Kawa (Ed.), *Polityka w opinii młodych. Idee – instytucje – obywatele* [Politics in the opinion of youth. Ideas – institutions – citizens] (pp. 121–137). Uniwersytet Śląski.

Kość, I. (2017). *Między obojętnością a zaangażowaniem. Źródła dylematów decyzji wyborczych studentów* [Between indifference and involvement. The sources of students' electoral decisions]. Wydawnictwo Naukowe Uniwersytetu Szczecińskiego.

Łada, A., & Schöler, G. (2017). *Love it, leave it or change it? Junge Europäer in Mittel- und Osteuropa bekennen sich zur EU, sehen aber Notwendigkeit der Reformen* [Young Europeans in Central and Eastern Europe are committed to the EU, but see a need for reform]. Bertelsmann Stiftung. https://www.bertelsmann-stiftung.de/en/publications/publication/did/flashlight-europe-022017-love-it-leave-it-or-change-it

Leszczuk-Fiedziukiewicz, A. (2019). Czy hejt i mowa nienawiści staną się normą? Społeczne uwarunkowania zachowań dewiacyjnych w Internecie [Will hate speech become the standard? Social determinants of deviant behavior on the Internet]. *Media – Kultura – Komunikacja Społeczna, 3*(14), 99–117.

Markowska-Manista, U. (2019). Migrant and refugee children in Polish schools in the face of social transformation. In C. Maier-Höfer (Ed.), *Die Vielfalt der Kindheit(en) und die Rechte der Kinder in der Gegenwart* (pp. 79–100). Springer.

Messyasz, K. (2015). *Postawy polityczne młodzieży polskiej w świetle adan empirycznych* [Political attitudes of Polish youth in the light of empirical studies]. Katedra Socjologii Polityki i Moralności, Wydział Ekonomiczno-Socjologiczny, Uniwersytet Łódzki.

Mikulska-Jolles, A. (2020). *Fake newsy i dezinformacja w kampaniach wyborczych w Polsce w 2019 roku – raport z obserwacji* [Fake news and disinformation in Poland's 2019 election campaigns – an observation report]. Helsińska Fundacja Praw Człowieka.

Moore, D. (2007). *Overcoming religious illiteracy. A cultural studies approach to the study of religion in secondary education.* Palgrave Macmillan.

Nowicka-Franczak, M. (2016). *Committee for the Defense of Democracy in Poland: Rebellion of the 'Beneficiaries of the Transformation'? Tr@nsit online.* Vienna: Institut für die Wissenschaften vom Menschen. https://www.iwm.at/transit-online/committee-for-the-defense-of-democracy-in-poland-rebellion-of-the-beneficiaries-of-the-transformation/

Pacewicz, P. (2016, June 29). Polexit? Nie! 77 proc. Polek i Polaków wolałoby zostać w Unii [Polexit? No! 77 percent of Poles would prefer to stay in the EU]. *OKO.press*. https://oko. press/polexit-nie/

Pacewicz, P. (2018, December 28). 51 proc. Polaków chce integracji UE i wzmocnienia KE, a tylko 35 \proc. Europy Kaczyńskiego i Orbana [51 percent of Poles would like EU integration and strengthening of EC, while only 35 percent want Kaczynski's and Orban's Europe]. *OKO.press*. https://oko.press/51-proc-polakow-chce-integracji-ue-i-wzmocnienia-ke-a-tylko-35-proc-europy-kaczynskiego-i-orbana/

Pędziwiatr, K. (2018). The catholic church in Poland on Muslims and Islam. *Patterns of Prejudice*, 52(5), 461–478. doi: 10.1080/0031322X.2018.1495376

Puchalski, P. (2022). *Poland in a colonial world order. Adjustments and aspirations, 1918–1939*. Routledge.

Stefaniak, A. (2015). *Postrzeganie muzułmanów w Polsce: Raport z badania sondażowego*. [Perceptions of Muslims in Poland: A survey report]. Centrum Badań nad Uprzedzeniami.

Szafraniec, K. (2005). 'Porzucona generacja' – polska młodzież wobec wyzwań społeczeństwa ryzyka ['The abandoned generation'. Polish youth towards the challenges of the risk society]. In M. Dziemianowicz, B. Gołębniak, & R. Kwaśnica (Eds.), *Przetrwanie i rozwój jako niezbywalne powinności wychowania* [Sustainability and growth as inalienable duties of education]. Wydawnictwo Naukowe DSWE TWP.

Wieniawski, M., Hansen, K., Bilewicz, M., Soral, W., Świderska, A., & Bulska, D. (2017). *Mowa nienawiści, mowa propagandy. Raport z badania przemocy werbalnej wobec grup mniejszościowych* [Hate speech, propaganda speech. A research report on verbal violence against minority groups]. Fundacja im. Stefana Batorego.

Włodarczyk J. (2014). Mowa nienawiści w Internecie w doświadczeniu polskiej młodzieży. Dziecko krzywdzone [Hate speech on the Internet as experienced by Polish youth. A child abused]. *Teoria, badania, praktyka*, 13(2), 122–158.

4

THE POLITICAL AND INTELLECTUAL DISCOURSE ON ISLAM AND MUSLIMS IN FLANDERS

ALEXANDER VAN LEUVEN, STEFAN MERTENS, LEEN D'HAENENS & ABDELWAHED MEKKI-BERRADA

Abstract

Over the last decade, the debate on the position of Islam in society has been quite fierce in Flanders, Belgium. This chapter explores the argumentations of the intellectuals inspiring the debate. Through the analysis of claims related to social institutions in the works of 19 authors, nine of whom represent centrist and right-wing politicians and so-called 'free thinkers' who take a rather *'culturalist' perspective* on the societal position of Islam, while the remaining ten, who are mostly academics and practicing or cultural Muslims themselves, take a more *social stance*. The former group thinks in terms of economised demographics, whereas the latter is more concerned with thoroughly explaining why the former group is 'culturalist' and often Islamophobic. Furthermore, the position of Islam is debated in terms of problems it allegedly poses. For the 'culturalist' group, these problems are due to an assumed latent Islamist totalitarianism, oppression of women and absence of Enlightenment in Islam. The 'social' group focuses strongly on the documented *othering* practice in the 'culturalists'' problematising and makes counterarguments based on both empirical data and personal experiences. Both groups share concerns about the employment rate of the Muslim demographic, although they explain it differently and in line with their own perspectives. Finally, the intellectuals under study agree on the fact that these tensions are not sustainable for Flemish society as they could lead to more polarisation and greater intolerance.

Keywords: anti-Muslim sentiment, anti-Muslim prejudice, racism, Islamophobia, Flanders, media

Aims and Scope

One of the features of a global society is that it promotes migration. How-ever, typical right-wing discourse calls for immigration to be reduced. An important consequence of this demographic trend towards an immigration society (Loobuyck & Jacobs, 2006) is that Flanders has increasingly become a meeting place for people of many different socio-cultural and religious backgrounds. That is why some authors tend to characterise Belgium as a diverse society: the phenomenon currently described in Flanders as an 'immigration movement' is already 60 years old. In time migration has become less of a government-sponsored international phenomenon, yet migrants have kept coming from various places, including Islamic countries. According to the American Pew Research Center (2017), 7.6 per cent of the Belgian population are Muslims. Belgian Muslims mostly live in Brussels (24.6 per cent of the city's population). In Flanders, 5.7 per cent of the population are Muslims, while in Wallonia, 5.3 per cent are Muslims. Population estimates predict that by 2050 the number of Muslims in Belgium will have risen to 15.1 per cent of the population (Pew Research Center, 2017). This growth of the Muslim population warrants increasing public and media interest. However, observers of the public debate in Flanders point out that negative media attention towards Islam has increased more than might be explained by demography. Sami Zemni (2009, p. 10) notes that we are 'immersed in the delusion that Islam is our country's biggest problem'.

This turn of events is not a purely Flemish or Belgian phenomenon, as it is linked to at least two major political trends of recent years. On the one hand, there is an increasing focus on national security and crime in many European countries, mostly driven by right-wing politicians, who tend to pass harsh judgement on Islam and Muslims. On the other hand, the image of Islam is also influenced by events in the Arab world, as well as an increasing characterisation of it as an enemy of the West. This characterisation was, of course, facilitated by political reactions to the 9/11 terrorist attacks.

To reconstruct the political and intellectual debate in Flanders, we read 20 books of which we present a synthesis in this chapter. These books were written by Flemish politicians and academics holding either left-wing, centrist or right-wing positions. Filip Dewinter (2019) is a far-right Flemish politician. On the right of the political spectrum, we also read books by language scholar and philosopher Wim Van Rooy (2015), as well as independent liberal politician Jean-Marie Dedecker (2009) and journalist Arthur van Amerongen (2015). We also read books by classic liberal politician Gwendolyn Rutten (2017), Christian Democratic politicians Koen Geens (2018) and Hendrik Bogaert

(2017), and Flemish-nationalist politician Bart De Wever (2019). Rutten, Geens, Bogaert and De Wever could be called the centrist voices in the debate. Darya Safai (2018) is a member of N-VA (Flemish-nationalist party). She is a dentist, Iranian refugee and an experienced expert. A third group of authors are political and social science authors, who are also experienced experts. These authors include Belgo-Tunisian political scientist and Middle East scholar Sami Zemni (2009), activist, fashion designer and entrepreneur Rachida Aziz (2017), former professor of political science and diplomat Bilal Benyaich (2013), politician Dyab Abou Jahjah (2016), lawyer Rachida Lamrabet (2017), anthropologist Nadia Fadil (2017) and political scientist Naima Charkaoui (2019). While not of an immigrant background, lecturer in new media and politics Ico Maly (2009), human rights scholar Eva Brems (2015), media specialist Kathleen De Ridder (2010) and anthropologist Martijn de Koning (2019) write from a similar perspective.

We analyse the debate around five recurring themes. The first one is the frequently raised issue of the proportionately lower labour market participation of people with a migration background, and their problematic integration in society. Some see this as a result of discrimination, while others point to perceived Islamic characteristics. A second issue is whether Islamist fundamentalism is a marginal phenomenon. A third theme focuses on the strategic exaggeration of (violent) extremism by some participants in the Islam debate. A fourth theme is the hijab or head scarf, and its various interpretations that feed the debate on Islam. Our fifth theme concerns benchmarks that can be put forward as shared values, such as the values of the Enlightenment.

Cultural and Social Explanations of Problematised Integration and Economic Inequality

Surveys (Van de Velden & Roelens, 2017) show that Flemings with a migration background are overrepresented in unemployment figures. Stumbling blocks to participation in the labour market include an often low level of education, and lack of knowledge of Dutch. According to the left-wing position, responsibility lies primarily with employers, who systematically shun workers with a non-Western appearance due to a more or less conscious Western superiority thinking. An unfamiliar name or a darker skin tone are a barrier to gaining a job interview. Culturalisation of the main causes of unemployment among people with a migration background also contributes to discrimination according to Aziz (2017), Charkaoui (2019), Lamrabet (2017) and Zemni (2009). Proponents of the 'social' explanation argue that the absence of a vigorous integration policy ensures that people of colour are not included as workers, but systematically and structurally excluded as the 'Other', the Muslim (Aziz, 2017; Lamrabet 2017; Zemni, 2009). In other words, what is at play is an 'othering' process that bars people with a migration background from entering the workforce based on a set of cultural characteristics. The right-wing position focuses on cultural factors (a lower willingness to work) that make Muslims less attractive workers in the eyes of local employers. Wim van Rooy (2015) blames this allegedly flawed work ethic on 'Muslim fatalism'. The 'culturalist' authors also have objections to some cultural and religious motivations Muslims might have, a case in point being men who refuse to work under women, who will not shake hands with their female colleagues or who tend to ignore women altogether. Another right-wing argument points to allegedly too generous welfare policies that tend to perpetuate lower participation in the labour market (Dedecker, 2009).

What is clear here is the different perspective on discrimination. While those in favour of 'social' explanations condemn discrimination based on colour or religion, and call on organisations such as the Belgian Interfederal Centre for Equal Opportunities (Unia) to take on this problem, 'culturalists' see no such discrimination. An example of this is provided by Rachida Lamrabet (2017, p. 52), who lost her job as a UNIA legal counsel after stating in her own name that 'a ban on face veiling is a far-reaching violation of women's rights', and subsequently that the 'human rights framework is universal and it cannot be deployed according to the state of mind of the majority'. According to the 'social' hypothesis, discrimination is the root cause of the lower employment rate of people with a migration background. This trend started in the 1960s and 1970s, when migrant workers were not viewed as workers but as Muslims (Aziz, 2017). It continues to this day with the exclusion of highly talented people of colour (Aziz, 2017; Charkaoui, 2019; Lamrabet, 2017).

However, the 'culturalist' point of view interprets the discrimination phenomenon very differently. First of all, Dedecker (2009) points to a sense of honour in Islam leading to false perceptions of inequality by Muslims' 'respectfulness' between people, which is, according to Dedecker, highly valorised among Muslims, but a negative side-effect of this value might be that people adhering to it too often might interpret negative decisions on the job market as a consequence of a lack of respectfulness. Second, the contention is that minorities, including Muslims, are not actually disadvantaged, but rather privileged, with the 'native' population being subject to reverse discrimination ('putting our own people last'; Van Rooy, 2016, p. 34). Third, discrimination against Muslims is actually recommended (Van Rooy, 2016) because the dangers associated with radical religion must be prevented in every way. 'Culturalists' argue that minorities get unemployment benefits without having to adjust to local culture, and that left-wing 'native' people approve of this.

Another difference lies in the perception of social security and welfare. Proponents of the 'social' explanation view rejection of the migrants' cultures as an excuse to reduce social security benefits. Social protection is being reduced to the detriment of those who desperately need it as the result of an 'us versus them' thinking. A more right-wing view states that social protection actually creates a vicious circle of 'welfare addiction'. Of course, this vicious circle cannot in itself be viewed as a cultural phenomenon since it has also been said to occur among people without a migration background.

Egoism is attributed to the other side by both the followers of the 'social' and the 'cultural' hypotheses. For example, reference can be made to migrant workers who came to Belgium in the 1950s and 1960s (Aziz, 2017). Back then they, their children and grandchildren experienced discrimination, which is recognised politically as a structural fact but ignored in terms of victimisation (Charkaoui, 2019).

In the culturalist hypothesis, those who criticise discrimination are accused of xenophilia – disproportionate concern for 'immigrants', neglect of their own cultural background, etc. Moreover, the 'xenophiles' are presented as condemning discrimination as a way to take the moral high ground, their concern for others as a mere expression of a desire to feel good and comfortable in a 'great equality' social setting (Dedecker, 2009).

In short, the two hypotheses are part of very different discourses. Theory of discourse teaches us that discourse does not only reflect the world: it actively contributes to the production of a social order. This contradicts the commonly held view that words and deeds are two very different things. This debate shows that both sides are aware of the power of words – not so much their own words as those of the other side. Many content analyses show that Muslims are mostly portrayed negatively by the media (Devroe, 2007; Ahmed & Matthes, 2016; Berbers et al., 2016). Conversely, the culturalist view is that the media are all too ready to portray Islamic minorities in a positive light (Van Rooy, 2016).

Yet it appears the media do not reflect diversity in society, which reinforces rejection of the other, for instance among employers. Kathleen De Ridder (2010) points out that the media should play a connecting function in a society where people of different cultural backgrounds are cut off from one another. Journalists need to break out of rigid interpretation frameworks that reflect deep divisions in society.

The Question of a Totalitarian Islam

In addition to the issue of economic inequality, there is a second, constantly recurring theme in the Flemish Islam debate: that of a violent, geopolitical Islam. This is a notion that encourages Western politicians to take anti-Muslim measures. Radicalised Islam has been a hot topic since 2004, when the term was introduced in scientific studies (Fadil, 2017). The totalitarian nature of this Islam, and its implications for Muslims (their freedom of action, their attitude to geopolitical violence), are apparent in crimes committed in the name of Islam, like the Charlie Hebdo and Bataclan terrorist attacks in France, and in crimes committed by far-right terrorists like Anders Breivik in Norway (Mekki-Berrada, 2019). The books we analysed look at the link between Islam, radicalisation and violence. They do not focus on far-right terrorists.

On the far right of the political spectrum, Filip Dewinter (2019, p. 11) states that we are 'at war with Islam', and that Europe is deluding itself with multi-culturalism notions while 'mass immigration' acts as a Trojan Horse for Islam. For Dewinter, Islam is a totalitarian system comparable to Nazism and Communism. Wim Van Rooy (2015) also views Islam as a totalitarian ideology, with Islam and Islamism being synonymous. He also sees Muslims as a homogeneous group when he refers to the umma (community of the faithful) and his interpretation of it: 'Touch one Muslim, touch them all' (Van Rooy, 2015, p. 181). According to him, Muslims have a double discourse: one for the West (more moderate in tone) and one for the faithful. His prediction is that as the numbers of Muslims grow in Western societies, Islamists will make increasingly stringent political demands, their goal being re-Islamisation. The author supports this thesis by citing the current situation in Turkey as an example (Van Rooy, 2015). Sami Zemni (2009) also points to this phenomenon in the Middle East. In Europe, it replaces re-Islamisation with a need for redefinition. Flemish right-liberal politician Jean-Marie Dedecker (2009) sees Muslims as a threat because the theocracy that Islam requires is incompatible with parliamentary democracy. He also takes a keen interest in the failing Belgian migration policy and does not believe in a direct link between poverty and terrorism, noting that no terrorists have come out of Sub-Saharan Africa and Latin America. Former Middle East correspondent Arthur van Amerongen (2015) recounts an 'experiment' that saw him spend a year incognito in the Brussels Marollen district with the aim of getting to know Islam from within. It is clear to him: 'Islamic culture goes hand in hand with social regression' (Van Amerongen, 2015, p. 130). In his quest for spirituality he found, in his own words, 'nothing but intolerance' (p. 161).

In her plea for the preservation of our freedoms and security, liberal politician Gwendolyn Rutten (2017) argues that a modern, rational Islam affords Muslims freedom of action, giving them a chance to openly and unequivocally oppose a minority that is dreaming of sharia and of a Caliphate. This freedom of action against an intolerant Islam that threatens to undermine the rule of law must therefore be defended. According to Rutten (2017), it is time to closely monitor Salafist organisations in Belgium, stem financial flows from the Gulf states, close radical mosques and expel hate preachers from the country.

Islamic fundamentalism is another concept, defined by the Dutch security service AIVD in the 1970s (Fadil, 2017). After the fall of European communism, a new global enemy has been defined (Fadil, 2017; Maly, 2009), but the group that 'Western' people fear most is systematically replaced by radical Islam, with the term 'activist' being reserved for left-wing groups (Fadil, 2017). Flemish-nationalist Bart De Wever (2019) sees Islamic fundamentalism as a backlash against the deconstruction of traditional social relations, the very notion of progress, the belief in rationalism and the loss of familiar and natural communities.

De Wever points to a sore point in Flemish society when stating that it has not managed to form a new 'we' with the Islamic communities that settled in Flanders in the last 60 years. People who were born in Islamic countries, and whose parents were born in Islamic countries, are still seen as immigrants, and would also see themselves as immigrants. 'After half a century we are all too often total strangers to each other who live in an actual apartheid system, with few transcultural connections' (De Wever, 2019, p. 103). Political Islam easily frightens the 'natives': 'People are wondering what is going on in the minds of the many Muslim fellow citizens they "do not know"' (De Wever, 2019, p. 103).

This gap is reinforced by the response of many European Muslims to their actual non-inclusion in society – starting with increased religiosity. De Wever (2019) looks at neighbouring countries and quotes the Dutch social cultural planning agency (SCP), according to which, since the 1980s Islam has been on the rise, and religion plays an increasingly important role: 85 per cent of Dutch Moroccan Muslims see themselves as devout, strictly practicing individuals. Prayer has become increasingly popular, as has going to the mosque and wearing a headscarf. In other Western European countries, we see the same trends.

Political scientist Bilal Benyaich (2013) describes how Islam came to Belgium along with migrant workers – not as a religion, but as a culture. Islamisation did not begin before the 1980s, as can be seen from the clothing worn in shops, restaurants, etc., as well as the presence of alcohol (Benyaich, 2013). He describes how Islam primarily spreads digitally, with an abundance of fatwas and videos about oppressed Muslims online (Benyaich, 2013).

Cultural Muslims feel alienated by this. Rachida Aziz (2017) notes that the alienation felt by guest workers can be ascribed to lack of recognition.

Othering and Strategic Exaggeration in the Flemish Islam Debate

In this section we highlight two themes that are situated at the meta-level. They are the 'elephants in the room', which we will first define and then illustrate. While the social scientists and authors adhering to the 'social' hypothesis find inspiration in their own experience, they also respond to the discourse of other authors – here we swap claims steeped in common sense, authority or emotion, for arguments based on history, logic and law. Analyses as part of the Islam debate pertain to its wider implications, i.e., the place of people of colour in society.

A first othering meta-theme is the ongoing dialectic between the self and the other, where the self is defined based both on its own characteristics and those of the other – that is, those characteristics the self does not possess. This brings us to the second meta-theme: that of strategic exaggeration, in which caricatures are made of the other. Aziz (2017, p. 151) writes that 'the Muslim problem was manufactured in 1981'. Zemni (2009) and Maly (2009) note that debates about Islam are about religion only formally. Substantially they are about Islam and Muslims as a virtual cultural group and their place in Western society. According to Maly (2009) the debate started around the collapse of the Soviet Union, and touches on 'philosophical principles' (Aziz, 2017; Fadil, 2017; Maly, 2009).

We started this literature study with Middle East expert Sami Zemni, who in 2009 took stock of the Islam debate (Zemni, 2009). We finished our study in 2019 with the work of anthropologist Martijn de Koning (2019), who summed up his observations on the Islam debate for the Flemish media platform Kif Kif. Ten years and many books later, Zemni's views of the Islam debate are still relevant. Regarding Flanders, Zemni laments the turn of this debate towards anger and aggression (Zemni, 2009) – a lack of nuance from people who view the world as a dangerous place and Islam as post-war fascism. Muslims are seen as inherently violent, and people fail to distinguish between violent jihadism and personal faith. According to Zemni, Islamophobia can be better defined as anti-Muslimism and racism, and there is only one solution: to strive to understand Islam and Muslims, through an anthropological approach. If we manage to do this, we will also see that Islam is evolving, being reframed and inspiring a new kind of entrepreneurship. So, what we see, according to him, is not a need for new conquests, but for a reframing (Zemni, 2009).

Authors who push 'social' explanations do not idealise Islam and acknowledge that criminal acts are being committed in Islamic countries, but they do not agree with the judgement of some other authors, such as that of criminologist Marion Van San (Van San & Leerkes, 2001). Although there is much research that contradicts this, she maintains that Islamic culture is the determinant of 'immigrant' crime. Maly (2009) points out that she has had more success in convincing politicians than scientists.

Rachida Lamrabet (2017) addresses human rights violations in Afghanistan, Saudi Arabia and Iran. She acknowledges that there are Muslims who are being oppressed in Afghanistan and in Belgium [sic], nevertheless warning against the danger of generalising (2017). Zemni also acknowledges the homophobia of many Muslims, which is in part product of their religion, while warning against any 'us versus them' sentiment that might develop as a result of such an acknowledgement (2009). According to Maly (2009), scientific research has been pushed aside in the Islam debate. Progressives are also caught into 'us versus them' thinking. Islam is much more diverse than is recognised in the debate, which mostly focuses on its radical elements. This is not just a matter of so-called homegrown radicalism (Abou Jahjah, 2016): it has to do with Muslims from Palestine, Iraq or Syria, who have become radicalised in response to Western geopolitical provocations (Abou Jahjah, 2016). Rachida Aziz shows (2017) how marginalised Muslim workers have become supporters of Wahhabism. Salafism (which grew out of Wahhabism) was not problematised before the fall of the Berlin Wall (see, for example, Maly, 2009; Zemni, 2009).

The question is, of course, what direction these opposing sides will take. Nadia Fadil (2017) states that the 22 March 2016 attacks make it painfully clear that we cannot go on like this. Rachida Lamrabet (2017) states that demographic changes will bring people with migrant roots in a majority position. She hopes that the democratic aspects of Belgian society will extend much deeper, embracing all that are part of it. Let the 'great replacement' (as explained, for instance, by Dewinter, 2019) remain a far-right fetish: Muslims will become the majority in Flanders, because they have families with more children. These (Lambaret versus Dewinter) are examples of the two opposing tendencies in the Islam debate in Flanders.

The Debate on the Islamic Veil (Hijab, or Headscarf)

The veil has become a symbol of a conquering Islam (Van Rooy, 2015), of the oppression of Muslim women, etc. (Aziz, 2017; Safai, 2018; Van Rooy, 2015; Dedecker, 2009). Ico Maly (2009) explains that these arguments are used in this way to 'sell' a book, a person or a party. Is the veil an instrument of oppression? Or is in fact banning it an act of oppression? These are leading questions in the Islam debate in Flanders.

Human rights specialist Eva Brems (2015) explains in legal terms that the veil should be seen as a religious sign not because it might be ordained from on high, but because some women choose to see it as religious. Counsel Rachida Lamrabet (2017) points out many inconsistencies in the treatment of the veil issue – with the garment deemed acceptable in some cases yet not in others. She argues that there is no difference between forcing women to wear certain clothes and prohibiting them from doing so. Christian Democratic politician Hendrik Bogaert (2017) wants to avoid outward religious signs to keep society balanced. He concludes that Islam should not be more visible than Judaism in the Flemish public sphere.

For liberal politician Gwendolyn Rutten (2017), religion is a purely private matter. She insists on individual freedom and does not want any ban or encouragement. She agrees with the academics and experience experts whose books we have read, and she defends the person beneath the veil rather than the act of wearing it (Aziz, 2017; Brems, 2015; Lamrabet, 2017; Zemni, 2009).

According to Rutten, by remaining 'neutral' and ensuring that both believers and non-believers respect the rule of law, the government guarantees the freedom of religion as a private matter. On a number of points, this need for neutrality is clear: in the courtroom, the absence of outward signs of personal beliefs (owing to the black toga, worn as a uniform) guarantees the judges' 'neutrality' that must stand for integrity, independence and objectivity. Rutten favours this neutrality approach over the Anglo-Saxon system, which lets police officers wear a turban, for instance. In Belgium things are different: throughout history, respect and neutrality have been the keys to living together regardless of beliefs and backgrounds. Rutten views this as the best solution today. Bart De Wever (2019) also opposes an Anglo-Saxon model in which police officers are allowed to wear headscarves or turbans in combination with their uniform – a symbolic violation of the secular status quo. For the politicians whose books we read (e.g., Safai, 2018) this sets the stage for the Islamisation of society. Koen Geens (2018) is an exception here. He argues that one cannot see a threat in Islam if one is strong enough in one's own identity.

Dyab Abou Jahjah (2016) sees a young, hijab-wearing generation as a standard-bearer for the dispossessed. For Dedecker (2009) and Van Rooy (2015), this runs counter to all feminist values. On the other hand, Rachida Aziz (2017) does not feel supported by feminists, arguing that 'neoliberal white feminists' thrive at the expense of others, deeming it impossible to reconcile antiracism and feminism. She cites as an example Sofie Peeters's documentary

Femme de la rue (2012), arguing that in dealing with the issue of sexual harass-ment of women in Brussels, it upholds the myth of the black rapist.

According to Sami Zemni (2009), women who are not allowed to wear the Islamic veil in public (at school or at work) are being discriminated against. Rather disingenuously, he reminds us of Christian women who managed to emancipate themselves without giving up their faith, calling such a ban an additional layer of discrimination. Aziz (2017) cites psychological studies on the link between unemployment and physical and mental complaints, noting that they do not mention the role of racism. Based on her many years of professional experience as a human rights specialist, Naima Charkaoui (2019) states that the potential impact of racism on individuals is not being acknowledged, and that insulting statements from authority figures can have a catastrophic impact – on social development, on a sense of belonging to society and on trust in the justice system and societal institutions. The debate on the veil is a strongly symbolic one. It pits a dominant group that feels threatened against a minority that feels unfairly targeted. It is worth noting that there is not much literature about the veil. Rachida Lamrabet (2017) wrote a book recounting her experience after her aforementioned discharge from Unia.

The Compass of the Enlightenment and the Need for an 'Aggiornamento': Looking for an Enlightened Islam

The question is: how can we overcome the impasse created by the opposition between the 'culturalist' and the 'social' group? Embracing the Enlighten-ment's compelling ideal – using it as a compass, while holding on to the belief that diversity is enriching, as long as it remains within the rule of law (Zemni, 2009; Lamrabet, 2017). When fundamental rights and freedoms collide, where do we draw the line? Are there any specific rights that we value more than others? How far are we willing to go in restricting the freedom of individuals to achieve more justice for the larger group? Based on Jeremy Bentham's utilitarian philosophy (1780/1999), Bogaert (2017) has based his book on the principle that the greatest possible advantages should be made available for as many people as possible. Bogaert does not follow the views of John Stuart Mill (1859, republished in 1975), another classical utilitarian, and proponent of absolute freedom of speech and religion. He argues there is instead a need for an adequate adjustment method to correctly balance socio-economic and identity themes.

In her manifesto on freedom, Rutten (2017, p. 18) advocates the pre-eminence of liberal democracy: 'while flawed, liberal democracy – in which every individual enjoys inalienable rights and freedoms – is the best possible form of society'. She wonders why we should find it acceptable for men to refuse to shake hands with a woman, for girls and boys not to be allowed to swim together, for homosexuals to be beaten up on the street, for hospitals to offer hymen restoration procedures, for there to be blood revenges and expulsions in Belgium (Rutten, 2017). She argues for an individualised version of Islam, viewed as a religion highly suited to establishing a personal relationship with the divine as it has no intermediate structure or hierarchy. That is the essence, everything else being about power and therefore freedom – and not about faith (Rutten, 2017).

Rutten also quotes British activist Maajid Nawaz (founding chairman of counter-extremist think tank Quilliam) and Sam Harris, authors of *Islam and the future of tolerance: A dialogue* (2015), who call for a liberalisation of Islam. This plea put Nawaz in danger after he was included on a list of anti-Muslim extremists by a US organisation for daring to criticise Islamist ideology in the name of liberal Muslims, gay Muslims, freethinkers and atheists of Muslim culture. Rutten also calls Ghent-based imam and researcher Brahim Laytouss a reformer. Laytouss once mentioned in progressive newspaper *De Morgen* in an interview with journalist De Ceulaer (2016) that a person's sexual life is between that person and God and does not concern him as an imam. Laytouss wishes for a 21st-century European Islam steeped in basic human rights and having done away with barbarous vestiges such as sharia law. Laytouss warns of a parallel society in ultra-conservative Muslim circles. He points to a need for role models: many Muslims support and embody the principles of the Enlightenment. Flemish Imams Platform President Khalid Benhaddou (whose ideas are familiar to Rutten, 2017, p. 80) says that true Islam is peaceful and rational, and that it supports European democratic values. As an imam in Ghent, he chooses to address young people in Dutch, not in Arabic. He must be supported, and so must be the many other modern Muslims who fight radicalisation with a progressive discourse.

According to Sami Zemni (2009), Islamic regimes are viewed as inferior to Western ones because they are based on obsolete tenets. Islam is seen as a throwback to a distant past where violence was seen as a legitimate framework for action. Zemni is inspired by Robert Kaplan's article *How Islam created Europe* (2016). It is often claimed as part of the Islam debate that contrary to Judeo-Christian tradition, Islam has had no Enlightenment, and that it is not part of the European identity. Islam has become an ideal scapegoat in connection with the construction of a purported European identity. According to Zemni (2009), Islam is demonised based on unenlightened thinking – from people who would be perceived as Enlightened but are clearly racist towards Muslims. He maintains that the Islam debate reduces Islam critics into reformers, only acknowledging them if they do not see religion as an emancipatory force (Zemni, 2009), and ignoring the voices of left-wing and progressive Muslims. However, Islam as a religion had its share of Enlightened thinkers (for instance, the Mu'tazila movement, which saw the Koran as the Uncreated Word, unlike the Sunnis view of it as the Word of God). But such social, political and economic forces were side-lined in the countries where Islam was a majority religion (Zemni, 2009). Rachida Aziz (2017) sees the discourse of the Enlightenment as a means of enforcing superiority, pointing out the irony of the fact that many people died in the name of the Enlightenment, and that homophobia and gender inequality are also alive in the West.

Flemish nationalist politician Bart De Wever (2019), the Mayor of Antwerp, the most diverse city in Flanders, maintains that there can be a positive link between individual and community as well as identity and citizenship, under one condition: identity must be subject to an open and dynamic process. De Wever (2019), whose line of thought we are following in the remainder of this paragraph, is inspired by Benedict Anderson's *Imagined communities* (1983). More than half of Antwerp's population is of immigrant origin, a share increasing by about one percentage point every year. For many citizens, this is an astonishing development. These people feel ill-treated when they hear from academic, political and public sector circles that they better embrace this reality, as it is never going away. Western cities are extremely diverse. This is indisputable and irreversible. We need to work with this reality in a positive way. Europeans view Islam as the real threat to modern identity according to De Wever (2019). They view Muslims with suspicion and fear – as a subversive group within European society bent on ultimately obliterating their culture. Throughout Europe and the Western world, radical right-wing forces feel that 'the natives' will be replaced if they fail to defend themselves.

De Wever (2019, pp. 106–107) calls this a madness that we can avoid if we understand that our age is not one of clashing civilisations. Radical Islam must be countered by a clear choice for Enlightenment in our identity experience: 'The compass of Enlightenment must once again clearly point to the direction in which our society wishes to move forward. The lighthouse of freedom and equality must shine its light, welcoming everyone who is born, grows up, lives, works and lives here.' According to De Wever (2019), a source code – a leading culture – is needed for the population to go beyond its confusion as to its identity and to discover itself as a community again. Without that shared source code, people cannot talk to one another because they lack a common reference framework.

A first principle of an Enlightened culture is government neutrality (De Wever, 2019). A second principle is mandatory use of the local community's language. The third principle is that it should be made clear that Enlightenment values are the software of our public culture: freedom, equality, solidarity, separation of church and state, the rule of law, sovereignty of the people. The fourth principle is the culmination of Enlightened culture: granting citizenship to newcomers having passed a citizenship test and celebrating with a ceremony the admission of the new member into the community.

Conclusion

Our analysis shows that very different views characterise the debate that is taking place in Flanders around Islam. We have tried to explore and synthesise opinions which express different ideological tendencies and which, to some extent, have been reflected in the media. There are many voices to be heard, several of which adhere to pragmatic explanations of social phenomena, while others ascribe social inequality to cultural determinants. Proponents of the *social thesis* argue that Muslims can be a full part of our society and that, ultimately, we must all stand together against current challenges. Exponents of the *cultural thesis* view integration as a threat, although their view on integration is different. What this boils down to is that in a globalised society, the loss of a majority position is assumed to be a threat.

These social and cultural theses inform all five themes we discussed. A first theme is the labour market position of people with a migration background – a lowly position that is explained rather differently on either side of the social/cultural divide. The first explanation focuses on the systematic discrimination of people of colour, particularly on the demand side of the labour market. The second explanation focuses on other issues that arise on the demand side of the labour market, particularly, culturally determined behaviours that allegedly limit one's participation in the job market. The second theme concerns the totalitarian characteristics attributed to Islam. For some authors radicalism and Islam are two sides of the same coin – a view that can be seen as distorting reality and contributing to the othering of Muslims. The third theme also highlights how both the Islam debate and the uncertainties of globalisation contribute to this othering. The fourth theme is the Islamic veil. Apparently, this is what oppression is about – wearing a veil or banning it. It can be said that what we have here is mostly a symbolic debate around the place of Islam in Western society. Finally, the fifth theme pertains to the ways Enlightenment values are being called upon in defence of either thesis, but also as a blueprint for the future.

References

Abou Jahjah, D. (2016). *Pleidooi voor radicalisering* [Plea for radicalisation]. De Bezige Bij.

Ahmed, S., & Matthes, J. (2016). Media representation of Muslims and Islam from 2000 to 2015: A meta-analysis. *International Communication Gazette, 79*(3), 219–244.

Anderson, B. (1983). *Imagined communities. Reflections on the origin and spread of nationalism.* Verso Books.

Aziz, R. (2017). *Niemand zal hier slapen vannacht* [No one will sleep here tonight]. EPO.

Bentham, J. (1999). *An introduction to the principles of morals and legislation.* Batoche Books. (Originally published 1780)

Benyaich, B. (2013). *Islam en radicalisme bij Marokkanen in Brussel* [Islam and radicalism among Moroccans in Brussels]. Van Halewyck.

Berbers, A. P. V., Koeman, J., & d'Haenens, L. (2016). Reception of media representation of Moroccan ethnicity and Islam in Belgium and the Netherlands: The case of the 'Syria fighters'. In S. Mertens & H. De Smaele (Eds.), *Representations of Islam in the news: A cross-cultural analysis* (pp. 157–174). Lexington Books.

Bogaert, H. (2017). *In vrijheid samenleven: Essay* [Living together in freedom: Essay]. Createspace Independent Publishing Platform.

Brems, E. (2011). *België gidsland: Een haalbare utopie* [Belgium as a guide country: An attainable utopia]. VUBPress.

Charkaoui, N. (2019). *Racisme. Over wonden en veerkracht* [Racism. On wounds and resilience]. EPO.

De Ceulaer, J. (2016). We moeten de geldstromen aanpakken [We need to address money flows]. *De Morgen.* Available through subscription at GoPress.be

De Koning, M. (2019). *Vijf mythen over islamofobie* [Five myths about Islamophobia]. Yunus Publishing/Kif Kif.

De Ridder, K. (2010). *De witte media: Of waarom 'allochtonen' altijd slecht nieuws* zijn [The white media: Or why 'immigrants' are always bad news]. LannooCampus.

De Wever, B. (2019). *Over identiteit* [On identity]. Borgerhoff & Lamberigt.

Dedecker, J.-M. (2009). *Hoofddoek of blinddoek? De migratie ontsluierd* [Headscarf or blindfold: Migration unveiled]. Van Halewyck.

Devroe, I. (2007). *Gekleurd nieuws? De voorstelling van etnische minderheden in het nieuws in Vlaanderen. Context, methodologische aspecten en onderzoeksresultaten* [Coloured news? The representation of ethnic minorities in the news in Flanders. Context, methodological aspects and research results] [Doctoral dissertation, University of Ghent]

Dewinter, F. (2019). *De-islamiseer Europa. 732* [De-islamise Europe. 732]. Egmont.

Fadil, N. (2017). *Tegen radicalisering. Pleidooi voor een postkoloniaal Europa* [Against radicalisation. Plea for a postcolonial Europe]. VUBPress.

Geens, K. (2019). *Wat ik ervan begrijp* [What I understand about it]. Polis.

Harris, S. & Nawaz, M. (2015). *Islam and the future of tolerance: A dialogue.* Harvard University Press.

Kaplan, R. (2016, May). How Islam created Europe. *The Atlantic.*

Lamrabet, R. (2017). *Zwijg, allochtoon!* [Shut up, immigrant!]. EPO.

Loobuyck, D., & Jacobs, D. (2006). The Flemish immigration society, political challenges on different levels. In L. d'Haenens, M. Hooghe, D. Vanheule, & H. Gezduci (Eds.), *'New' citizens, new policies? Developments in diversity policy in Canada and Flanders* (pp. 105–123). Academia Press.

Maly, I. (2009). *De beschavingsmachine: Wij en de islam* [The civilising machine: Us and Islam]. EPO.

Mekki-Berrada, A. (2019). Islamophobie viriliste et radicalisation islamophobe [Virilist Islamo-phobia and radicalisation]. *Religiologiques, 39*, 5–49.

Mill, J. S. (1975). *On liberty.* Oxford University. (Originally published 1859)

Peeters, S. (2012). *Femme de la rue* [Woman of the streets] [Audiovisual documentary]. RICTS.

Pew Research Center. (2017). *Europe's growing Muslim population.* Pew Research Center: https://www.pewforum.org/2017/11/29/europes-growing-muslim-population/

Rutten, G. (2017). *Nieuwe vrijheid* [New freedom]. Polis. (e-book version)

Safai, D. (2018). *Plots mocht ik niet meer lachen: Hoe de islam vrouwen onderdrukt* [Suddenly I wasn't allowed to laugh: How Islam oppresses women]. Borgerhoff & Lamberigts.

Van Amerongen, A. (2015). *Brussel Eurabia* [Brussels Eurabia]. Atlas.

Van de Velden, W., & Roelens, T. (2017). Een op drie werklozen in Vlaanderen is allochtoon [One in three unemployed people in Flanders is an immigrant]. *De Tijd.* https://www.tijd.be/politiek-economie/belgie/vlaanderen/een-op-drie-werklozen-in-vlaanderen-is-allochtoon/10196441.html

Van Rooy, W. (2015). *Waarover men niet spreekt: Bezonken gedachten over postmodernisme, Europa, islam* [What people don't talk about: Pondered thoughts on postmodernism, Europe, Islam]. De Blauwe Tijger.

Van San, M., & Leerkes, A. (2001). *Criminalité et criminalisation: les jeunes allochtones en Belgique. Rapport pour le Ministre de la Justice* [Criminality and criminalisation: Young allochthones in Belgium. Report for the Minister of Justice]. Amsterdam School for Social Science Research.

Zemni, S. (2009). *Het islamdebat* [The debate on Islam]. EPO.

5

ISLAMOPHOBIA IN GERMANY, STILL A DEBATE?

LUIS MANUEL HERNÁNDEZ AGUILAR

Abstract

As in many other European countries, the existence of Islamophobia in Germany is a highly debated and contested topic, despite mounting empirical evidence detailing the scope and spread of the phenomenon. However, in recent years, there has been a slow process of recognition that Muslims and those perceived as such are facing several forms of discrimination, stereotyping and violence. Such recognition, though, can be seen as influenced by extreme and violent manifestations of Islamophobia, like the Hanau shootings in February 2020. The present contribution charts contemporary discussions of Islamophobia in Germany, zooming in on state-led discussions of the issue. It also discusses the Hanau shootings against the background of population replacement conspiracy theories, and makes a case for situating Islamophobia as one of the empirical faces of racism currently entangled with conspiracy theories.

Keywords: Islamophobia, Germany, anti-Muslim racism, Hanau, conspiracy theories

Introduction

On 19 February 2020, the news of a terrorist attack committed by a 'lone wolf' far-right extremist in the city of Hanau shocked Germany. The terrorist targeted two shisha bars, killing nine people. He also killed his own mother, and, in the end, took his own life. The motivation behind his attacks was laid out in a 20-page manifesto detailing a racial Weltanschauung, conspiracy theories, misogyny and a particular hatred towards Muslims. The shisha bars were purportedly targeted because they have been deemed 'oriental' spaces within the Western landscape (Kaiser & Färber, 2019), 'plagued' by 'foreign criminality' (*Ausländerkriminalität*) and 'clan criminality' (mxx/dpa, 2020), well before the attack. The Hanau terrorist attack also made the spatial dimension of Islamophobia's racial formation visible.

Just some months before the Hanau shootings, on 9 October 2019, a far-right terrorist attempted to enter and attack the Jewish community centre and synagogue in Halle during Yom Kippur. After this failed attempt, the perpetrator shot a passerby and then headed towards a kebab restaurant, where he killed another person and injured two more. Eventually he was caught by the police. In his manifesto, this perpetrator had also declared considering attacking either a mosque or antifa headquarters. By and large, the perpetrator expressed hatred towards all those he deemed as non-White Germans.

The reconstructions of these two events so far have indicated antisemitism as the driving force behind the Halle attack, and Islamophobia or xenophobia behind the one in Hanau. However, a closer examination of the atrocities reveals common ideological grounds driving political terrorist violence, including, among others discussed below, racism towards 'non-White Germans'. These attacks brought the issues of racial violence in particular, and racism in Germany in general, into the limelight. But how could these atrocious acts have happened in a country where public discourses announced the end of racism decades ago?

This contribution centres on reading racial violence against the dominant framework of Germany as a post-racial society, by analysing how Islamophobia as a form of racism has been discussed from the state perspective. The first part of this chapter discusses the myth of post-racial Germany, paying particular attention to state discourses emanated from the German Islam Conference. The second part juxtaposes a post-racial understanding of the nation and the realities of conspiratorial racial violence, showing such an understanding is rather schematic, and centres on the function of conspiracy theories in the operation of racism, in particular of Islamophobia and antisemitism.

Post-racial Germany?

As in many other European countries, the myth of a post-racial society (Goldberg, 2015; Lentin, 2008) has taken a strong hold in German narratives on the nation. However, in contradistinction to other European nations, post-raciality occupies a central position in Germany, as it has been linked to the reconstruction of the German nation and identity since the aftermath of the Second World War (Räthzel, 1991; Räthzel & Kalpaka, 1986; Terkessidis, 2004). The myth of a post-racial society reconstructs Germany as a new rising nation learning from, and overcoming, its racial and murderous past, but only in relation to one of many empirical manifestations of racism: antisemitism.[1] The myth does not entail the inexistence of racial formations in the country, but rather operates as a narrative disguising racial ideas on belonging and otherness as well as racial practices of discrimination and violence. Furthermore, the myth of a post-racial Germany has deeply influenced the conceptual language through which different forms of discrimination, based on racial characterisations, are minimised at best, denied at worst.

As Nora Räthzel and Anita Kalpaka (1986) already pointed out in the 1980s, public discourse refrained from using the concept of racism, and instead relied on terminology such as xenophobia (*Fremdenfeindlichkeit, Ausländerfeindlichkeit*) to describe ideas, practices and violence that were racist. Talking about contemporary forms of racism in Germany is still a taboo (Attia, 2007; Terkessidis, 2004). A similar pattern can be discerned with relation to Islamophobia or anti-Muslim racism, where the preferred terminology has been 'hostility against Muslims' (*Muslimfeindlichkeit*) and 'hostility against Islam' (*Islamfeindlichkeit*). However, the issue is not only a matter of etymology. Not naming racism has crucial social and political consequences (Lentin, 2008), as it allows to displace and disavow racial constructions, practices and violence from the historical construction of the German nation and identity; it attenuates the extent of the phenomenon, and imposes restrictions upon anti-racist practices and projects. In recent decades, this process has been particularly salient in public discussions on Islamophobia.

Ever since its reappearance and dissemination in the public sphere, the term 'Islamophobia' has been highly contested.[2] Critics of the term have argued that the concept can be used to shield Muslim communities from criticism (see Halliday, 1999); others blast the etymological imprecision of the term (López, 2011); other positions hold that being fearful of Muslims and Islam was an understandable reaction towards violence committed in the name of Islam, and the so-called growing radicalisation of Muslims (Kelle, 2021; see also Schneiders, 2010). And yet, as Salman Sayyid (2014, p. 11) has argued with regard to the dissemination of the concept, 'its continual circulation in public debate testifies to ways in which it hints at something that needs to be addressed'. And the issue that needs to be addressed pertains to the different ways in which Muslims are discursively constructed as alien populations in Europe (Bracke & Hernandez Aguilar, 2020; Fekete, 2004) – inferior in terms of historical development (Hernández Aguilar, 2018), and potentially, if not inherently, violent (Kundnani, 2014) – and to how they are discriminated against for being Muslims in labour and housing markets (Bayrakli & Hafez, 2017, 2018; Šeta, 2016), as well as access to health services (Bartig et al., 2021).

Furthermore, Muslims suffer harassment and different forms of violence (Attia & Shooman, 2010; Deutscher Bundestag, 2017, 2018; Yegane Arani, 2015), and have been positioned at the centre of racial conspiracy theories (Bangstad, 2013; Bracke & Hernandez Aguilar, 2020; Carr, 2006; Zia-Ebrahimi, 2018). In short, the concept of Islamophobia expresses and denotes a reality in which Muslims are routinely and ubiquitously problematised for being 'Muslims'. And this reality, despite mounting empirical evidence confirming it, has been constantly denied.[3]

In Germany too, Islamophobia has been contested and minimised. Particularly troubling in public debate has been the proposition of Islamophobia as a manifestation of racism, since it is argued that Islam is not a race (for a critique, see Keskinkılıç, 2019), as if race is a biological reality. Paradigmatic in this regard has been the position of the German Islam Conference (Deutsche Islam Konferenz (DIK)), the institution of the German state in charge of 'Muslim affairs'.

Founded in 2006 at the initiative of the Federal Ministry of the Interior (BMI) and embedded in the Federal Office for Migration and Refuges (BAMF), the DIK's purpose is to solve a series of 'issues' associated with Islam and Muslims (Deutsche Islam Konferenz, 2008). These problems include the construction of mosques, the training of imams, questions of national security related to extremism, radicalisation and Islamism, as well as debates on gender inequality and antisemitism. By and large, the DIK can be seen as the institutional frame of the German state problematising Muslims' presence and existence in the country. In other words, it turns Muslims into problems that politics must solve, echoing Michel Foucault's (1984) concept of problematisation.

The DIK was presented as a forum for dialogue, to foster and enhance the integration of Muslims, even though national security concerns have been foundational since its beginnings. Different scholars have analysed this institution as a technology of power geared towards reforming Muslims and Islam (Amir-Moazami, 2011a, 2011b; Hernández Aguilar, 2017; Peter, 2010; Schiffauer, 2014; Tezcan, 2008, 2012), while being a key agent in matters of national security (Hernández Aguilar, 2016; Rodatz & Scheuring, 2011; Schiffauer, 2006). In short, while the DIK was presented and lauded as a forum for dialogue, that dialogue was always dictated by state prerogatives, and overwhelmingly focused on solving 'problems' arising from the presence of Muslims in the country (Amir-Moazami, 2011b; Schiffauer & Bojadžijev, 2009). However, in 2011, the state-led dialogue finally started to include the concerns of Islamic organisations about stereotyping, hatred and discrimination against Muslims. It is important to highlight that some political events, like the so-called Sarrazin debate and the killings of 'migrants' by the Nationalist Socialist Underground (NSU), influenced the positioning of the issue in the DIK's agenda. Islamic organisations partaking in the DIK had been pushing for the inclusion of the topic in the debate since 2007; it was not until 2011 that the issue was finally addressed.

A working group was then set up to discuss and address the issue, but in conjunction with so-called Muslim antisemitism and Islamism. As such, from the outset, the concerns of Islamic organisations were accepted on the condition that the 'problems' caused by Muslims were addressed too (Deutsche Islam Konferenz, 2011). The working group drew the following conclusions. First, a concept was needed to name the phenomenon, and 'hostility against Muslims' (*Muslimfeindlichkeit*) was chosen, since, according to the working group, 'racism' was a concept too inflammatory, that could potentially polarise the public debate. Furthermore, the working group objected to the concept 'racism', as using it might be subjected to criminal penalties.[4] Finally, the working group also considered it unfair to use the word 'racism', as 'many people, who perhaps feel a vague uneasiness about Muslims, would surely consider it unjust if they were considered to be almost racist from the outset' (Deutsche Islam Konferenz, 2011, p. 4). In short, a discussion on the lived experiences of Muslims with racial discrimination turned into an argument about the sensibilities of an imagined audience's unease about Muslims. No action plans, strategies, recommendations or policies were advanced to thwart the 'hostility'. *Muslimfeindlichkeit*, in effect, became the official term to address hatred against Muslims in the German Islam Conference's protocols (Deutsche Islam Konferenz, 2011, p. 4; for a critique, see Hernández Aguilar, 2017).

Besides naming Islamophobia as a form of racism, counting, assessing and making its spread visible was another issue in the German context. For instance, and despite mounting pressure from different national and international fronts, hate crimes against Muslims were not systematically recorded as politically motivated crimes by the federal government system until 2017. From that year onward, these types of crimes have been categorised under the label 'hostility against Islam' (*Islamfeindlichkeit*). As in the DIK's position, this concept does not relate the phenomenon to the operations of racism, yet the existence of official statistics on the spread of the phenomenon represents an important yet overdue first step in the fight against racial discrimination. To summarise this section, the establishment of the concept of Islamophobia as a form of racism has been met with reluctance from the state point of view, and a different terminology has been put forward instead. In the next section, we make a case for insisting on appraising and conceptualising Islamophobia as a form of racism.

Conspiratorial Racial Violence

Briefly defined, racism is the discourse and practice of crafting differences and hierarchies within humanity. It can use different visual and non-visual markers, such as skin colour, hair texture, dress, culture and cultural competences, language and religion to elaborate such differences in a hierarchical system (Du Bois, 2005; Medovoi, 2012; Meer & Modood, 2009; Stoler, 1995; Topolski, 2018, 2020). There have been many historical modalities of racism, and Islamophobia has been one of them. Conceptually, Islamophobia, according to Salman Sayyid (2014), can be better defined through its range of deployments, that is, by understanding how it manifests itself: sporadic and organised violence, individual and institutional discrimination, denigration in the media and on the streets, and dehumanisation, as well as special policies seeking to regulate or de-Islamise Muslims. Furthermore, all these deployments are predicated upon the construction of Muslims as 'Muslims'. 'Muslims', with quotation marks, refers to the racial fabrication of the figure of the Muslim. It encapsulates all the stereotypes and racial characterisations imposed onto Muslims, the violent, atavistic, patriarchal, criminal, antisemitic, fanatic, homophobe, etc. In short, historical racial constructions have produced the figure of the 'Muslim', and this is a discursive operation through which some conspiracy theories operate and spread, as the history of European antisemitism has shown (Benz, 2007; Cohn, 1996; De Michelis, 2004; Soyer, 2019; Webman, 2011).

Against this background, conspiracism, as a tradition of explanation (Butter & Knight, 2020; Byford, 2011),[5] needs to be included in the range of Islamophobic deployments. Muslims have been the subject of conspiracy theories, the most prominent so far being Eurabia (Bangstad, 2012, 2013; Carr, 2006; Larsson, 2012; Zia-Ebrahimi, 2018), the Great Replacement (Bracke & Hernandez Aguilar, 2020; Davey & Ebner, 2019) and Islamisation (Hafez, 2019; Schmuck & Matthes, 2019; Uenal, 2016). In general terms, these conspiracy theories postulate Muslims as agents of destruction seeking to transform Europe into an Islamic continent via migration as infiltration, and the combative use of higher birthrates as a long-term strategy to replace 'native Europeans' with Muslims. The presence of Muslims, in this view, is tantamount to the extinction of White Europeans. At times, such conspiracy theories about replacement have also reworked classic antisemitic tropes of world domination, as they assumed that the replacement is being 'orchestrated by Jews' (ADL, 2017).[6] Furthermore, conspiracy theories about population replacement operate through a Manichean and combative view of the world, where the survival of White Europe is in jeopardy.

Recently, different scholars have pointed out the use of conspiracy theories as a shared characteristic of antisemitism in its classical and novel forms, as well as of Islamophobia or anti-Muslim racism (Hafez, 2019; Zia-Ebrahimi, 2018). These scholars argue that conspiracy theories are among the many components of the racial characterisation of religious communities like Jews and Muslims. Both the Hanau and Halle shootings were acts of terrorist political violence inspired by antisemitic and racial conspiracy theories on population replacement.

The Halle perpetrator confessed believing that a Jewish plot was behind his personal failures. He too subscribed to the conspiracy of a population replacement in Europe via migration and higher birthrates, and the belief that Jews were orchestrating such an 'evil process' (see Koehler, 2019). The perpetrator of the Hanau shooting also subscribed to the conspiracy theory of replacement, in particular, he appraised migration as a deleterious process geared towards the extinction of the German White race (see Crawford & Keen, 2021). In both atrocious instances conspiracy theories and racism merged into a warrant for political violence, as the perpetrators – just like those of the Utøya massacre and Oslo bombing as well as the Christchurch mosque shootings – saw violence as the only way to stop the replacement of White populations.

In Germany, the conspiracy theory of Islamisation has been present in the public sphere for at least a decade, and is by no means restricted to the far-right fringes. Former senator of Finance in Berlin and executive member of the Bundesbank Thilo Sarrazin can be credited with mainstreaming the Islamisation conspiracy in 2011, with his book *Germany abolishing/undoing itself: How we're putting our country in jeopardy* (2010). Sarrazin played a crucial role in mainstreaming racial thinking and the Islamisation conspiracy theory, and catapulting them into the public sphere as acceptable topics of discussion, particularly in relation to Muslims, whom he saw as slowly eroding the German nation and identity. Although racism never disappeared from the German landscape, despite vociferous arguments claiming otherwise (see, for instance, the map of these negations, Chin et al., 2009), racial slurs, violence and overall racial thinking became mainstream through the debates about Sarrazin's arguments on an impending 'dilution' of the German Volk due to 'native' Germans' lower rates of fertility vis-à-vis Muslims and foreigners, a process that in the long term would have the Islamisation of German life as an outcome.

Nevertheless, Sarrazin was not alone in advancing this conspiracy theory. In Dresden, Pegida (Patriotic Europeans Against the Islamisation of the Occident) arose as an anti-social movement whose objective was to stop

gn.ро888

the process described by Sarrazin, that is, the Islamisation of the country.[7] The local success of Pegida swiftly prompted the creation of other branches in Germany and some other European countries (Druxes & Simpson, 2016; Schmidt, 2017). Meanwhile, the far-right political party Alternative for Germany (AfD) has made stopping the Islamisation of Germany a key tenet of its political platform and manifesto (AfD, n.d., 2016), and in 2019 campaigned to stop the fulfilment of Eurabia (Fröhlich, 2019). In other words, conspiracy theories about population replacement have been present in German public discourse, at least during the last decade. The Hanau and Halle perpetrators did not invent the ideologies upon which they acted; instead, population replacement conspiracy theories have become established topics in discussions about Muslims and Islam in Germany. The formation, spread and circulation of population replacement racial conspiracy theories and their violent consequences testify to the lasting presence of racism in the country, a reality that, rather than being denied, needs to be reckoned with.

Conclusion

The conspiratorial terrorist violence in Hanau and Halle put racism in Germany into the spotlight, while highlighting the extent to which far-right racial violence had not been seriously addressed by the government. Spokespersons from different religious communities and minorities in Germany expressed such concerns in the aftermath of the Hanau attacks: Jewish, Muslim, Kurdish and Roma representatives stressed that, for quite long, racism in general, and racial violence in particular, had not been seriously addressed. Furthermore, discussing the Hanau attack, Blyth Crawford and Florence Keen (2021) made an important argument by stressing the need to further understand the elements underpinning this type of violence, specifically 'the interconnected relationship between racial hate and conspiracy theory … an understanding of both remains crucial to understanding this fresh wave of far-right, lone-actor attacks in the normalizing age of social media' (Crawford & Keen, 2021, p. 2).

Immediately after the Hanau attack, major media outlets as well as high-profile politicians condemned the attack and mourned the victims. Notoriously, chancellor Angela Merkel declared: 'Racism is poison. Hatred is poison' (Die Bundeskanzlerin, 2021), while poignantly linking Hanau's attack to a list of high-profile cases of far-right racial violence: the NSU, the murder of Walter Lübeck and the terrorist attack in the Halle synagogue in 2019 (Die Bundeskanzlerin, 2021). The statements and position of the chancellor represent so far one of the most important and influential political standings regarding racism in Germany: it acknowledges the reality of racism, links it to previous racial violence and sends out a clear message against racism. Strategies, action plans and policies to thwart racism and racial conspiracy theories are the next necessary step to take.

Notes

1. The mythical denazification process and the 'zero hour' as historical events (Räthzel, 1991) worked as historical devices whereby the German society could (re)imagine itself exempt from the racial antisemitic terror of the past.
2. 'Islamophobia' as a concept was first developed during the 1920s in the French colonial empire (Sayyid, 2014, p. 12). Later Edward W. Saïd (1985) linked it to the operation of the Orientalism discourse. In current debates on the concept, its origin is situated in 1997, when the Runnymede Trust published *Islamophobia: A challenge for all of us* (Runnymede Trust, 1997). Following Sayyid (2014), one of the effects caused by the Trust report was an advancing of the concept of Islamophobia as a neologism, as if it was addressing an emergent reality. Furthermore, the reception of the report created the impression that the commission coined the term. Yet, as Vakil (2010, p. 34) has argued, the term Islamophobia was already circulating among some Muslim communities in Britain during the 1980s.
3. According to Sayyid (2014, p. 11) the denial of the existence of Islamophobia can be seen as a political response arising from the context in which it appears, a contested field where questions about national security, social cohesion and cultural belonging are played out. It is this field in which the relationship between national majorities and the post-colonial, ethnically marked minorities is being forged.
4. 'Racist stigmatisation must not be encouraged but must be rejected (and in extreme cases, if necessary, be subject to criminal penalties). Precisely for this reason therefore, the term "racism" must not be used in an excessive manner under any circumstances' (Deutsche Islam Konferenz, 2011, p. 5).
5. Scholars of conspiracy theories have defined conspiracism as a 'distinct culture … which encompasses a specific system of beliefs, values, practices and rituals shared by communities of people' (Byford, 2011, p. 5; Dyrendal et al., 2018). Furthermore, such a distinct culture operates through the assumption that 'the fate of governments, institutions and society as a whole is secretly determined by a small group of individuals bound by a common purpose and interests' (Soyer, 2019, p. 7).
6. Elsewhere, Sarah Bracke and I have conceptualised these conspiracy theories as the biopolitical dimension of the 'Muslim Question', that is, how the systematic problematisation of Muslims in Europe centres on constructing an 'alien' population threatening the socio-political body (Bracke & Hernández Aguilar, 2020).
7. Pegida is a far-right anti-Islam organisation that describes itself as a group of 'concerned and angry citizens', formed in the city of Dresden at the end of 2014.

References

ADL. (2017). *White Supremacists Adopt New Slogan: 'You Will Not Replace Us.'* Anti Defamation League. Retrieved November 20, 2021, from https://www.adl.org/blog/white-supremacists-adopt-new-slogan-you-will-not-replace-us

AfD. (n.d.). *Islamisierung | AfD Kompakt.* Alternative Fur Deutschland [Islamisation | AfD Compact. Alternative For Germany]. Retrieved January 24, 2021, from https://afdkompakt.de/tag/islamisierung/

AfD. (2016). *Manifesto for Germany: The political programme of the Alternative for Germany.* AfD.

Amir-Moazami, S. (2011a). Dialogue as a governmental technique: Managing gendered Islam in Germany. *Feminist Review, 98,* 9–27.

Amir-Moazami, S. (2011b). Pitfalls of consensus-orientated dialogue: The German Islam Conference (Deutsche Islam Konferenz). *Approaching Religion, 1,* 2–15.

Attia, I. (2007). Kulturrassismus und Gesellschaftskritik [Cultural racism and social criticism]. In I. Attia (Ed.), *Orient- und Islambilder. Interdisziplinäre Beiträge zu Orientalismus und antimuslimischem Rassismus* (pp. 5–30). UNRAST Verlag.

Attia, Iman, & Shooman, Y. (2010). The reception of the murder of Marwa el-Sherbini in German print media and German weblogs. *Jahrbuch Für Islamophobieforschung,* 23–46.

Bangstad, S. (2012). Terror in Norway. *American Anthropologist, 114*(2), 351–352.

Bangstad, S. (2013). Eurabia Comes to Norway. *Islam and Christian–Muslim relations, 24*(3), 369–391. https://doi.org/10.1080/09596410.2013.783969

Bartig, S., Kalkum, D., Le, H. M., & Lewicki, A. (2021). *Diskriminierungsrisiken und Diskriminierungsschutz im Gesundheitswesen – Wissens-stand und Forschungsbedarf für die Antidiskriminierungs-forschung* [Discrimination risks and discrimination protection in health care – State of knowledge and research needs for antidiscrimination research]. Antidiskriminierungsstelle des Bundes.

Bayrakli, E., & Hafez, F. (Eds.). (2017). *European Islamophobia Report 2016.* SETA.

Bayrakli, E., & Hafez, F. (Eds.). (2018). *European Islamophobia Report 2017.* SETA.

Benz, W. (2007). *Die Protokolle der Weisen von Zion* [The protocols of the wise men of Zion]. C. H. Beck.

Bracke, S., & Hernandez Aguilar, L. M. (2020). 'They love death as we love life', The 'Muslim Question' and the biopolitics of replacement. *British Journal of Sociology, 71*(4), 680–701.

Butter, M., & Knight, P. (Eds.). (2020). *Routledge handbook of conspiracy theories.* Routledge.

Byford, J. (2011). *Conspiracy theories: A critical introduction.* Palgrave Macmillan.

Carr, M. (2006). You are now entering Eurabia. *Race & Class, 48*(1), 1–22. https://doi.org/10.1177/0306396806066636

Chin, R., Fehrenbach, H., Eley, G., & Grossmann, A. (2009). *After the Nazi racial state. Difference and democracy in Germany and Europe.* The University of Michigan Press.

Cohn, N. (1996). *Warrant for genocide. The myth of the Jewish world conspiracy and the protocols of the elders of Zion.* Serif.

Crawford, B., & Keen, F. (2021). The Hanau terrorist attack: How race hate and conspiracy theories are fueling global far-right violence. *CTC Sentinel, 13*(3), 1–9. https://ctc.usma.edu/hanau-terrorist-attack-race-hate-conspiracy-theories-fueling-global-far-right-violence/

Davey, J., & Ebner, J. (2019). *'The Great Replacement': The violent consequences of mainstreamed extremism.* Institute for Strategic Dialogue.

De Michelis, C. (2004). *The non-existent manuscript: A study of the protocols of the sages of Zion.* University of Nebraska Press.

Deutscher Bundestag. (2017). *Drucksache 19/148* [Printed Matter 19/148]. https://doi.org/10.1111/cobi.12656.Dar

Deutscher Bundestag. (2018). *Drucksache 19/987* [Printed Matter 19/987].

Deutsche Islam Konferenz. (2008). *Interim résumé by the Working Groups and the round table. Paper for the 3rd Plenary Session of the German Islam Conference 13 March 2008*. DIK.

Deutsche Islam Konferenz. (2011). *Zwischenbericht über die Arbeit der Arbeitsgruppe 'Präventionsarbeit mit Jugendliche'*. [Interim Report on the Work of the Working Group on 'Prevention Work with Youth'.]. DIK.

Die Bundeskanzlerin (2021). *Kanzlerin Merkel: „Rassismus ist ein Gift. Der Hass ist ein Gift'* [Chancellor Merkel: 'Racism is a poison. Hate is a poison']. Die Bundeskanzlerin. Retrieved November 20, 2021, from https://www.bundeskanzlerin.de/bkin-de/mediathek/bundeskanzlerin-merkel-aktuell/podcast-jahrestag-hanau-1853552

Druxes, H., & Simpson, P. A. (2016). Introduction: Pegida as a European far-right populist movement. *German Politics and Society, 34*(4), 1–16. https://doi.org/10.3167/gps.2016.340401

Du Bois, W. E. B. (2005). *The souls of Black folk*. Bantam Books.

Dyrendal, A., Robertson, D. G., & Asprem, E. (2018). *Handbook of conspiracy theory and contemporary religion*. Brill.

Fekete, L. (2004). Anti-Muslim racism and the European security state. *Race & Class, 46*(1), 3–29. http://rac.sagepub.com/cgi/doi/10.1177/0306396804045512

Foucault, M. (1984). Polemics, politics, and problematizations. In P. Rabinow (Ed.), *The Foucault reader: An introduction to Foucault's thought* (pp. 381–390). Penguin Books.

Fröhlich, A. (2019). *AfD-Europawahlkampf in Berlin: Die nackte Frau und die bösen Turbanträger* [AfD European Election Campaign in Berlin: The naked woman and the evil]. Tagesspiegel. Retrieved November 20, 2021, from https://www.tagesspiegel.de/berlin/afd-europawahlkampf-in-berlin-die-nackte-frau-und-die-boesen-turbantraeger/24214994.html

Goldberg, D. T. (2015). *Are we all postracial yet? Debating race*. Polity Press.

Hafez, F. (2019). From 'Jewification' to 'Islamization': Anti-semitism and Islamophobia in Austrian politics then and now. *ReOrient, 4*(2), 197–220. https://doi.org/10.13169/reorient.4.2.0197

Halliday, F. (1999). Islamophobia reconsidered. *Ethnic and Racial Studies, 22*(5), 892–902.

Hernández Aguilar, L. M. (2016). The imam of the future on racism and the German Islam conference. *Islamophobia Studies Yearbook, 7*, 66–85.

Hernández Aguilar, L. M. (2017). Suffering rights and incorporation. The German Islam conference and the integration of Muslims as a discursive means of their racialization. *European Societies, 19*(5), 623–644. https://doi.org/10.1080/14616696.2017.1334950

Hernández Aguilar, L. M. (2018). *Governing Muslims and Islam in contemporary Germany*. Brill.

Kaiser, L., & Färber, A. (2019). *Kulturwissenschaftlerin über Shisha-Bars: „Das Gift der Anderen"* [Cultural scientist about shisha bars: 'The poison of the others']. https://taz.de/Kulturwissenschaftlerin-ueber-Shisha-Bars/!5564000/

Kelle, B. (2021). *Islam: Kritik an Muslimen ist keine Krankheit und Religion keine Rasse* [Islam: Criticism of Muslims is not a disease and religion is not a race]. FOCUS Online. https://www.focus.de/politik/experten/gastbeitrag-von-birgit-kelle-es-gibt-keine-islamophobie-aber-sicher-einen-terror-im-namen-des-islam_id_12601630.html

Keskinkılıç, O. (2019). Aber Islam ist doch keine Rasse… – Leugnungs- und Abwehrstrategien im antimuslimischen Rassismus [But Islam is not a race … – Denial and defense strategies in anti-Muslim racism]. In P. Baron & A. Drücker (Eds.), *Antimuslimischer Rassismus und Muslimische Jugendarbeit in der Migrationsgesellschaf* (pp. 12–16). IDA-NRW.

Koehler, D. (2019). The Halle, Germany, Synagogue attack and the evolution of the far-right terror threat – Combating Terrorism Center at West Point. *CTC Sentinel, 12*(1). https://ctc.usma.edu/halle-germany-synagogue-attack-evolution-far-right-terror-threat/

Kundnani, A. (2014). *The Muslims are coming! Islamophobia, extremism, and the domestic war on terror.* Verso.

Larsson, G. (2012). The fear of small numbers: Eurabia literature and censuses on religious belonging. *Journal of Muslims in Europe, 1*(2), 142–165. https://doi.org/10.1163/22117954-12341237

Lentin, A. (2008). Europe and the silence about race. *European Journal of Social Theory, 11*(4), 487–503. https://doi.org/10.1177/1368431008097008

López, F. B. (2011). Towards a definition of Islamophobia: Approximations of the early twentieth century. *Ethnic and Racial Studies, 34*(4), 556–573.

Medovoi, L. (2012). Dogma-line racism: Islamophobia and the second axis of race. *Social Text, 30*(2), 43–74. https://doi.org/10.1215/01642472-1541754

Meer, N., & Modood, T. (2009). Refutations of racism in the 'Muslim question'. *Patterns of Prejudice, 43*(3–4), 335–354. https://doi.org/10.1080/00313220903109250

mxx/dpa. (2020). *Polizei gegen Clans: 'Wir durchbrechen den Mythos der Unangreifbarkeit'* [Police against Clans: 'We are breaking the myth of unassailability']. *Der Spiegel.* Spiegel Panorama. Retrieved November 20, 2021, from https://www.spiegel.de/panorama/justiz/berlin-polizei-erfolge-gegen-clans-die-fuehlen-sich-gestoert-a-1303331.html

Peter, F. (2010). Welcoming Muslims into the nation. Tolerance politics and integration in Germany. In J. Cesari (Ed.), *Muslims in Europe and the United States since 9/11* (pp. 119–144). Routledge. https://doi.org/10.4324/9780203863961

Räthzel, N. (1991). Germany: One race, one nation? *Race & Class, 32*(3), 29–48. https://doi.org/10.1177/030639689103200305

Räthzel, N., & Kalpaka, A. (1986). *Die Schwierigkeit, nicht rassistisch zu sein* [The difficulty of not being racist]. Express Edition.

Rodatz, M., & Scheuring, J. (2011). Integration als Extremismusprävention Rassistische Effekte der wehrhaften Demokratie bei der Konstruktion eines islamischen Extremismus [Integration as extremism prevention racist effects of defensible democracy in the construction of Islamic extremism]. In F. für kritische Rechtsextremismusforschung (Ed.), *Ordnung. Macht. Extremismus* (pp. 163–190). VS Verlag für Sozialwissenschaften. https://doi.org/10.1007/978-3-531-93281-1

Runnymede Trust. (1997). *Islamophobia: A challenge for us all: Report of the Runnymede Trust Commission on British Muslims and Islamophobia.* Runnymede Trust.

Saïd, E. W. (1985). Orientalism reconsidered. *Race & Class, 27,* 1–15. https://doi.org/10.1177/030639688502700201

Sarrazin, T. (2010). *Deutschland schafft sich ab: Wie wir unser Land aufs Spiel setzen* [Germany abolishing/undoing itself: how we're putting our country in jeopardy]. Deutsche Verlags-Anstalt.

Sayyid, S. (2014). A measure of Islamophobia. *Islamophobia Studies Journal, 2*(1), 10–25.

Schiffauer, W. (2006). Enemies within the gates. The debate about the citizenship of Muslims in Germany. In T. Modood, A. Triandafyllidou, & R. Zapata-Barrero (Eds.), *Multiculturalism, Muslims and citizenship. A European approach* (pp. 94–116). Routledge.

Schiffauer, W. (2014). The irresponsible Muslim: Islam in German public culture. In F. Peter & R. Ortega (Eds.), *Islamic movements of Europe. Public religion and Islamophobia in the modern world* (pp. 344–350). I. B. Tauris.

Schiffauer, W., & Bojadžijev, M. (2009). Es geht nicht um einen Dialog. Integrationsgipfel, Islamkonferenz und Anti-Islamismus [Germany is doing away with itself: How we are putting our country at risk]. In S. Hess, J. Binder, & J. Moser (Eds.), *No Integration?!* (pp. 171–186). Transcript Verlag.

Schmidt, I. (2017). Pegida: A hybrid form of a populist right movement. *German Politics and Society, 35*(4), 105–117. https://doi.org/10.3167/gps.2017.350405

Schmuck, D., & Matthes, J. (2019). Voting 'against Islamization'? How anti-Islamic right-wing, populist political campaign ads influence explicit and implicit attitudes toward Muslims as well as voting preferences. *Political Psychology, 40*(4), 739–757. https://doi.org/10.1111/pops.12557

Schneiders, T. G. (2010). *Islamfeindlichkeit : wenn die Grenzen der Kritik verschwimmen* [Islamophobia: When the boundaries of criticism become blurred]. VS Verlag.

Šeta, D. (2016). *Forgotten women: The impact of Islamophobia on Muslim women.* ENAR. www.enar-eu.org

Soyer, F. (2019). *Antisemitic conspiracy theories in the early modern Iberian world.* Brill.

Stoler, A. L. (1995). *Race and the education of desire. Foucault's history of sexuality and the colonial order of things.* Duke University Press.

Terkessidis, M. (2004). *Die Banalität des Rassismus Migranten zweiter Generation entwickeln eine neue Perspektive* [The banality of racism. Second generation migrants develop a new perspective]. Transcript Verlag.

Tezcan, L. (2008). Governmentality, pastoral care and integration. In A. Al-Hamarneh & J. Thielmann (Eds.), *Islam and Muslims in Germany* (pp. 119–133). Brill.

Tezcan, L. (2012). *Das Muslimische Subjekt. Verfangen im Dialog der Deutschen Islam Konferenz* [The Muslim subject. Trapped in the dialogue of the German Islam Conference]. Konstanz University Press.

Topolski, A. (2018). The race-religion constellation: A European contribution to the critical philosophy of race. *Critical Philosophy of Race, 1*(6), 58–81.

Topolski, A. (2020). Nation-states, the race-religion constellation, and diasporic political communities: Hannah Arendt, Judith Butler, and Paul Gilroy. *European Legacy, 25*(3), 266–281. https://doi.org/10.1080/10848770.2020.1741264

Uenal, F. (2016). The 'secret Islamization' of Europe: Exploring integrated threat theory for predicting Islamophobic conspiracy stereotypes. *International Journal of Conflict and Violence, 10*(1), 93–108. https://doi.org/10.41119/UNIBI/ijcv.499

Vakil, A. (2010). Is the Islam in Islamophobia the same as the Islam in anti-Islam; or when is it Islamophobia time? In S. Sayyid & A. Vakil (Eds.), *Thinking through Islamophobia: Global Perspectives* (pp. 23–43). Hurst & Company.

Webman, E. (Ed.). (2011). *The global impact of the 'Protocols of the Elders of Zion': A century-old myth.* Routledge.

Yegane Arani, A. (2015). *Anti-Muslim racism and Islamophobia in Germany. Alternative report on the 19th – 22nd state report of the Federal Republic of Germany in accordance with Article 9 of the International Convention on the Elimination of All Forms of Racial Discrimination.* The Network Against Discrimination and Islamophobia, Inssan e.V.

Zia-Ebrahimi, R. (2018). When the Elders of Zion relocated to Eurabia: Conspiratorial racialization in antisemitism and Islamophobia. *Patterns of Prejudice, 52*(4), 314–337. https://doi.org/10.1080/0031322X.2018.1493876

PART III

MEDIA PRACTICES

6

ISLAMOPHOBIA IN THE MEDIA IN THE PROVINCE OF QUÉBEC, CANADA: A CORPUS-ASSISTED CRITICAL DISCOURSE ANALYSIS[1]

VIVEK VENKATESH, ABDELWAHED MEKKI-BERRADA, JIHÈNE HICHRI, RAWDA HARB & ASHLEY MONTGOMERY

Abstract

The chapter employs corpus-assisted critical discourse analyses to identify and describe how themes related to Islamophobia are relayed by columnists and editorial writers in eight of the most widely read dailies in the Province of Québec, Canada from 2010 to 2020. Collocation analyses of more than 3 million words followed by inductive content analyses yielded two major themes: Debates about Islamophobia in the popular media and scholars' perspectives of Islamophobia as relayed by the media. Results are discussed in light of sociological frames of xenophobia and media studies. Policy options to include multiple stakeholders in addressing hateful conduct enabled through Islamophobia are discussed.

Keywords: Islamophobia, Québec, Canada, popular media, corpus-assisted critical discourse analysis, content analysis, grounded theory

Introduction

Let us note at the outset that the notion of Islamophobia remains controversial, and this for several reasons, the most widespread of which is that it would necessarily be a liberticidal notion aiming to proscribe any criticism of Islam and Muslims (Mekki-Berrada, 2019). The most conservative-leaning of Muslims and their acolytes – who represent a minority of the 1.7 billion people who identify as Muslim – seek to prohibit any criticism of Islam, in the Muslim world as much as in the West. However, as in any democracy where freedom of expression is an inalienable and non-negotiable right, prohibiting criticism is simply unthinkable. But, as the historian of secularism and sociologist Jean Baubérot (2012) rightly points out in a video address, 'a clear distinction must be made between the right to criticism and hate speech or advocacy of hatred', and 'while criticism is a matter of free debate, hate speech and advocacy of hatred are a matter for justice'.

Context

The notion of Islamophobia in this chapter refers to a discursive, socio-political strategy of violent psychological and physical assaults, hate speech, exclusion and discrimination against Muslims because they are Muslims, and wherein Islam tends to be constructed as 'a lasting trauma' (Said, 2003, p. 76). Islamophobia is part of a relationship of social domination accompanied by an attempt at ontological inferiorisation, dehumanisation and animalisation of the Muslim 'other'. Islamophobia is first and foremost a matter of power (see the introductory chapter to this book by Mekki-Berrada and d'Haenens). It is, in the Foucauldian sense of the term, a form of 'governmentality of Muslim alterity' (Mekki-Berrada, 2018a, p. 24, 2019). At the centre of this governing technique, Islamophobia is primarily aimed at Muslim women whose bodies form a political and ideological battleground.

The 2010s in Québec were marked, among other events highlighted in the introduction to this book (Mekki-Berrada & d'Haenens), by three major events that shook both the Canadian political class and the Canadian population. These events need to be briefly recalled here, because they allow for a better contextualisation of the results discussed in this chapter. They are (1) the introduction of the so-called 'Quebec Charter of Values', (2) *Bill 21* and (3) the first mass murder perpetrated in a mosque in the West, in contemporary history. 'The Charter of Quebec Values', as it was clumsily titled by its advocates and the media, refers to *Bill 60: A Charter Affirming the Values of Secularism and Religious Neutrality of the State and of Equality between Women and Men and framing Requests for Accommodation*. It was tabled in the National Assembly by the then provincial government (in minority power) in November 2013. A source of tension and social polarisation that spread among the population like a burning powder train, Bill 60 sought, among other things, to prohibit the wearing of religious 'ostentatious signs' (e.g., hijab, turban, kirpa, kippa, cross) in public service. This was seen by some commentators as essentially stigmatising and discriminating against

Muslims in general, and Muslim women in particular. Bill 60 was also seen as implementing at least two processes, including the 'catho-laicisation' (*catho-laïcité*, a combination of rejection of historical religious practices alongside the establishment of laicity) of the state (Baubérot, 2006, 2007) and the securitisation of immigration in general, in particular of its Muslim component (Mekki-Berrada, 2014, 2018a, 2018b).

The intense social and political tensions generated in such a turmoil contributed to the fall of the government in April 2014, less than 20 months after its election. It was not until June 2019, and this is the second major event, that another government, this time with a strong majority, imposed Bill 21, titled *An Act respecting the laicity of the State*, which builds on the platform created by Bill 60. Bill 21 rekindled the social, cultural, religious and political tensions simmering in the province. In the context of the introduction and eventual adoption of Bill 21 in 2019 it is important to frame the third major event, which occurred on 29 January 2017, when an avowed right-wing extremist of 27 years of age shot and killed six Muslim worshippers and injured 19 others in a terrorist attack at La Grande Mosquée in Québec City.

In light of these tumultuous events, the notion of Islamophobia remains young and semantically immature – especially in Québec – yet it refers to a 'moral panic' (Cohen, 2002) that tends to be aroused in the West by the idea of the Muslim-existential threat, and by Islam as a threat both to 'the political and symbolic gains of cultural "majorities"' (Helly, 2015, p. 5) and to 'secular patterns of thought' (Helly, 2015, p. 7; Sayyid, 2014). There are also essayists and social science commentators whose works form 'a direct symptom of the existence, in academic circles, of a "scholarly Islamophobia" that distills hostile language under the guise of science' (Bibeau, 2017, p. 41; Said, 2003). This pseudo-scholarly Islamophobia is maintained by its 'experts', media stars for the most part, and still deeply imbued with the primitive orientalism of the 18th and 19th centuries. It is relayed today in the media as well as in European, North American and Asian extreme-right spaces (Mekki-Berrada, 2019; Saïd, 2003). The present chapter consists, in this context, in analysing Islamophobia as a concept and as a social reality as it is treated by Québec daily newspapers, both in the English and French language.

The central objective of the present project[2] is to identify and describe how themes related to Islamophobia are relayed by columnists and editorial writers in some of the most widely read dailies in the Province of Québec.

Methodology[3]

We sourced articles from eight dailies (two of which are English-language dailies: *The Globe and Mail*, and *The Montreal Gazette*) available provincially in Québec, using the keywords 'islamophobia', 'islam', 'islamist', 'islam', 'islamism', 'muslim', and its variant terms from the years 2010 to 2020. Our sampling yielded 1,515 online articles, opinion pieces and related publications (readers' online comments on the articles) from the following sources:

- *Le Journal de Montréal*: 555 articles
- *Le Journal de Québec*: 125 articles
- *La Presse*: 18 articles.
- *Le Soleil*: 102 articles
- *The Montreal Gazette*: 102 articles
- *The Globe and Mail*: 177 articles
- *L'Actualité*: 149 articles
- *Le Devoir*: 287 articles.

Our sampling strategy yielded a main corpus of 3,254,346 words, with 2,503,620 words in French, and 750,726 words in English. Note that in the results section we provide exemplars of texts from some dailies, but, due to space constraints, we do not provide extracts from all the above sources.

To analyse our corpus of more than 3.25 million words, we employed an innovative mixed methodology, namely, corpus-assisted critical discourse analysis (CACDA) (Thomas, 2015). As an analytical technique, CACDA provides both a quantitative portrait of data in terms of word frequency information and associative textual patterns, and a qualitative interpretation of the discursive context surrounding significant word associations measured through collocations. As the nomenclature suggests, CACDA combines transitional corpus linguistic techniques (Hunston, 2002) with critical discourse analysis (Fairclough, 2003). The quantitative techniques associated with corpus linguistics can help to reveal the focus of a given corpus. For example, frequency counts and dispersion analysis with the help of plots and clusters can reveal the use and distribution of important concepts within a corpus. Concordance analysis can be used to reveal not only the frequency of particular keywords within a corpus, but can also facilitate detailed analysis of the context surrounding each instance of the terms, which can expose certain discursive constructions. Collocation analysis, which was used extensively in this research, can help to reveal the strength of the relationship between two or more words.

We used a rigorously developed and widely used software, Sketch Engine, to conduct the frequency, concordance, and collocation analyses for our project. Owing to the large size of the corpus, we split up the main corpus into four component corpora of manageable size (approximately 700,000 words each). For each of these component corpora, our collocation analyses were conducted as follows. Based on frequency counts, we entered a series of keywords (or lemmas as they are termed in corpus linguistics) one at a time into Sketch Engine's Word Sketch function. From there, the software identified collocates (terms associated with the keyword/lemma at a statistically significant level) from a span of ten words on either side of the keyword.

Statistical significance of relational strength was determined by the logDice value: a statistic that combines the relative frequencies of two words – X and Y – appearing close to each other within a corpus alongside the frequencies of those same two words – X and Y – appearing largely independent of each other within that corpus (derived from Rychlý, 2008). The logDice statistic carries a theoretical maximum value of 14, in cases where 'all occurrences of X co-occur with Y and all occurrences of Y co-occur with X' (Rychlý, 2008, p. 9). For example, the collocation 'discourse analysis' would carry a logDice value of 14 if every time the lemma 'discourse' appears within a text it appears alongside 'analysis', and vice versa. Usually, however, logDice values are less than 10. The calculation of logDice is based solely on the frequency of the lemma and the collocate and the frequency of the whole collocation (co-occurrence of the lemma and collocate). The value of logDice is independent of the size of the corpus and, therefore, can be used to compare scores between different corpora. A detailed mathematical explanation of the calculation of logDice can be found in Kilgarriff et al. (2014).

Once a series of collocates were identified for each keyword, we employed a critical discourse analysis to examine the discursive context immediately surrounding the collocates with a logDice value of 10 or greater. This threshold of 10 was chosen because logDice holds a theoretical minimum of 0 and maximum of 14; it is widely accepted that collocations that carry a logDice value of 10 or greater reveal particularly strong discursive relationships (Baker et al., 2013; Rychlý, 2008). Qualitatively, we employ constructivist grounded theory principles (Charmaz, 2014) with a constant comparative inductive analysis (Spiggle, 1994) of source data in the corpus. Our chosen methodology allows us to (1) refer to existing theoretical frameworks; (2) account for themes already discussed in existing literature; and (3) allow theoretical presuppositions and empirical evidence discussed in the literature to interact with emergent themes from the data. Using open in vivo coding, we will ensure that only codes that repeat themselves across multiple component corpora are used to construct themes discussed in the results, thereby enabling triangulation and an approximation of theoretical saturation.

Results

Following the quantitative analysis produced by Sketch Engine, we examined the context in which word pairs appear to better understand the nature of the discourses. We then grouped the main concepts that were associated into themes using our constant comparative method. We identified a series of concepts under two main themes that were mainly discussed:

1.   The concepts 'Islam', 'Muslim', 'radical', 'moderate', 'value', 'culture', 'minority', 'politics', 'Islamism', 'veil', 'criticism', 'Islamophobia', 'fundamentalist', 'racist', 'terrorist', 'hatred', 'propaganda', 'racism', 'multiculturalism', 'value', 'identity', 'fundamentalist', etc., and some names of activists like 'Adil Charkaoui' and 'Dalila Awada', were the basis of the theme 'The representation of Islam and Muslims and the debate on the concept of Islamophobia in the media'.

2.   The concepts 'Islam', 'secularism', 'neutrality', 'right', 'freedom', 'equality', 'sociologist', 'intellectual', 'book', 'scientist', 'political scientist', and the names of writers, intellectuals and specialists such as 'Gérard Bouchard', 'Taylor', 'El-Mabrouk', 'Fatima Houda-Pepin', 'Abdennour Bidar', 'Anne-Marie Delcambre', 'Tariq Ramadan', 'Caroline Valentin' and so on formed the basis of the theme 'Scholars' perspectives of Islamophobia as relayed by the media'.

The Representation of Islam and Muslims and the Debate on the Concept of Islamophobia in the Media

Definition of Islamophobia. The results show in a general way that the term Islamophobia is presented by the columnists and editorialists as a notion up for debate. Our analysis reveals a certain instability in the conception of this word. Several columnists and editorialists try to conceive the meaning of this term starting from their own opinions, but also based on scientific, political and media discourses.

> The word 'Islamophobia' is banned in the Parti Québécois (PQ), which prefers to use the expression 'anti-Muslim sentiment' instead. The semantic prowess does not pass the test of common sense. Would we accept to speak

of anti-gay sentiment instead of homophobia? Anti-Jewish sentiment instead of anti-Semitism? The PQ justifies its position by the fact that the term 'Islamophobia' is being used by Muslim fundamentalists, which is true. But fundamentalists do not have a monopoly on the use of this term, which is widely used in popular discourse and scientific research. To deny the very idea of a debate on Islamophobia is to deny the freedom of those most affected to name things as they feel them.' (So that they did not die in vain, bis in *Le Devoir* by Brian Myles, 27 January 2018)

Islamophobia, freedom of expression or racism? We note that the frequency of appearance of the terms 'Islamophobia' and 'Islamophobic' is quite high, but this can be explained in part by the importance of the number of articles analysed on the one hand, and the use of this term by readers in their comments that are part of the data analysed. The significant co-occurrence of the words 'criticism', 'racism' and 'freedom of expression' reveals a multiplicity of efforts to distinguish these terms, or to link them to the notion of Islamophobia. Some columnists and editorialists distinguish between 'Islamophobia' and 'freedom of expression' when it comes to assessing their words, but this logic is reversed when it comes to the words of an imam, activist or intellectual defending Islam and Muslims. Their words are frequently associated with 'racism' and 'sexism', but not with 'freedom of expression'.

> Why link Quebec to a tragedy on the other side of the world [the Christchurch, New Zealand mosque shooting in March 2019]? To fuel the victimisation of Muslims here? Or to attack the freedoms of the host society? Let's be clear, when Ms. Torres adds 'Islamophobia and hatred are a poison. It is up to everyone not to propagate it in any way', she wishes to stop criticising Islam as a religion and Islamism as a political posture. (Ravary, 2019)

The context of the appearance of the two terms 'freedom' and 'criticism' shows a denunciation of the use of the concept of Islamophobia, which is considered a semantic manipulation aiming at hindering the exercise of 'freedom of expression' and 'criticism' of Islam and Muslims. We note that some columnists, especially in *Le Journal de Montréal* and *Le Devoir*, tend to adopt a contradictory discourse that opposes the logic of racism without expressing a condemnation of this phenomenon. Furthermore, we note that their discourse is oriented towards a criticism of anti-racist or anti-Islamophobic groups.

> A religion frozen in its dogmas becomes sclerotic, it becomes fanaticism, it becomes unbearable towards its followers and aggressive towards

unbelievers, it responds to criticism with anathema and excommunication: whoever allows himself, for example, to point out the incompatibility of Islam with the autonomy of individuals or with the freedom of women is immediately, and without appeal, accused of Islamophobia. In this regard, the term 'Islamophobia' is, today, used wrongly. There is Islamophobia when Islam and Muslims are the target of hate speech and victims of criminal acts, not when the Koranic doctrine is subject to various interpretations that do not please this or that fundamentalist. Furthermore, any generalisation is likely to strain relations between adherents of various beliefs: just because one individual murders Muslims at prayer does not mean that all of Quebec should be branded with the seal of infamy. (Haroun, 2018)

We also note that some columnists propose an articulation of the two terms 'Islamophobia' and 'racism' as two related phenomena. Thus, criticism is addressed to their colleagues who refuse to conceive Islamophobia as a form of racism and to denounce racist and Islamophobic situations that Muslims face. These journalists (of whom there are very few) recognise that this minority of Muslims is a victim of negative stereotypes and prejudices.

Islamophobia does exist in Quebec. There are individuals who express Islamophobic ideas. There are also hate crimes that target the Muslim community … without making Quebec an Islamophobic nation. Let us be clear, there is absolutely nothing intolerant about debating Islamism, as has been done in Quebec for years. There is nothing Islamophobic about militating for secularism, opposing the full veil or criticizing radical fundamentalism. Islamophobia is much more than that: it is the irrational fear, the visceral aversion, the hostility against Muslims. It is the pig's head placed in front of a mosque. It's the burning of a Muslim's car. It's the multiplication of hateful gestures. (Cardinal, 2018)

Perceptions of Islam. Our analyses show that there is a considerable place given to the qualification of 'Islam' by the words 'political', 'radical', 'Islamism', etc. The recurrent use of certain terms such as 'charter', 'veil', 'religious', 'Islamist', 'woman', 'secularism', 'values', 'Al-Qaeda' and 'Daesh' shows a certain strategy used to describe the different dimensions and characteristics related to this religion to reach a conclusion that defends or condemns Islam and Muslims. In other words, these words are presented as pieces of a larger puzzle to build a picture of Islam supporting the opinion of the columnist. The frequent association of the word 'Islam' with the words 'political' and 'radical', and the very frequent use of the words 'Islamists' and 'Islamism' also reveal a preconceived opinion about Islam and Muslims, in particular about veiled women, who are perceived as a real danger linked to the spread of radical forms of Islam. The Muslim is presented by some columnists as a potential invader, barbarian or even terrorist. This image, which serves to argue and justify the fear and rejection of Islam, is conveyed through events that reveal a 'fundamentalist Islamism'.

> Radical Islam is a social regression. Freedom of religion as defined by the Canadian Charter of Rights and Freedoms cannot become a Trojan horse for destabilising claims that put citizens in fear. And no one should be gagged by the risk of being labelled Islamophobic. It would be intolerable if Islam could escape the severe criticism that is applied to Christianity and Judaism in our society. Furthermore, who dares to say that anti-Semitism is part of the culture of Islam, because it is written in the Koran? And all Islamists, not all Muslims, carry within them a hatred of Jews. The rise of Islamophobia in our country is directly related to the abuses perpetrated by the Taliban, Al Qaeda and Daesh, and the attacks committed by other religious nuts. Our politicians have a responsibility to speak out in a way that does not encourage unbalanced and intolerant people to take the step to hate Muslims. But they must in no way allow themselves to be contaminated by the guilt and angelic quality that resides in Justin Trudeau. (Bombardier, 2018)

There is an emphasis in several articles on the links between Islam in Québec and Islam in France. Certain examples of incidents, statistics or study results are put forward by some columnists and editorialists to confirm and validate an opinion on Islam and Muslims. Generally, these examples are manipulated to support the negative connotation, presenting Islam as a danger that threatens the Western world as illustrated by the following excerpt:

> It's been more than thirty years that we close our eyes to these propagandists of a misogynistic, homophobic and retrograde Islam that are rampant with impunity in schools and mosques in France. The first to sound the alarm, as early as 2002, were the authors of the book *Les territoires perdus de la République* (Mille et une nuits) edited by the historian Georges Bensoussan. Since then, all studies have confirmed the thesis of an increasingly massive Islamisation of the French suburbs. (Rioux, 2020)

Perception of Muslims. Our analyses reveal that a distinction is made between Muslims who wish to integrate into Québec society by respecting the 'values' of the majority Franco-Québec population and who are in favour of Law 21 (which, among other restrictions, forbids the wearing of religious garb by certain employees of the State), and Muslims who are less inclined to do so. Muslims who integrate are valued, as illustrated by the following excerpt:

> Furthermore, Muslims do not escape the vindictiveness of Islamic fundamentalists. In our country, courageous Muslim women such as Fatima Houda-Pepin, Nadia El-Mabrouk and Djemila Benhabib are themselves called Islamophobes. And because they are women, Islamists attack them with fury and contempt. They are Quebec heroines before whom we should bow. (Bombardier, 2018)

We also note that even if some columnists avoid lumping together all Muslims as fundamentalists, they still emphasise the danger posed by certain 'Islamists' even though the latter represent a minority.

> The problem is that the dominant terrorist movement is not only loosely linked to Muslims. It claims to act in the name of a 'fighting' Islam. The most barbaric groups base their propaganda on a supposed religious justification. Who can answer this, if not the legitimate representatives of the Muslim faith? Yesterday, Syed Soharwardy, a Calgary imam who founded Muslims Against Terrorism, said we need to mobilise Muslim leaders in Canada to keep an eye especially on new converts. (Boisvert, 2014)

There are frequent uses of the conjunction 'but', which serves to warn readers to not underestimate the Islamist danger, even if it is propagated by a minority, as illustrated by the following excerpts.

> Muslims do not have to bear the guilt of terrorist or psychiatric aberrations committed in the name of Allah. But as things stand, they do have an additional responsibility to counter them. The vast majority of peaceful Muslims unjustly bear the burden of violent Islam. And of the one that justifies violence. Or encourages it. Or excuses it. But this other Islam has its representatives or sympathisers in the flesh, right here in Canada. (Boisvert, 2014)

Meaning of the veil. Religious symbols, in particular the Islamic veil, were also the subject of debate in the articles analysed, with positions differing between columnists. The issue is generally approached from different angles. For example, from a secular point of view, the veil is seen as a form of proselytising, Islamisation and an attack on the neutrality of state institutions. However, from the principle of equality between men and women, the veil is a form of oppression and submission that is incompatible with Western values. Some columnists tend to associate the veil with 'political Islam', 'fundamentalism' and the oppression of women, presenting an image of Muslim women oppressed by Islamists and forced to wear the veil to dominate and invade Western countries.

> Marks & Spencer, Dolce & Gabbana, H&M and Uniqlo are now offering hijabs, veils, long tunics and swimsuits that cover the entire body. It's like being in Michel Houellebecq's *Soumission* … By 'glamorizing' the veil, by saying loudly and clearly that it is only a fashion accessory like any other, the designers are participating in trivializing the misogynistic discourse of religious fundamentalists. (Martineau, 2016)

Other columnists denounce the ban on the veil because they believe that the veil is an individual freedom that should not be interpreted as a symbol of fundamentalism. It can be seen that columnists and editorialists who oppose the veil ban tend to follow a strategy to present their arguments without offending their readers. They first put forward a discourse that the majority 'obviously' agree with, such as the legitimacy of fighting radical Islamism, terrorism, fundamentalism, etc. They then couch their opposition to the veil ban as one that pits the tension between liberty and equality in liberal democracies.

> Should we fight religious fundamentalism? Absolutely! Because fundamentalism is a step backwards in relation to the secular advances made in Quebec and Canada, thanks to which the governance of the State is no longer guided by religious norms. However, we must not designate as fundamentalism what is not. Is the veil a symbol of fundamentalism? A girl wearing a veil who attends a Quebec school is not a fundamentalist. Neither is a woman wearing a veil who works in a Quebec public institution; it can be assumed that she at least shares the common values of the society. The majority of women who wear the veil in Quebec adopt orthodox behaviors, such as eating halal, but they do not respect religious norms at all times – especially the young ones. We are not at all in fundamentalist logics. (Dubé, 2014)

Scholars' Perspectives of Islamophobia as Relayed by the Media

As already pointed out, several columnists and editorialists emphasise the contentious definitions of Islamophobia in books, articles and other published sources. Some columnists and editorialists from *Journal de Montréal, Le Devoir, La Presse* an' *L'Actualité* reference intellectuals or essayists who frame Islamophobia as a strategy used to curb criticism of Islam. In particular, the essayist Pascal Bruckner, who sees Islamophobia as an 'imaginary racism' (*racisme imaginaire*) to prevent any criticism of Islam, is often referenced by these columnists.

> A new word had been invented to allow the blind to remain blind: Islamophobia. To criticise the militant violence of this religion in its contemporary incarnation was considered fanaticism. – Salman Rushdie. There was a time in Quebec when books on the index circulated under the cloak. Will the same be true of Pascal Bruckner's latest book, *Un racisme imaginaire, islamophobie et culpabilité* (Grasset)? (Rioux, 2017)

This columnist, Christian Rioux, goes on to present testimonies of appreciation for the book of Pascal Bruckner that are made by intellectuals and politicians. Later, Rioux points out that Bruckner acknowledges in his book the existence of various forms of discrimination against Muslims and racism against Arabs living in France. This discrimination is quickly mitigated by the columnist by questioning whether it is 'allegedly systemic'. Rioux then proceeds to distinguish opposing views of Islam by pitting those who he sees as fundamentalist, and, in Rioux's words, 'nihilistic', versus those who are more moderate.

> The main interest of this book lies in the brilliance with which the author demonstrates to what extent this crime of Islamophobia serves first and foremost to condemn those who, from within Islam itself, seek to reform this religion. In short, to fight the reformists who claim the right to exegesis in an Islam too often dominated by a nihilistic culture of death. In our countries, the mere fact of evoking a 'Muslim problem' and the rise of fundamentalism is today worth witch hunts that target intellectuals like Michel Houellebecq, Georges Bensoussan, Jeannette Bougrab, Djemila Benhabib and Pascal Bruckner himself. Not to mention the cartoonists of Charlie Hebdo. Through a meticulous analysis, the author demonstrates how, thanks to the new victim competition, Islamophobia has by successive shifts tried to occupy the place that anti-Semitism occupied at the end of the war. (Rioux, 2017)

Based on the writings of certain intellectuals and essayists, some columnists and editorialists consider Islamophobia as an unreasoned fear of Islam and Muslims. This fear can be manifested by aversion, hatred or rejection, and finally generate a new form of racism. This conception of Islamophobia is based on definitions proposed by certain intellectuals and essayists such as Michel Seymour and Frédéric Castel. For example, the journalist Jean-Benoit Nadeau distinguishes between the terms 'fundamentalist' and 'radicalist' as presented by Frédéric Castel:

> The fundamentalist has a conservative reading of religious texts, but is not violent. He is almost always reacting to the dominant group of his religion, which he considers too conciliatory. The radicalist, on the other hand, is more sectarian; he pushes the withdrawal and the disengagement further. He condemns the outside world, including his co-religionists who do not adhere to his ideas. (Nadeau, 2015)

Last but not least, it is worth noting that some columnists and essayists of Muslim origin such as Fatima Houda-Pepin, Abdenour Bidar and Nadia El-Mabrouk are often referenced by other columnists because they contest the silence of Muslims in the face of radical Islamism and fight against the racism and hate speech of Islamists and the 'jihadist violence' against 'unbelievers'. These columnists also applaud essayists' analyses that reference the tensions and weakening of social order in Québec because of the rise of religious communitarians and their incessant demands for inclusion.

Discussion of Policy Options

In this final section, we choose to depart from the traditional paradigmatic style of propositions for future research, and instead point to specific policy options for stakeholders in government, big technology and related institutions.

1.   Human rights issues associated with addressing the rise of polarisations must employ multi-stakeholder policy development that encourages collaboration among sectors such as research, pedagogy, communications and media, big technology, social services, public safety and criminal justice. This can ensure that protection of rights and equalities through public education programmes are approached in a holistic fashion.
2.   Canada's legal system must review, and, where necessary, adopt clear, precise and delimited definitions of hate speech and related phenomena such as xenophobia, discrimination and prejudice to ensure clarity in

development of any policies pertaining to prevention of hate speech, including those that might be classified as Islamophobic.

3. Curricular programmes that focus on human rights preservation should draw from multiple theoretical frameworks including civic and citizen education, critical thinking, pluralism, empathy and perspective-taking, multi-culturalism and religion, peace education, social justice, social pedagogy, violence prevention, digital literacy, enquiry-based learning, as well as media and information literacy, among others.

4. Evaluation of initiatives that ensure preservation of human rights requires careful planning and should ideally be conducted through regulatory and policy-making bodies. Multiple sources of triangulated data must be collected including, for instance, the frequency of incidents of human rights violation, analyses of codes and policies, as well as monitoring and documentation of behaviours, academic outcomes and pedagogical practices in curricular contexts. A more concerted effort must be made to identify specific societally beneficial programmes that preserve human rights, and to promote best practices for sustainably evaluating these from both a formative and summative standpoint.

Concluding Remarks

Our analyses of texts using the innovative model of both corpus statistics and critical discourse analysis provide a detailed description of how Islamophobia has been framed, justified and deliberated in the sphere of popular media in Québec from 2010 to 2020. We acknowledge that these analyses must be complemented with further work on the public's opinions on the issue of Islamophobia, both in reaction to popular media as well as on open online forums such as Reddit, YouTube, Facebook and Twitter, where the potential for exposure to multiplicities of viewpoints is still possible despite the existence of so-called echo chambers (Nelson & Venkatesh, 2021).

Notes

1.   The research for this chapter stems from a project mainly funded by the Social Sciences and Humanities Research Council (SSHRC): *Scholarly and mediatic Islamophobia: A transnational study of discourses and their impact* (Original French title *Islamophobie savante et médiatique: Étude transnationale des discours et de leur impact*; SSHRC 2019-2023, #890-2018-0016), for which Abdelwahed Mekki-Berrada is the Principal Investigator.

2.   The research reported in this chapter is funded by a Partnership Development Grant award-
      ed by the Social Sciences and Humanities Research Council of Canada titled 'Islamophobia
      in Scholarship and the Media: A Cross-National Study of Discourses and Their Impact'
      (Grant #890-2018-0016), for which chapter co-author Abdelwahed Mekki-Berrada is the
      principal investigator and for which chapter co-author Vivek Venkatesh is a co-applicant.
3.   Detailed descriptive statistical analyses of keyword counts and outputs of logDice values
      of collocations can be procured by writing to the principal author at vivek.venkatesh@
      concordia.ca. Space restrictions prevented the authors from providing a detailed appendix
      of statistical output.

References

Baker, P., Gabrielatos, C., & McEnery, T. (2013). Sketching Muslims: A corpus driven analysis of
      representations around the word 'Muslim' in the British press 1998–2009. *Applied Linguistics,*
      34(3), 255–278.

Baubérot, J. (2006). *L'intégrisme républicain contre la laïcité* [Republican Fundamentalism versus
      Secularism]. Éditions de l'Aube.

Baubérot, J. (2007). Transferts culturels et identité nationale dans la laïcité française [Cultural
      transfers and national identity in French secularism]. *Diogène, 2*(218), 18–27.

Baubérot, J. (2012, March 1). *Islam et laïcité* [Islam and laicity] [Video]. YouTube. https://www.
      youtube.com/watch?v=9N_ehXIyYYk&feature=youtu.be

Bibeau G. (2017). *Andalucía, l'histoire à rebours* [Andalusia, history in reverse]. Mémoire d'encrier.

Boisvert, Y. (2014, October 24). Islam de paix, Islam de guerre [Islam of war, Islam of peace].
      La Presse.

Bombardier, D. (2018, February 2). Justin Trudeau et l'islamophobie [Justin Trudeau and
      Islamophobia]. *Le Journal de Montréal.*

Cardinal, F. (2018, January 11). *Biffer l'islamophobie … pour en taire l'existence* [Strike out
      Islamophobia … to silence its existence]. La Presse.

Charmaz, K. (2014). *Constructing grounded theory.* Sage.

Cohen, S. (2002). *Folk devil and moral panics: The creation of the mods and rockers* (3rd ed.).
      Routledge.

Dubé, C. (2014, February 19). Comment la Charte des valeurs risque de favoriser l'intégrisme au
      lieu de le combattre ! [How the Charter of Values risks encouraging fundamentalism instead
      of fighting it!]. *L'Actualité.*

Fairclough, N. (2003). *Analysing discourse: Textual analysis for social research.* Routledge.

Haroun, S. (2018, February 22). La liberté de religion passe par la liberté de critiquer la religion
      [Freedom of religion requires freedom to criticise religion]. *Le Devoir.*

Helly, D. (2015). La peur de l'Islam [Fear of Islam]. *SociologieS.* http://sociologies.revues.org/4900

Hunston, S. (2002). *Corpora in applied linguistics.* Cambridge University Press.

Kilgarriff, A., Baisa, V., Bušta, J., Jakubíček, M., Ková`r, V., Michelfeit, J., Rychlý, P., & Suchomel,
      J. (2014). The sketch engine: Ten years on. *Lexicography, 1*(1), 7–36.

Martineau, R. (2016, April 4). Le voile, c'est chic ! [The veil is chic!]. *La Presse.*

Mekki-Berrada, A. (2014). La charte des valeurs québécoises: Co-exister (exister ensemble) dans
      la catho-laïcité de l'État et la sécurisation de l'immigration [The Quebec Charter of Values:
      Co-existing (existing together) in the catholic secularism of the State and the securitisation
      of immigration]. *Diversité canadienne/Canadian Diversity, 10*(2), 5–10.

Mekki-Berrada, A. (2018a). Femmes et subjectivations musulmanes: Prolégomènes [Women and Muslim subjectivities: Prolegomena]. *Anthropologie et sociétés, 42*(1), 9–33.

Mekki-Berrada, A. (2018b). Ayn mika: Traumatic experience, social invisibility, an0d emotional distress of sub-Saharan women with precarious status in Morocco. *Transcultural Psychiatry.* https://doi.org/10.1177/1363461518757798

Mekki-Berrada, A. (2019). Prolégomènes à une réhabilitation de la notion d'islamophobie [Prolegomena to a rehabilitation of the notion of Islamophobia]. *Religiologiques, 39,* 5–49.

Myles, B. (2018, January 27). Pour qu'ils ne soient pas morts en vain, bis [So that they did not die in vain, bis]. *Le Devoir.*

Nadeau, J. (2015, April 1). Une mosquée ou un « musallâ » ? [A mosque or a 'musallâ'?]. *L'Actualité.*

Nelson, B. J., & Venkatesh, V. (2021). Manifeste pour une pédagogie sociale par l'inclusivité réflexive [Manifesto for a social pedagogy through reflexive inclusiveness]. In D. Morin, S. Aoun, & S. Al-Baba Douaihy (Eds.), *Le nouvel âge des extrêmes ? Les démocraties occidentales, la radicalisation et l'extrémisme violent* [The new age of extremes? Western democracies, radicalisation and violent extremism] (pp. 483–504). Presses de l'Université de Montréal.

Ravary, L. (2019, March 18). *Racisme à géographie variable* [Racism with variable geography]. *Le Journal de Montréal.*

Rioux, C. (2017, February 17). Un racisme imaginaire? [An imagined racism?]. *Le Devoir.*

Rioux, C. (2020, February 21). Le séparatisme islamiste [The Islamist separatism]. *Le Devoir.*

Rychlý, P. (2008). A lexicographer-friendly association score. In P. Sojka & A. Horák (Eds.), *Proceedings of recent advances in Slavonic national language processing* (pp. 6–9). Masaryk University.

Saïd, E. W. (2003). *L'orientalisme. L'orient créé par l'Occident* [Orientalism. The East created by the West]. Seuil.

Sayyid, S. (2014). A measure of Islamophobia. *Islamophobia Studies Journal, 2*(1), 10–25.

Spiggle, S. (1994). Analysis and interpretation of qualitative data in consumer research. *Journal of Consumer Research, 21,* 491–503. https://doi.org/10.1086/209413

Thomas, T. (2015). *Analyzing online discourses of Canadian citizenship: O Canada! True north, strong and free?* [Doctoral dissertation, Concordia University]

7

THE VEIL IN FRANCE: TWENTY YEARS OF MEDIA COVERAGE (1989-2010)

CAMILA ARÊAS & ABDELWAHED MEKKI-BERRADA

Abstract

This chapter[1] analyses public debates around the 'headscarf affair' (1989–2004) and the 'burqa affair' (2009–2010) in France by questioning the mediatisation of the Islamic signs-symbols based on notions of visibility and spatiality. Ranging from news stories to the enactment of laws, these public debates mark the transition from a social visibility to a media visibility of the veil, putting into evidence the transformation of media controversies into national affairs and public issues. Based on the study of the coverage of the French national press, this chapter traces the genealogy of discourses that constructed the media visibility of the veil in France from 1989 to 2010. By means of a semiotic approach, it analyses the images and discourses that have constituted the sources of meaning of recent public debates on Islam in France. The aim of this study is to demonstrate how media coverage constructed a degraded and stigmatised visibility of the veil ('ostensible', 'over-visible', sign of 'proselytising' act of 'concealment'), legitimising thereby a geographic extension of the ban on the veil from schools to the streets. The analysis of the prohibitionist discourses of veil public debates reveals the construction of norms of Islamic visibility ('ostentation' vs. 'neutrality'; 'transparency' vs. 'concealment'), as well as a new political management of public appearances ('marked-unmarked'; 'illicit-licit'; 'minority-majority'). We argue then that the increasing media visibility of the Islamic veil contributes to a legal redefinition of French public space. This chapter seeks to contribute to a broader reflection on the transformation of contemporary public spaces with regard to the increasing media visibility of the veil and, more broadly, of Islam, a reflection that is particularly suitable for the European context.

Keywords: Islamophobia, Islam, veil, headscarf, burqa, media, France, visibility, spatiality, public space

Introduction

This chapter reports on a semiotic analysis of two public debates in France known as the 'headscarf affair' (1989–2004) and the 'burqa affair' (2009–2010), conducted to interrogate, through the notions of visibility and spatiality, the mediatisation of Islam. From the initial news coverage to the enactment of legal bans, these two 'affairs' marked the transition from social visibility to media visibility of the veil, while also highlighting the elevation of the controversies themselves into the realm of national 'affairs' or public issues. In the French and European contexts, these debates provide insight into how legal, political and/or media agendas regarding the Islamic veil are constructed, which in turn raises new questions about the *visibility* and *spatiality* of Islamic symbols. They remain relevant today, well after 2010. In France, examples of debates include those regarding women and girls wearing veils on school trips (2007–2013), in daycare centres (2008–2015), in universities (2013–2016), on beaches (2016) and in corporate settings (2013–2017). With the election season underway at the time of writing (January 2022), these debates, as well as the social polarisation surrounding them, persist. Within Europe, they are particularly salient in French-speaking countries.

Against this backdrop, this chapter intends to highlight how the media visibility of the Islamic veil is contributing to the transformation of our concepts of visibility and spatiality, which we have been presently defining in a broader sense, in the context of veil bans in France. How is it that the 'headscarf affair' in 1989 introduced an 'issue' regarding Islamic *visibility*, whereas the 'burqa affair' and the banning of the niqab from the street in 2009 raised new questions regarding public spaces? How, in the space of 20 years, did the illegitimate *visibility* of the headscarf become illegal *spatiality* of the niqab? How are public spaces, in France and in Europe, being legally redefined, politically regulated and socially re-signified, as a result of the changing media visibility of the headscarf and other Islamic symbols?

To answer these questions, we apply a semiotic method of analysis to both academic (scholarly journals in the field of Humanities and Social Sciences) and journalistic (national and regional press) output related to these public debates, with the goal of drawing a genealogy of the discourses that shaped France's 'veil affairs' from the 1990s to 2010. Our aim is to explore the ways in which the media coverage of these two affairs resulted in a denigrated and stigmatised form of visibility of the veil ('ostensible', 'overly visible', a sign of 'proselytising', an act of 'concealment'), which in turn legitimised a spatial expansion of the ban of the veil from the school to the street, in the name of public order. In other words, we aim to examine *how* and *to what extent* the veil-focused media debates contributed to the legitimisation of a new definition – at once legal, political and social – of the notion of public space, understood in an expansive sense.

We start by analysing scholarly work on the 'headscarf affair'. The corpus gathered for this analysis includes all scholarly articles related to the 'headscarf affair' published during the period of the debates (1989–2009) in journals qualified by the Agency for the Evaluation of Research and Higher Education (Agence d'évaluation de la recherche et de l'enseignement supérieur). It consists of 48 articles published by 42 researchers in 28 journals, as well as three thematic journal issues on either the 'headscarf affair' (*Droit et Société*, 2008, 'The Veil on Trial' [Le voile en procès]) or secularism in public schools (*Pouvoirs,* 75, 1995, 'Secularism' [La Laïcité]; *Mots*, 1991, 'Secularism' [Laïcité]). Through the analysis of this corpus, we highlight the emergence of an issue regarding the *visible*, which can be understood as a process involving the construction of the norms of visibility (ostentation–neutrality, transparency–concealment), and of the political management of public appearances (marked–unmarked, illicit–licit, minority–majority).

As a second step, we study the emergence of a *spatial* issue in the press coverage of the 'burqa affair'. The corpus selected for this analysis includes all articles published in the *Libération*, *Le Monde*, *Le Figaro* and *Le Parisien* newspapers from 16 June 2009 to 31 October 2010 (n = 126, out of a total of 17,013 articles published during this period), as well as all those published by the *Ouest France* and *Presse Océan* newspapers from 2 April 2010 to 31 December 2010 (n = 45, out of a total of 225 articles). The goal of this corpus analysis is to illustrate how the 'public space' term was conceptualised, appropriated and re-signified *in* and *by* this media debate.

This chapter intends to show, based on this French case study, how public places are currently being redefined through the prism of increased news media visibility of Islam and its distinctive symbols (veils, minarets) and practices (halal meat, Ramadan, prayer). We then seek to contribute to a broader reflection – applicable to the European context – regarding the transformation of contemporary public spaces in light of the increasing news media visibility of the veil and, more broadly, Islam.

The Media Construction of the Visibility of the Islamic Veil (1989-2004)

In the case of the 'headscarf affair', the visibility issue is apparent from the very start. The beginning of the 1989 school year was marked by the expulsion of two young, veiled girls from the Gabriel-Havez College in Creil. However, the schoolgirls had been veiled in the previous year's class photo, which at that time had not been a problem (Baubérot, 1996; Bowen, 2008; Monnet, 1990). Thus, the beginning of the 1989 school year marked the transition from the headscarf's symbolic 'invisibility' to a new and exposed visibility. But what form did this new visibility take: media, social or empirical visibility?

In the scholarly corpus, the young schoolgirls' headscarves are framed as a tangible index of broader historical transformations, namely the postcolonial immigration of Muslims and their ensuing social integration. By approaching the 'headscarf affair' within sociological and historical studies on immigration, integration and secularisation, researchers in the Humanities and Social Sciences suggested that the 'headscarf affair' marked the transition from the 'invisibility' that resulted from the silent settling of Muslim immigrants (1950–1980) to their 'visibility', as a way of demanding recognition from 1980 onwards (Gaspard, 2006; De Galembert, 2009; Cohen, 2000). The young girls' headscarves were empirically 'visible' when they entered into the French republican school system. This was a form of social visibility, constructed via daily practical interactions. Then, starting with the Creil affair in 1989, the landscape changed.

From that point on, the regular staging of similar incidents in the news media over the ensuing 15 years of public debate resulted in a new, symbolic visibility of the veil. In this case, it was specifically a media visibility, experienced as a mediated interaction occurring on a national scale. The exponential multiplication of images and speeches regarding the headscarf from the 1990s onwards created the impression of a proliferation of 'empirical headscarves' (Rochefort, 2002; Lorcerie, 2007; Baubérot, 1996).

This is how the social and media visibilities of the headscarf interrelate: while the headscarf's social visibility is at the origin of its media visibility, the latter in turn contributes to its social visibility. In doing so, it shifts the perception and meaning that this religious symbol (often viewed as a symptom of an integration model in crisis) acquires in the course of practical everyday interactions. Thus, for the construction of this new Islamic visibility in France, interdependence between the social and media spheres was required. A product of the time, but also of the communication technologies of the period

(Thompson, 2000; Voirol, 2005; Heinich, 2012), this new Islamic visibility came to symbolise the turn of the century's shifting sociopolitical reality, made tangible by the young schoolgirls' headscarves.

The Headscarf Affair: From an 'Invisible' Symbol to an 'Ostensible' One

Studying the 'headscarf affair' through scholarly journals allows us to register in time each of the semiotic turning points – discursive and visual – that defined the veil's journey of meaning from 1989 to 2004. On the visual level, these semiotic turns refer to the various shifts and overlaps of international images and frames of reference that appeared between 1989 (Iranian), 2001 (Afghan), and 2004 (Algerian) in the media arena. On the level of discourse, which is what interests us here, the meaning of the headscarf was consolidated over 15 years of public debates, particularly through political (circulars, parliamentary reports) and legal texts.

Semiotic analysis of these texts allows us to trace the trajectory of the meaning ascribed to young girls' headscarves that, from 1989 to 2004, shifted from representing 'neutrality' or invisibility to 'ostensible' over-visibility. This semiotic journey corresponds to the processes of mediatisation, politicisation and juridicisation of the veil issue in France (Lorcerie, 2007; De Galembert, 2009).

To begin, we note that the 'ostentation' term first appeared in the public arena in a 1989 advice from the Council of State.[2] In this text, 'ostentation' referred to a form of usage demarcating the threshold of tolerance for the expression of religious affiliation in schools. The term was then taken up in the 1994 Bayrou Circular,[3] which argued that the Islamic headscarf, in itself described as an 'ostentatious' symbol, was in radical opposition to the 'neutrality' of public education. In the advice of the Council of State (1989) and the Bayrou Circular (1994), 'ostentation' came to denote a qualifier of religious/political expressions deemed to present a threat to public order.

Subsequently, in the Debré Mission and Stasi Commission reports (2003),[4] the legal characterisation of the headscarf, as both a political and religious symbol functioned as a matrix that generated meaning and values. In addition, the Debré report introduced the 'visibly wearing' phrase, the pragmatic effect of which was to widen the scope of the ban to any publicly visible religious or political symbol. In the Stasi report, a distinction was made between religious 'dress' and 'symbols', though the report advocated a broad and general ban in both cases.

Based on these reports, Law no. 2004-228 of March 15, 2004[5] finally enshrined the notion of 'ostentation' by determining, in 'the application of the principle of secularism', that 'in public schools, colleges and high schools, the wearing of symbols or outfits by which students ostensibly manifest a religious affiliation is prohibited' (our translation). Note the problematic nature of this notion of 'ostentation': it is used in its adverbial form, classifying a certain manner of religious expression (in the phenomenological sense) as overly visible. The semiotic importance of this prohibition, implemented by the 2004 law, is that it legally defines the meaning ('ostentatious') and classification ('illegal') of the young schoolgirls' headscarves. The law reaffirms the principle of 'the educational institution's neutrality'. Here, 'neutrality' is understood as uniformity of appearances in line with the republican ideal of 'equality' of citizens (shift in meaning).

As public and performative speech acts (Kerbrat-Orecchioni, 2008), these political and legal texts serve as linguistic evidence of a larger ongoing sociopolitical process regarding the visibility of the Islamic religion, as governed by specific normative bases. These textual devices define what can be viewed as legitimate republican discursiveness regarding this Islamic symbol, thus setting out a certain 'order of discourse' (Foucault, 1971). These texts underline concretisations of meaning that, over time, configure the visibility of the Islamic veil (how it will be seen) in the French context as an 'ostensible', 'overly visible' and 'proselytising' symbol.

The notion of 'ostentation' relates to notions of 'inclusion–exclusion', 'compatibility–incompatibility' or even 'lawfulness–unlawfulness'. These notions are essential to republican visibility regime. As configured by the 2004 law, any political use (proselytising) of religious symbols is ostentatious and, therefore, illicit. Conversely, the concealment of religious symbols in the secular school space is licit, and therefore legitimate. Following this semantic and legal framework, we see that the notion of 'ostentation' is in opposition to that of 'neutrality', which is intended to be the empirical and visible materialisation of the republican ideal of citizen 'equality'. In the repertoire of republican grammar dealing with the scope of legitimate visibilities, the 'neutrality' concept is closely related to those of 'uniformity', 'homogeneity', 'conformity', 'erasure' and 'egalitarianism'.

From a micro-sociological perspective, the principle of 'neutrality' ties in with Erving Goffman's (2013, p. 11) notion of 'fitting into a situation': 'The rule of behavior that seems to be common to all situations, and exclusive to them, is the one obliging participants to "fit in" … [and] not attract undue attention to themselves … The individual must be "good" and not cause a scene or disturbance … He must keep within the spirit or ethos of the situation; he must not be *too much* or out of place.'

This semantic and legal pattern, whereby the 'ostentation' notion is situated in opposition to the 'neutrality' notion, can be understood through the perspective of Wayne Brekhus's (2005) 'markedness' concept, which establishes a distinction between extraordinary or holy (marked) behaviours, and mundane or secular (unmarked) attitudes. While the 'marked' is actively emphasised, the 'unmarked' refers to the vast expanse of social reality passively defined as unremarkable. In the case of the 'headscarf affair', the normative principle of 'neutrality', which denotes 'normality', becomes the threshold at which any unusual and/or 'abnormal' symbol becomes a potential threat. The characterisation of a symbol as 'ostensible' or 'neutral' refers to the question of normativity (*normativité*) – 'illicit' or 'licit' – and of otherness – 'minority' or 'majority'. This sociological analysis allows us to view the 'headscarf affair' as a key moment in the evolution of the political management of public visibilities, as it sheds light on what was considered a regular appearance, as well as on the large number of symbols considered marked within the public educational space. The symbolic threat supposedly embodied by the headscarf thus lies in its potential to overturn the markedness hierarchy.

As expressions of these sociopolitical issues, the 'ostensible', 'overly visible' and 'symbol of proselytism' terms, frequently used in the case of the 'headscarf affair', shed light on the discursive construction of a kind of republican normativity related to the visible and the management of public appearances. This semantic field came to constitute a matrix of meaning, shaping subsequent public debates around the veil (2010–2020) that interrogated the legal limits of religious expression in the French public space.

The Burqa Affair: The Full Veil as a Symbol of an Opaque Identity

Six years later, this republican vocabulary centred on the 'visible' became the groundwork for the 'legitimisation' of the 'burqa affair' and the ensuing 2010 law prohibiting 'face concealment in the public space'. On a legal level, the notion of 'concealment' was associated with secrecy and lies, functioning as the antithesis of the concept of 'transparency', which was linked to the notions of truth and authenticity.

Notably, the visibility issue emerges from the discursive analysis of the values and meanings the 'national identity' concept acquired in the news media coverage of the 'burqa affair'. Among the three republican key concepts at the time – secularism (*laïcité*), the Republic and national identity – the notion of national identity was often signified through the prism of 'visibility' and 'transparency'. Analysis of the prohibitionist discourses in this press debate reveals an argumentative dynamic of signifying the full veil as an 'identitarian opacity' or 'iconocrisis' (Arêas, 2015) that compartmentalises social relationships and hinders social interaction. Within this prohibitionist discursiveness, we note a characterisation of the niqab as an impediment to the subjectivation of Muslim women (Mekki-Berrada, 2018).

This line of argument, whereby the niqab is understood through the prism of identity, is central to the discursive construction of visibility norms. For example, in 2009 President Nicolas Sarkozy (UMP) stated that 'in our country we cannot accept that women are imprisoned behind a grid, cut off from all social life, deprived of all identity' (Gabizon, 2009, our translation). UMP Members of Parliament Jean-François Copé, Nicole Ameline, François Baroin and Éric Raoult described the niqab as a 'mask' that severs women 'from any social life', and stated that 'permanently hiding one's face in the public space is not an expression of individual freedom. It is a negation of oneself, a negation of the other, a negation of life in a society' (De Malet, 2009, our translation). PS Members of Parliament Manuel Valls, Aurélie Filipetti and Philippe Esnol described the full veil as 'an attack on human dignity' that 'places women in a subordinate position. Because a woman whose facial expressions cannot be read loses her humanity' (*Libération*, 2009, our translation). PCF Member of Parliament André Gerin said that 'because it denies women the right to assert their identity in the public sphere, the full veil represents the very negation of their citizenship' (*Libération*, 2010, our translation). UMP Minister Xavier Darcos's slogan 'la République à visage découvert' ('the Republic with faces uncovered', Auffray & Coroller, 2009) was repeated several times in this debate. A final example comes from philosopher Michel Serres:

> What is identity? How do we recognise a person? By their face: the very word means that they see AND are seen. The expression 'with faces uncovered' means loyal, without lying or hiding. The niqab showed us the decisive role the face plays in the construction of the collective and of public law because those who can be recognised by their face pass from the status of private persons to that of public persons. Forcing a person to cover her face amounts to reducing her to a private person, to depriving her of all public existence and of her status as a subject of the law. It turns her into a ghost, without responsibility or security. The face is the foundation of civil society. (Serres, 2010, n.p., our translation)

The above statements show how politicians in favour of the veil-banning law employed a hermeneutic and performative ruse to signify the full veil as a barrier – both physical and symbolic – to identification, socialisation, citizenship, and thus, to the very existence of fully veiled women within French society. Via this prism-of-identity interpretation, the quoted actors emphasise that the full veil imposes on women a loss of face, identity and humanity. The 'uncovered face' is thus constructed as a central aspect of the French conception of identity, in contrast to the opacity of the full veil. Xavier Darcos's phrase 'the Republic with uncovered faces' captures the stakes of this argument. Embraced by politicians seeking to legitimise the law banning the full veil and quoted numerous times in all the newspapers we examined, the phrase owes its success and semiotic force to its concise and semantically charged nature, as well as to the fact that it carries a singular argument: the transparency of the face as a powerful feature of the republican profile. Thus, the full veil, a symbol of 'concealment', is constructed as being contrary to the principle of 'transparency' advocated for by the French republican visibility regime.

In Michel Serres's quote, it is interesting to note that the meaning of disloyalty attributed to the veil, based on the idea that 'to hide is to lie', presupposes the classical philosophical idea that truth resides in appearance. We thus see the emergence of a conception of truth based on the transparency of the face. Serres touches on the issue when he outlines a conception of the 'public' anchored on the face, the function of which, according to him, is to act as a pathway from the private domain to the public one. The title of the *Libération* article containing his interview clearly reflects the issue of identity visibility: 'Without a face, there is no social contract.'

Analysis of the 'burqa affair' shows then that, within the republican visibility regime, the concept of 'transparency' is understood as the conformity between inner/intimate and outer/public spaces. It thus approaches the notion of 'authenticity', according to which nothing should be hidden, and hiding comes with a risk of being accused of concealment or lying. This conception of 'transparency' is therefore in opposition to the facial 'concealment' imposed by the full veil, which would be closer to 'lying'. The moral and ethical dimension in this case lies in the fact that the negative nature of the hidden and the secret (the intimate, the self) is reaffirmed in normative terms. The 2010 law, in turn, prohibits the opaque, shadowy or invisible areas that precisely give meaning and value to the 'visible'. As a result of this context of meaning, wherein the logic of the all-visible prevails, the 'invisible' and the 'unspeakable' are interpreted as either symbols of weakness or pathological symptoms.

In an interesting analysis of the 'transparency' and 'neutrality' concepts, Claudine Haroche argues that they underlie a

> pejorative representation of diversity, of the heterogeneous, of difference…
> This representation has as a corollary the dramatisation of differences,

and as a consequence, a fear of the other… [*In the internalised culture of the transparency to oneself [« Dans la culture intériorisée de la transparence à soi-même*], which assumes that everything can be seen, it is the other that one can no longer see. (Haroche, 2004, p. 148, our translation)

The author feels that contemporary democracies have suppressed 'unequal attentions' and imposed 'equal inattention': 'The fact of being "equally looked at" would involve that of being watched with inattention and indifference' (Haroche, 2004, p. 148). Through this reflection, we can understand the principle of republican neutrality to be a refusal of differences. Specifically, one that imposes a homogenisation and an 'equal inattention', and can result in a denial of recognition of the other.

We thus see the extent to which the construction of the contemporary republican citizen is contingent on this set of beliefs regarding appearances in public places. This leads us to interrogate religious visibility from the perspective of a space-related issue.

The Reconfiguration of Contemporary Public Spaces (2009–2010)

While the spatial issue, which was necessarily linked to the visibility issue, was already a component of the framework of the 'headscarf affair' by way of sociogeographic[6] calculus, the 2004 law's veil ban was limited to the institutional educational setting. Five years later, the 2010 law shifted the landscape, introducing a new, unprecedented spatial issue by prohibiting the wearing of the niqab in the public thoroughfare, on the street and in places open to the public as part of an expansive interpretation of the concept of public space.

Analysis of the national press coverage of the 'burqa affair' shows the salience of the issue of spatial norms in particular. As the notion of public space had been legally redefined in the terms of the 2010 law, which stipulated that 'no one may, in the public space, wear clothing intended to conceal their face', we paid particular attention to potential avenues for understanding the process that resulted in this redefinition of the concept of public space. Specifically, the analysis of mediatised interaction and rhetorical confrontations of press discourses (Amossy & Burger, 2011) allowed us to reconstruct the public and collective process through which the law was written.

Through this analysis, we found that a political and legal conversation centred on the notion of public space had been initiated by both politicians at the forefront of the parliamentary scene, as well as specialists interviewed by national newspapers. This shed light on how the concept of public space had been reconsidered, reappropriated and re-signified in the context of this public debate. The notion appears to have been an object of discursive controversy among the actors who disputed its meaning based on their respective political interests and strategies. We then observed that the legality, legitimacy and applicability of the concept of public space had been questioned and negotiated throughout the press coverage of the affair.

In our lexico-metric analysis of the corpus, we inventoried 176 articles containing the term *'espace public'* (public space), 116 containing *'rue'* (street), 75 containing *'territoire'* (territory) and 47 containing *'voie publique'* (public thoroughfare). We found that the central role of the concept of public space in this debate was contrasted by a lack of precision, as well as a vagueness of meaning surrounding the notion. The sustained presence of the public space notion in the news coverage expanded its spectrum of meaning and practical values. As such, these findings help us identify important semiotic issues: the conceptual indeterminacy and the malleability of the meaning of the notion of public space.

In December 2009, following six months of work and interviews with more than 50 specialists, the Parliamentary Mission of Information on the wearing of the full veil in France met for the last time to hear ministers Brice Hortefeux, Éric Besson and Xavier Darcos, and to conclude its work. On this occasion, it became clear that, while a consensus among members of Parliament existed regarding the need for legislation on the full veil, the scope of this legal application remained a matter of dispute.

Public institutions, public services, hospitals, universities, public transport, the street, the public thoroughfare: to what extent would it be legitimate and constitutional to apply a ban on the full veil? In other words: how should the concept of public space be defined, and which spaces should be included? Or again: what place (physical and symbolic) was to be reserved for Islam in French society? What kind of normativity emerges from these discourses on space?

During this final parliamentary session, the three ministers presented various solutions for banning the niqab, focusing on three distinct understandings of the concept of public space reflective of the political and legal stakes of the debate. Defending the more 'cautious' approach (Gabizon, 2009), Xavier Darcos, Minister of Labour, suggested that Parliament pass a resolution, rather than a law, limiting the ban to town halls, prefectures, post offices and social security offices. Noting that a ban on wearing the niqab on the street would be subject to legal controversy, the minister recommended 'caution to those who would be tempted to follow the precedent of the 2004 law on the prohibition of religious symbols in schools', because if 'the expression of a religious belief in schools contradicts the secular character of the educational institution, the wearing of the full veil, on the other hand, takes place in an indeterminate space where the expression of an opinion, even a religious one, remains a fundamental right' (Auffray & Coroller, 2009, our translation). Interior Minister Brice Hortefeux advocated a 'minimal solution', proposing a law banning the niqab in public services (post offices, prefectures, public transport) so as to avoid the risk of unconstitutionality where the Constitutional Council and the European Court of Human Rights were concerned. More categorically, Eric Besson, Minister of Immigration, promoted a general ban of the niqab in 'the whole of the public space', i.e., in public services and buildings open to the public, but also on the street. While saying that he was 'aware' of the legal constraints a complete ban faced, he suggested that the ban be based 'on the imperative of public order', following a similar proposal by Jean-François Copé (Auffray & Coroller, 2009). Thus, the spectre of a threat to public security was rhetorically brandished to justify calls for exceptional measures.

Torn between these three understandings of the concept of public space, a large number of ministers sided – following several parliamentary sessions – with the all-encompassing conception of public space and its associated proposal for a general ban, as suggested by Éric Besson. A text, co-signed by UMP deputies Jean-François Copé, Nicole Ameline, François Baroin and Éric Raoult is a telling illustration of this position. These government-majority representatives, who co-chaired the parliamentary mission, defined the spatial perimeter of the proposed ban as follows:

> It is obvious that the burqa has no place in public services and public build-
> ings or in private places open to the public, such as shops… The question
> of a general ban on the public thoroughfare remains. For some, it would be
> disproportionate or would risk being misunderstood. Some legal experts
> also point to the legal obstacles. The ban must be based on the imperative
> of public order: imagine the danger of a city where everyone is permanently
> masked and dressed the same way. (De Malet, 2009)

On the left of the political spectrum, the socialist deputies in favour of the law, Manuel Valls, Aurélie Filipetti, and Philippe Esnol, advocated the banning of the niqab in 'the public space and its associated service locations (town halls, schools, prefectures, social security offices) as well in the whole of the public thorough-fare'. Noting the phrase 'with uncovered faces' as a public order imperative, they described a complete ban on the niqab as a necessary measure 'in a democratic society, for public security, for the protection of order … or the protection of the rights and freedoms of others' (*Libération*, 2009, our translation).

As revealed in these discourses, the semantic elasticity of the public space notion – its conceptual indeterminacy and malleability of meaning – supported an expansive interpretation of the concept. The discursive battlefield formed by these various understandings of public places, as illustrated in this section, ended up benefitting prohibitionist discursiveness. From a critical perspective, this semantic blurring can be interpreted both as a performative speech act and as a political action strategy. As a result, this extensive interpretation of the public space concept can be considered a 'linguistic event' (Moirand, 2011).

Of note, at the time of the government's publication of the text of the proposed law, which stipulated that 'no one may, in the public space, wear clothing intended to conceal his or her face' under penalty of a 'second-class fine of up to 150 euro',[7] the State Councillor and former rapporteur of the Stasi Commission on secularism in schools, Rémy Schwartz, issued a public statement that was picked up by all the newspapers included in this study:

> A crucial difference exists between rules that can be enacted in public services and the constraints that can be imposed on citizens in the public space, for, in the latter case, freedom is the principle, and restriction, let alone prohibition, is the exception. The government has the right to prohibit its employees and students in public schools from ostensibly showing their religion. However, ... Parliament cannot invoke secularism to prohibit women from wearing full veils in the street. (Perrault, 2010, our translation)

The report published by the Parliamentary Mission of Information on the full veil (2010), written by Éric Raoult and André Gerin, is also illustrative in this respect. The matter of the legitimate argument (*argument légitime*) and the issue of the broad definition of the public space notion can be grasped, respectively, from the summary report headings (our translation):

B. BANNING THE FULL VEIL IN THE PUBLIC SPACE?[8]
2. Would a ban be possible under the Constitution and the ECHR?
a) Laicity, an inoperative basis
b) The dignity of the human person, a concept of uncertain meaning
c) Public order, the least risky path

C. SUPPORTING PUBLIC SERVICE OFFICERS AND ALL PEOPLE IN CONTACT WITH THE PUBLIC
2. Adopt a general provision to support public service employees
3. An extension to other establishments open to the public?

a) Restrictions can already be placed on the wearing of the full veil in these establishments
b) … if they are not based on a discriminatory ground

As the terms used in this report illustrate, the various categories of space that emerged from the public debate not only reflected an expansive interpretation of the notion of public space, but also, and more importantly, a discursive strategy for dealing with the legal constraints on mobilising the concept under the terms of the 2010 law. If the primary legal constraint to a broadened interpretation of the public space notion was the inclusion of the 'public thoroughfare' and 'street' in the category of 'public spaces' subject to state control and legally defined by the principle of laicity (neutrality of the public service), actors in favour of a ban used both the 'public order' argument and 'the uncovered face' imperative to circumvent this constraint and legitimise the 2010 law. In other words, a rhetorical strategy aimed at legitimising the legal redefinition of free-movement spaces governed by the principle of freedom. We can thus speak of a concerted, but nonetheless polemical, re-signification of the public space concept in the specific context of this press debate.

The spatial issue introduced by the 'burqa affair' was unprecedented: it marked the first time in contemporary French history that a ban on religious symbols was applied outside the institutional public spaces of the Republic, such as schools, public administration buildings and hospitals. Thus, the debate on the full veil presented a different problem from that of the 'headscarf affair' and the 2004 law, particularly due to the geographical scope of the 2010 law. Over time, the secular issue raised by the 'headscarf affair' expanded beyond the school setting to challenge the republican nature of other public spaces. From the 'headscarf affair' to the 'burqa affair', there has been a shift towards a more broadly defined conception of public space.

The new legal reality established by the 2010 law has since determined the meaning and practical value of these free movement spaces. It is no longer the principle of 'laicity', but that of 'order' that defines the public quality of republican spaces. The meaning of this new public space is thus closer to matters of security and moral order than to those of social order (a space for living together through relationships of mutual recognition). This definition then has the effect of shifting the meaning of the 'public' notion further to the side of the republican state and its power, than to that of civilians and the common good. Through this rationale, we can understand the 2010 law as a legal device that reinforces the binary distribution of space, cutting across divides such as public/private, male/female, religiosity/secularism and threat/security.

Furthermore, it is important to emphasise that, through this broad interpretation of the public space concept, the 2010 law constructed a new meaning for the veil and its visibility. The prohibitionist discourses construct the many ways the visibility and spatiality of Islam in France can be perceived (classifying), judged (attributing value) and managed (discrimination). If, prior to the law, the full veil was represented as a politically suspicious and religiously radical symbol, after the law, it came to be seen as dangerous, and wearing the full veil is now considered an illicit practice. We therefore argue that the 2010 law legally defined the spatial perimeter of Islamic visibility, while also symbolically demarcating the limited social acceptance of the full veil in France. In this case, the legal interpretation of public space served as a basis for a re-signification of the full veil, based on the matters of recognition (social, symbolic) and the relationship between the law and morals.

Conclusion

In 1989, the 'headscarf affair' introduced into the public arena a new issue related to Islamic visibility, when the headscarf became qualified as an 'ostensible' symbol that was contrary to the republican principle of 'neutrality' of appearances. Five years later, the 'burqa affair' concerned an Islamic visibility that was no longer new, but was becoming emphasised by the figure of the full veil, which was understood as a sign of 'concealment'. The 2010 law introduced a new spatial issue by prohibiting the niqab in the public thoroughfare, based on a broadened interpretation of the public space concept. In the space of 20 years, there was a shift from a new media 'visibility' to a new legal 'spatiality' for Islamic veils. We can thus argue that the media coverage of the 'headscarf affair' produced a denigrated and stigmatised visibility for the veil, which came to legitimise the broadening of the niqab ban to the thoroughfare. This raises the question of whether the niqab ban could have been implemented in such a short time (June 2009 to September 2010) without 15 years of prior debates about the headscarf in schools (October 1989 to March 2004).

Notes

1.   The research for this chapter stems from a project mainly funded by the Social Sciences and Humanities Research Council (SSHRC): *Scholarly and mediatic Islamophobia: A transnational study of discourses and their impact* (Original French title *Islamophobie savante et médiatique: Étude transnationale des discours et de leur impact*; SSHRC 2019-2023, #890-2018-0016), for which Abdelwahed Mekki-Berrada is the Principal Investigator.
2.   https://www.senat.fr/rap/l03-219/l03-2193.html
3.   https://www.assemblee-nationale.fr/12/dossiers/documents-laicite/document-3.pdf. François Bayrou was the minister of national education (1993–1997); the Bayrou Circular (*Circulaire Bayrou*) refers to a circular he addressed to the public education officials and entitled 'Neutrality of public education: Wearing ostentatious signs in schools'.
4.   https://www.assemblee-nationale.fr/12/dossiers/laicite.asp
5.   https://www.assemblee-nationale.fr/12/dossiers/laicite.asp
6.   Unlike their mothers' headscarves, which were confined to the private sphere of the home (1950–1980), young girls' headscarves became controversial when they were introduced into the school environment in 1980. The headscarf was perceived as out of place in the school space, as its meaning was linked to an ethnic or cultural origin, thus embodying a conception of identity that did not fit in with the republican representation of secular public spaces and the principle of 'neutrality'.
7.   https://www.legifrance.gouv.fr/dossierlegislatif/JORFDOLE000022234691/
8.   https://www.assemblee-nationale.fr/13/dossiers/voile_integral.asp

References

Amossy, R. & Burger, M. (2011). Introduction: La polémique médiatisée [Introduction: The media controversy]. *Semen, 31,* 7–24.
Arêas, C. (2015). Construction médiatique de la visibilité religieuse de l'islam en France à travers « l'affaire de la burqa »: Sur le primat du « visage » et le voilement intégral comme signe « d'iconocrise » [Media construction of the religious visibility of Islam in France through the 'burqa affair': On the primacy of the 'face' and the full veil as a sign of 'iconocrisis']. *Canadian Journal of Communication, 40*(1), 29–50.
Brekhus, W. (2005). Une sociologie de l'« invisibilité »: Réorienter notre regard [A sociology of 'invisibility': Reorienting our gaze]. *Réseaux, 1–2*(129–130), 244–272.
De Koning, M. (2019). *Vijf mythen over islamofobie* [Five myths about Islamophobia]. Yunus Publishing/Kif Kif.
Foucault, M. (1971). *L'ordre du discours* [The order of discourse]. Gallimard.
Goffman, E. (2013). *Comment se conduire dans les lieux publics* [How to behave in public places]. Economica.
Haroche, C. (2004). Manières de regarder dans les sociétés démocratiques contemporaines [Ways of looking in contemporary democratic societies]. *Communications, 75,* 147–169.
Heinich, N. (2012). *De la visibilité. Excellence et singularité en régime médiatique* [Visibility. Excellence and singularity in the media regime]. Gallimard.
Kerbrat-Orecchioni, C. (2008). *Les actes de langage dans le discours* [Speech acts in the discourse]. Armand Colin.

Mekki-Berrada, A. (2018). Femmes et subjectivations musulmanes: Prolégomènes [Women and Muslim subjectivations: Background]. *Anthropologie et sociétés, 42*(1), 9–33.

Moirand, S. (2011). *Les discours de la presse quotidienne. Observer, analyser, comprendre* [Discourses in the daily press. Observe, analyse, understand]. Presses Universitaires de France.

Thompson, J. B. (2000). Transformation de la visibilité [Transformation of visibility]. *Réseaux, 18*(100), 187–213.

Voirol, O. (2005). Les luttes pour la visibilité: Esquisse d'une problématique [Struggles for visibility: An outline of a problematic]. *Réseaux, 23*(129–130), 89–120.

Scholarly journal *corpus*

Baubérot, J. (1996). L'affaire des foulards et la laïcité à la française [The headscarf affair and French secularism]. *L'Homme et la société, 120*(2), 9–16.

Bowen, J. R. (2008). Why did the French rally to a law against scarves in schools? *Droit et société, 6*(1), 33–52.

Cohen, M. (2000). Juifs et Musulmans en France: Le modèle républicain d'intégration en question [Jews and Muslims in France: The Republican model of integration in question]. *Sociétés contemporaines, 37*, 89–120.

De Galembert, C. (2009). Cause du voile et lutte pour la parole musulmane légitime [Cause of the veil and the struggle for legitimate Muslim speech]. *Sociétés contemporaines, 2*(74), 19–47.

Gaspard, F. (2006). Le foulard de la dispute [The headscarf of the dispute]. *Cahiers du Genre, 3*, 75–93.

Lorcerie, F. (2007). L'islam comme contre-identification française: Trois moments [Islam as French counter-identification: Three moments]. *L'Année du Maghreb 2005–2006*, 509–538.

Monnet, J. F. (1990). À Creil, l'origine de « l'affaire des foulards » [In Creil, the origin of the 'headscarf affair']. *Hérodote, 56*, 45–54.

Rochefort, F. (2002). Foulard, genre et laïcité en 1989 [Headscarf, gender and secularism in 1989]. *Vingtième Siècle. Revue d'histoire, 3*(75), 145–156.

News media *corpus*

Auffray, A., & Coroller, C. (2009, December 17). Ministres en mission sur le voile [Ministers on a mission on the veil]. *Libération*.

De Koning, M. (2019). *Vijf mythen over islamofobie* [Five myths about Islamophobia]. Yunus Publishing/Kif Kif.

De Malet, C. (2009, December 16). Voile intégral: Une loi indispensable [Full veil: A necessary law]. *Le Figaro*.

Gabizon, C. (2009, June 26). Sarkozy: 'La burqa n'est pas la bienvenue' [Sarkozy: 'The burqa is not welcome']. *Le Figaro*.

Gabizon, C. (2009, December 16). Les députés UMP souhaitent une interdiction totale de la burqa [UMP MPs want a total ban on the burqa]. *Le Figaro*.

Libération (anonymous). (2009, December 16). Il faut bannir la burqa de l'espace public [The burqa must be banned from public spaces].

Libération (anonymous). (2010, March 26). Forum de Rennes. Le bonheur une idée neuve ! Le voile sape-t-il la citoyenneté des femmes ? [Rennes Forum. Happiness is a new idea! Does the veil undermine women's citizenship?]. *Libération.*

Perrault, G. (2010, April 23). La dignité de la femme, base juridique du futur texte [Women's dignity as a legal basis for the future text]. *Le Figaro.*

Serres, M. (2010, March 19). Sans visage, pas de contrat social [No face, no social contract]. *Libération.*

8
FROM PEN TO PERCEPTION: DOES NEWS REPORTING ADVANCE TERRORISTS' AGENDAS?

STEFAN MERTENS, DAVID DE CONINCK & LEEN D'HAENENS

Abstract

Although historically newspapers and their audiences in Flanders, Belgium, have reflected economic left–right differences in society, they have grown closer together in recent decades. However, a new left–right dimension related to attitudes towards various topics such as refugees, immigration, Islam and terrorism gained influence in the 2000s. This chapter presents two studies: a first one on how two Flemish newspapers, one historically left-leaning and the other historically right-leaning, currently differ in the representation of terrorism (study 1); a second one on whether this difference is reflected in fear of terrorism among their readers (study 2). In the left-wing newspaper, contextual themes such as the family background and religious experience of terrorists are discussed more; the readers of that newspaper also hold lower levels of fear of terrorism. The audience of the right-wing newspaper holds a greater fear of terrorism, which may be explained by the fact that this newspaper uses a vocabulary that is more about crime and political intervention. Both the content and audience perspectives show divergence rather than homogenisation.

Keywords: terrorism, newspapers, lexical analysis, audience survey, Belgium

Radicalisation in Society and Media Polarisation

In 2004, Hallin and Mancini noted that European newspapers are part of a tradition of political parallelism, that is the degree to which the structure of the media system parallels that of the party system, structural ties between political actors and media organisations and the extent to which the latter reflect political divisions (De Albuquerque, 2018). Yet they also observed that European newspapers had become more homogenised in terms of content. In the 2010s, the debate about ideological polarisation moved from the supply side to the demand side, suggesting that readers might have become entrapped in so-called filter bubbles (Pariser, 2011), taking in only information that confirms their own biases. Proponents of the (online) filter bubble theory stress that within non-diverse, closed discussion/ readership groups leaving no room for alternative voices, opinions tend to swirl around like sound in an echo chamber, locking users into their own – possibly false, but certainly biased – beliefs. This theory more often applies to online news media (Dubois & Blank, 2018; Flaxman et al., 2016; Haim et al., 2018; Vaccari et al., 2016) but is rarely tested on newspaper data. We aim to fill this gap.

In Flanders (the northern part of Belgium) we see a similar evolution from political parallelism to homogenisation of content in newspapers. Raeijmaekers (2018) studied this evolution through case studies on the coverage of austerity programmes at five moments in Flemish history: 1960, 1977, 1993, 2005 and 2014. The first case study (1960) concerns a segregated political landscape with newspapers that each represented an ideological pillar (liberal, socialist or catholic). The second case took place with respect to a semi-pillarised society. The last three cases take place in a society where pillars increasingly lost influence.

Within Flanders there were many catholic newspapers, but both liberals and socialists had just one newspaper that held left-wing and right-wing economic views, respectively. The newspapers were *De Morgen* (DM) (socialist) and *Het Laatste Nieuws* (HLN) (liberal). However, these two newspapers, as Raeijmaekers's (2018) study shows, have shifted in each other's direction, and the coverage of economic politics has become more and more similar in both newspapers as the process of de-pillarisation progressed, and media adopted a homogenised journalistic culture of objective professionalism.

As the economic orientation of both newspapers converged, a new left–right distinction emerged between defenders of an open society with a lot of room for immigration, and the defenders of a closed society in which nationalism prevails and immigration is restricted. The emergence of this new cleavage was identified as early as 1994 in Flanders by Elchardus (1994) and echoes the distinction between openness and closedness that was later discussed in *The Economist* (2016) as an international phenomenon.

Radicalisation, Terrorism and Islam

There has been much ideological discussion on the representation of ethnic minorities lately, starting with the radicalisation process of ethnic minority youngsters, i.e., young people with a Muslim background – home-grown potential terrorists who might have fought in the Syrian war or recruited to carry out terrorist attacks in various countries. Earlier studies (Berbers et al., 2016) suggest that left-wing and broadsheet newspapers tend to insist that terrorists are the products of very specific backgrounds, while right-wing and tabloid newspapers focus on the crimes committed, with little concern for the criminals' backgrounds. This supposed ideological difference between broadsheets and tabloids on terrorism-related topics such as the representation of radicalisation will be investigated further on in this chapter.

The September 11, 2001 suicide attacks against New York's World Trade Center sparked increasingly negative sentiment towards Muslims and Islam in the Western world. The 9/11 attacks were followed by several mass killings in Europe (Madrid 2004, London 2005), culminating with a spate of attacks in Paris in 2015, including the slaughter of the Charlie Hebdo editorial staff on 7 January and coordinated attacks against a concert hall, restaurants, and a sporting venue on 13 November. Because they took place in neighbouring France, these attacks, and the 2016 Bastille Day killings in Nice, were a shock for the Belgian public. A series of attacks in Belgium itself on 22 March 2016, was even more terrifying as they occurred closer to home.

Terrorism thrives in an atmosphere of crisis and fear – an atmosphere in part created by the media, which largely set the agenda for public debate. While right-wing conspiracy theorists (Bump, 2017) may suggest that a large number of terrorist attacks against the West are kept unreported to control racism among populations, it is partly through relentless media coverage of violent attacks that the goal of terrorists – to promote fear – is reached. As early as 2009, Sami Zemni (2009, p. 10) noted that Belgian citizens, and especially the Flemish, are 'immersed in the delusion that Islam is our country's biggest problem'. The 2016 attacks only aggravated this perception. Van Gorp (2005) identified two frames in the reporting of asylum seekers in Flanders in the early years of the 21st century. Asylum seekers were either portrayed as innocent victims who need help, or as intruders who present a threat to society. In this research, DM appeared to be more left-wing in as much as this is indicated by a statistically significant overrepresentation of the victim frame. In HLN, the intruder frame emphasising asylum seekers as a threat was more prominent.

According to cultivation theory (Gerbner & Gross, 1976), the more time spent on (news) media consumption, the greater the belief that the mediated world aligns with reality. It can be argued that constantly reading/hearing about terrorism will convince the public that terrorism has become a fact of life. Increased media consumption may provoke more fear, and the way terrorist attacks are represented and interpreted might also have an impact on feelings of fear. Pomerantsev et al. (2019, p. 11) observe that 'in an environment where trust in traditional journalism is fragile, where populist politicians and "alternative" news sites are constantly pushing inaccurate narratives and provocative policies to deliberately polarise and toxify public discourse, newsrooms need to be more aware of the potential impact of their content on the quality of engagement'.

Research (Slaets et al., 2020) shows that Flemish news consumers aged 24 to 45 are less likely than younger news users to find themselves cut off from reality in media echo chambers of their own making than described in extreme versions of the filter bubble scenario, thanks to relatively diverse media consumption patterns. This audience is not homogeneous. We can roughly distinguish two profiles: those who favour 'high-brow' media (the so-called quality media), and those who prefer 'low-brow', popular media. The former lean more to the political left, and the latter more to the right.

The tabloids have often been accused of fuelling readers' negative perceptions by conflating migrants and refugees with terrorists, as right-wing politicians are wont to do. Their modus operandi being to emphasise sensational and negative events, usually crime and violence, we could expect them to provide more of the same (Greussing & Boomgaarden, 2017) with respect to radicalised youngsters. And as shown by earlier research (e.g., Zhu et al., 2018), consumption of sensationalistic crime coverage goes hand in hand with an increased fear of crime.

Hypotheses

This chapter presents two studies[1], one on media supply and another on audience perceptions (i.e., fear of terrorism). Study 1 analytically tests hypotheses using the Sketch Engine tool, based on corpora that integrate all routine radicalisation coverage done by two Flemish newspapers from 2016 to 2019: *De Morgen* (DM, a left-leaning broadsheet) and *Het Laatste Nieuws* (HLN, a right-leaning tabloid). This thematic corpus is complemented with a smaller 'crisis coverage' corpus of articles about radicalisation published from 22 March 2016 (the day of the Brussels terrorist attacks) and 21 August (five months after the attacks), the rationale being that media coverage may take a different approach in the case of unexpected key events such as political scandals or terrorist attacks (Beckers & Van Aelst, 2019, p. 736).

H1: Analysis of the used language will identify more 'journalistically differentiated' news on terrorism in the historically left-wing broadsheet newspaper DM and less 'journalistically differentiated' news in the historically right-wing tabloid newspaper HLN. ('News differentiation' occurs when a distinction is made between Muslims and terrorists (Matthes et al., 2019). If no such distinction is made, we call the news undifferentiated.)

H2: Fear of terrorism is more pronounced among readers of the historically right-wing tabloid newspaper HLN, and less pronounced among readers of the historically left-wing newspaper DM.

By looking at the actual content of media through vocabulary analysis, this study complements the study by Rashid and Olofsson (2021) that measures media coverage as a quantity of published articles. Furthermore, it complements Williamson et al. (2019), who argue that an active mode of engagement with news articles is more likely to enhance the cultivation of fear when compared with passive media consumption, but who do not look at actual lexical choices within media content.

Study 2 deals with the impact such differences in news supply/content may have on fear of terrorism among broadsheet and tabloid readers. Research has shown that attitudes towards immigration and refugees are associated with fear of terrorism in Belgium (De Coninck, 2020). Hence, fear of terrorism is one of the potential tokens of right-leaning political choices. If the readership of both DM and HLN is still divided along divisions between left-wing and right-wing orientations, this might result in higher fear of terrorism among the readership of HLN, and lower fear of terrorism among the readership of DM. Furthermore, the difference between the audiences might coexist alongside differences in the content of both newspapers.

Study 1: The News Media Supply Side

Data and Method: A Lexical Analysis

Our first study deals with the representation of radicalisation in newspapers, through a lexical analysis of pieces published by DM and HLN. The first aspect we looked at was the word count of any article containing the word 'radicalisering' ('radicalisation'). To this end, we entered this word as a search term in the GoPress Belgian media archive, which includes all articles published by our two newspapers in the time frame of interest, that is, the years 2016 through

2019. The search yielded a corpus of 422,817 words in DM, and a corpus of only 237,470 words in HLN. In other words, radicalisation received more attention in DM than in HLN, as also demonstrated by a comparison of the two, smaller, 'crisis' corpora. While in the wake of the attacks we might have expected a barrage of radicalisation coverage from HLN owing to this newspaper's sensationalistic profile, DM's coverage (92,451 words) was in fact much higher than HLN's (37,151 words).

In a second step, we focused on meaning rather than text volume. Searching for the meaning of a word can be done through dictionary research, but as noted by Lin (1998), a word's meaning can also be derived from context. When analysing larger bodies of texts, we obtain many words with many collocations. As manually analysing such large quantities of text is quite labour-intensive, we used SketchEngine to identify which words collocate with other words more often than they would if their joint appearance was purely a matter of chance (a similar approach was also taken in chapter 6 of this book).

A 'collocation' (Lexico, s.d.) can be defined as the habitual juxtaposition of a given word with one or more words with a frequency greater than may be ascribed to chance. To provide an overview of all such collocative patterns SketchEngine generates 'word sketches' – overviews of the ways words happen to be associated with others in various grammatical relations. In this chapter, we also use the 'thesaurus score'. This score (ranging from 0 to 1) is based on an assessment of the percentage of word sketches shared among various words and their own word sketches. We drew up lists of words that had a high thesaurus score when compared with other words: 'As similar words appear in a similar context, their word sketches will be similar, so the similarity of two words can be obtained by calculating the intersection of the word sketches of the two words' (Herman et al., 2019, p. 87).

We generated a list of the 15 most frequent collocations with the words 'radicalisation' and 'Islam' in both corpora under study, following the computer-assisted approach, while adding an extra layer of qualitative assessment. Our results show how words from the collocations lists can be grouped under the heading of overarching themes. The categories to which we assign the words are not the result of calculations (such as the thesaurus score) but are part of an interpretation that we present as such in the results section. While the SketchEngine programme is also able to regroup collocating words into clusters based on their objective proximity, we opted for a reasoned classification, which provides more meaningful results as their appearance among the 15 selected words already is an indicator of objective proximity.

Results

To provide sufficient breadth of analysis combined with sufficient clarity, we limited ourselves to our 15-word lists with the highest thesaurus scores in both newspapers. The results, with an interpretation of the words and their thesaurus scores, are discussed below.

Table 8.1: 'Islam' in DM and HLN in the crisis corpus

Lemma HLN	English translation	Thesaurus score	Lemma DM	English translation	Thesaurus score
Staats-veiligheid	National security	0.277	Probleem	Problem	0.218
Politiek	Politics	0.274	Burger	Citizen	0.206
N-VA	N-VA	0.252	Strand	Beach	0.201
Imam	Imam	0.239	Denker	Thinker	0.200
Regering	Government	0.238	Gezin	Family	0.196
Ouder	Parent	0.234	Jongere	Youngster	0.195
School	School	0.230	Feit	Fact	0.194
Herdenking	Commemo-ration	0.222	School	School	0.193
Opdracht	Order	0.222	Onderzoek	Research	0.186
Wijk	Neighbour-hood	0.220	Debat	Debate	0.185
Angst	Fear	0.214	Punt	Point	0.183
Plaats	Place	0.212	Moskee	Mosque	0.179
Slachtoffer	Victim	0.211	Stap	Step	0.178
Hoofdstad	Capital	0.209	Stem	Voice	0.177
Gemeente	Township	0.206	Huis	House	0.176

Looking at the word lists (Table 8.1) generated by a thesaurus search on 'Islam' in the crisis corpus, we come across remarkable differences. A first difference is merely quantitative: the thesaurus scores of words most associated with Islam are generally higher for HLN than for DM, implying a stronger collocation between Islam and the preferred lexical choices.

Second, the words in HLN carry a different discourse compared to the DM corpus. Let us look at the three highest scoring words in the HLN corpus: 'national security', 'politics' and 'N-VA' (Flanders's largest separatist party). These words can be considered part of a 'government' discourse that associates Islam with the terrorist attacks in Belgium and stresses a need for action on the part of the government. The word in fifth place, 'government', could also belong to this semantic field.

Let us compare this with the first three words in the DM corpus: 'problem', 'citizen' and 'beach'. While irrelevant on the face of it, the latter refers to a debate regarding the 'burkini', an Islamist women's bathing suit, the use of which on beaches and in swimming pools remains controversial. This word does not directly refer to government action, but rather to a debate about Islam. The word 'problem' also refers to a debate about a situation in need of change. 'Citizens' are said to take part in the debate, rather than governments taking action. This 'debate' focus can also be associated with some other words further down the list, such as 'thinker', 'fact', 'research', 'debate', 'point', 'step' or 'voice'.

Next to words relating to government action, the word list includes terms that refer to geographical places: 'neighbourhood', 'place', 'capital', 'township' and the like. Such words do not appear in the DM hit list of words most collocated with the word 'Islam'. Another frequently occurring semantic field in the HLN corpus relates to violence. Words such as 'fear' and 'victim' directly refer to terrorist attacks. A 'commemoration' is also an event related to terrorism – a direct consequence.

A further distinction between our two corpora is the more frequent appearance of words related to family in the DM corpus, such as 'family', 'youngster', 'school' and 'house', although two words related to this field also appear in HLN. This 'family' discourse focuses on the families of radicalised youngsters. To complete the overview, we should also mention that each corpus has only one strictly religious word in its top-15 collocations: 'imam' for HLN, and 'mosque' for DM, suggesting that neither newspaper explicitly links terrorism to religion.

To conclude our description of the crisis corpus on 'Islam', we can see patterns that confirm a more personal approach (family and debate oriented) on the part of DM, and a more crime-oriented one (focused on government action and violence) on the part of HLN. This pattern is in line with the higher journalistic differentiation in DM predicted by hypothesis 1.

Table 8.2: 'Radicalisation' in DM and HLN in the crisis corpus

Lemma HLN	English translation	Thesaurus score	Lemma DM	English translation	Thesaurus score
Terreur	Terrorism	0.239	Familie	Family	0.259
Geval	Case	0.235	Kind	Child	0.241
Jongere	Youngster	0.229	Centrum	Centre	0.235
Vrouw	Woman	0.220	Gemeenschap	Community	0.234
Probleem	Problem	0.208	Ouder	Parent	0.232
Dag	Day	0.200	Hoofd	Head	0.231
Mens	Human	0.198	Strijd	Struggle	0.220
Herdenking	Commemoration	0.193	Identiteit	Identity	0.217
Opdracht	Order	0.193	Boek	Book	0.207
Politie	Police	0.193	Huis	House	0.204
Plaats	Place	0.190	Leerling(e)	Pupil (male or female)	0.204
Beeld	Image	0.190	Cel	Cell	0.201
Slachtoffer	Victim	0.185	Weg	Way	0.199
Terrorist	Terrorist	0.184	Broer	Brother	0.198
Voorzitter	President	0.182	Partij	Party	0.197

When looking at the word clouds surrounding the word 'radicalisation', we observe some other connotations. The thesaurus scores (Table 8.2) in both corpora strongly suggest a similar trend as in Table 8.1, i.e., a focus on 'terrorist attacks' on the part of HLN versus one on 'family context' on the part of DM.

Almost all other words in the DM word cloud refer to a similar focus on families and community institutions, like 'centre' and 'community', 'child', 'parent', 'pupil' and 'brother'. In addition to this focus on family there is once again a focus on debate, as illustrated by words such as 'book', 'struggle' for 'identity' and the 'way' to go. On the other hand, a word such as 'party' directly pertains to politics, while 'cell' refers to prison, the place where terrorists belong. This reduces the difference between the two lexical clouds somewhat.

The HLN word cloud includes many words also found in the word clouds on 'Islam', such as 'commemoration', 'police' and 'victim', albeit with lower thesaurus scores. These words are also accompanied by words that are more in line with 'debates' and 'family': 'case', 'problem', 'image', etc. 'Youngster', 'woman', and 'human' refer to aspects such as demographics and family. Finally, the word 'president' is the only reference to politics in the HLN corpus.

Altogether these results indicate that Hypothesis 1 is confirmed by data regarding the term 'radicalisation' in a crisis corpus, but in a less definite manner than in relation to 'Islam'.

Table 8.3: 'Islam' in DM and HLN in a routine corpus

Lemma HLN	English translation	Thesaurus score	Lemma DM	English translation	Thesaurus score
Probleem	Problem	0.137	Moslim	Muslim	0.198
Controle	Control	0.136	Idee	Idea	0.137
Baas	Boss	0.112	Staat	State	0.134
Vrouw	Woman	0.110	Radicalisering	Radicalisation	0.134
Dader	Perpetrator	0.109	Religie	Religion	0.133
Jongere	Youngster	0.108	Partij	Party	0.132
Druk	Pressure	0.106	Moskee	Mosque	0.132
Leerling(e)	Pupil (male/female)	0.104	Ideologie	Ideology	0.131
Kleuter	Toddler	0.103	Jongere	Youngster	0.128
Man	Man	0.099	Week	Week	0.124
Persoon	Person	0.097	Politicus	Politician	0.124
Oplossing	Solution	0.097	Kind	Child	0.123
Kind	Child	0.097	Politie	Police	0.120
Cel	Cell	0.097	Samenleving	Society	0.118
Vorm	Form	0.095	Vrouw	Woman	0.116

Further analysis of the co-occurrences of the word 'Islam' in a routine corpus points to a blurring of the vocabularies in each newspaper (Table 8.3). The differences between them are less pronounced in routine corpora on radicalisation than in the crisis corpus.

The HLN corpus includes many demography-related terms such as 'woman', 'youngster', 'pupil', 'toddler', 'man', 'person', or 'child', as well as debate-oriented terms such as 'problem', 'control', 'solution' and 'form'. 'Perpetrator' and 'cell' are still more violence-oriented words, and a 'boss' exerting 'pressure' may be viewed as an instance of power being wielded.

In the DM corpus we identify some strictly religious words such as 'Muslim' (which tops the list) or 'religion' and 'mosque', next to others that pertain to the context of the intellectual debate on radicalisation, such as 'ideas', 'radicalisation', 'ideology' and 'society'. There are also a number of demography-related words such as 'youngster', 'child' or 'woman'. Finally, we come across words with a political or law and order connotation such as 'state', 'politician' and 'police'.

We must conclude that differences between both newspapers as found in the crisis corpus are less pronounced in the routine coverage. Hence hypothesis 1 is more strongly confirmed in the crisis corpus.

Table 8.4: 'Radicalisation' in DM and HLN in the routine corpus

Lemma HLN	English translation	Thesaurus score	Lemma DM	English translation	Thesaurus score
Kind	Child	0.109	Islam	Islam	0.134
Jongere	Youngster	0.100	Kind	Child	0.126
Jaar	Year	0.098	Idee	Idea	0.125
Aanslag	Attack	0.098	Mens	Human	0.124
Radicalisme	Radicalism	0.096	Moslim	Muslim	0.120
Vrouw	Woman	0.092	Verantwoor-delijkheid	Responsi-bility	0.118
Wapen	Weapon	0.091	Partij	Party	0.114
Probleem	Problem	0.090	Leven	Life	0.114
Man	Man	0.087	Verhaal	Story	0.112
Extremisme	Extremism	0.087	Geloof	Belief	0.111
Terreur	Terrorism	0.086	Familie	Family	0.107
Boek	Book	0.085	Boek	Book	0.106
Werk	Work	0.084	Aanslag	Attack	0.106
Politie	Police	0.078	Extremisme	Extremism	0.104
Taak	Task	0.078	Visie	Vision	0.104

Finally, we look at the collocations of the word 'radicalisation' in both newspapers in the routine corpus (Table 8.4). Religion is a clear focus in the DM corpus, with terms such as 'Islam', 'Muslims' and 'belief'. A focus on debate ('idea', 'responsibility', 'vision') and family ('human', 'family') is also apparent, and we also come across words such as 'party' (which pertain to politics), or 'attack' and 'extremism', which refer to violence. 'Life' is among the more neutral words in the DM corpus.

Again, the HLN corpus includes words linked to violence ('attack', 'weapon', 'extremism', 'terrorism' and 'police'), but this is mixed with family-oriented words (with 'child' and 'youngster' topping the list, ahead of 'woman' and 'man') and words that refer to the existence of a debate, such as 'radicalism', 'problem' and 'book'. More neutral words such as 'year' and 'work' also appear.

Altogether, we can conclude that in HLN, a right-wing tabloid, reporting on radicalisation and Islam is likely to be lexically framed in the context of 'governmentality', 'violence' and 'locality', while frames on debating, families of radicalised youngsters and religious descriptors occur more frequently in DM, a left-leaning broadsheet. Our hypotheses predicting such frames in DM (H1a) and HLN (H2a) in a crisis corpus are confirmed. Our parallel hypotheses suggesting similar tendencies in routine corpora (H1b and 2b) are confirmed as well, but less strongly.

Study 2: Fear of Terrorism among Audiences

Our second study investigates the extent to which consumption of our two newspapers is related to a person's fear of terrorism. As Study 1 showed, in the years following the 2016 terror attack in Belgium, both HLN and DM published many stories containing the words 'radicalisation' and 'Islam', which chimes with the perceived importance of these themes among public and policy makers at the time. Although DM had more stories using these words, such words were more strongly associated with violence-related terms such as 'terrorism', 'attack' and 'perpetrator' in HLN, both in the crisis and routine corpus. Given the different ways in which these newspapers report on Islam and radicalisation, we expect they will have a different impact on audience perceptions about terrorism. More specifically, we posit that reading HLN will heighten fear of terrorism.

Data

We distributed an online questionnaire to adults aged 18 to 65 in Flanders in September and October of 2017 (N = 878). The polling agency we worked with drew a sample from its panel with heterogeneity in terms of age and gender. The response rate was about 35 per cent, and responses were weighted by gender and age to ensure that the data were representative for these characteristics in Flanders. Respondents were contacted through e-mail with the request to cooperate in a study. No specific subject was specified in the e-mail to respondents to avoid priming. The actual survey was distributed via the polling agency's own survey tool, in Dutch, Flanders's official language. Skipping a question was not possible, but a few did have a 'no answer' option. Each question appeared on its own page, and respondents did not have the option to return to previous questions in order to change their answers.

Measures

Fear of terrorism. We used the fear of terrorism scale developed by Nellis and Savage (2012), with a few changes. The scale consists of six hypothetical scenarios ('Someday I may witness a terror attack', 'Someday my family or close friends may be the victim of a terror attack', etc.), with answer categories ranging from 1 ('not likely at all') to 11 ('very likely'). While the original scale measured fear of terrorism based on separate scenarios ('I could be on a plane that is hijacked', 'I could be on a subway or bus that is hijacked'), we aggregated these into a single item ('Someday I may be on a plane/subway/bus that is bombed'). Part of the original wording was adjusted as well. Principal component analysis indicates that a single factor is present, with high internal consistency (Cronbach's alpha = .98).

Newspaper consumption and trust. Respondents were asked about their newspaper consumption pattern in the past month, with answer categories from 1 ('never') to 8 ('every day'). We presented respondents with eight of the most read newspapers in Flanders, asking them, for each paper, how often they had read it over the past month. Regarding their trust in each newspaper type, respondents were asked the extent to which they trusted news on quality newspapers (with DM as an example) and tabloids (with HLN as an example), with answers ranging from 1 ('untrustworthy') to 5 ('trustworthy').

Demographics. Respondents were asked about their gender (1 = male, 2 = female), age, educational attainment (1 = no education, 6 = university education) and religious denomination (1 = Christian, 2 = Muslim, 3 = other religion, 4 = not religious) (Table 8.5).

Results: Survey Analysis

All respondents were residents of Flanders, the northern region of Belgium. Descriptive results include a mean score of 4.87 (out of a possible 11) on the fear of terrorism scale, indicating moderate fear. In terms of newspaper consumption, we found that respondents read HLN (M = 2.46, SE = 2.48) more frequently than DM (M = 1.40; SE = 1.37). This difference in consumption is in line with the readership numbers of these two newspapers in Flanders: in 2018–2019, HLN had 1,382,400 readers, while DM had only 294,400 (CIM, 2019).

Table 8.5: Descriptive statistics in Study 2

Variables	Mean (SD)	1	2	3	4	5	6	7	8
1. Age	48.16 (12.47)	1							
2. Gender	1.53 (0.50)	-.10**	1						
3. Education	4.32 (1.14)	-.40**	-.01	1					
4. Reading *De Morgen*	1.40 (1.37)	.06	-.03	.12*	1				
5. Reading *Het Laatste Nieuws*	2.46 (2.48)	.12**	-.04	-.12**	.05	1			
6. Trust quality newspapers	3.75 (0.90)	-.17**	.06	.26**	.08*	-.10**	1		
7. Trust popular newspapers	3.48 (0.90)	.06	.04	-.11**	-.17**	.15**	.40**	1	
8. Fear of terrorism	4.99 (2.53)	.00	.26**	-.23**	-.07*	.14**	-.18**	.05	1

Note: *N* = 878. Gender was coded as male = 1, female = 2. * p < .05, ** p < .01.

The regression included four independent variables (reading DM, reading HLN, trust in quality newspapers, trust in tabloids), which were added in two steps (Table 8.6). Covariates included age, gender, educational attainment and religious denomination. Two-way interactions between readership and trust indicators were modelled but did not yield any significant results. The results revealed two significant main effects: reading HLN (B = .11, SE = .01, p = .001) and trust, and more specifically lack thereof, in quality newspapers

(B = -.17, SE = .04, p = .000). At the same time, trust in tabloids (B = .06, SE = .04, p = .083) and reading DM (B = .01, SE = .02, p = .828) were not significantly related to fear of terrorism.

Table 8.6: Stepwise linear regression of fear of terrorism, with standardised coefficients of predictors

	Model 1	Model 2	Model 3	Full model
Age	-.10**	-.11**	-.10**	-.12***
	(.00)	(.00)	(.00)	(.00)
Gender (ref. = male)				
Female	.24***	.25***	.26***	.25***
	(.05)	(.05)	(.05)	(.05)
Educational attainment	-.27***	-.25***	-.20**	-.21***
	(.03)	(.03)	(.03)	(.03)
Religious denomination (ref. = Christian)				
Muslim	-.09**	-.08**	-.09**	-.09**
	(.46)	(.46)	(.43)	(.46)
Other religion	-.04	-.03	-.03	-.03
	(.10)	(.10)	(.10)	(.10)
Not religious	-.11***	-.11**	-.11**	-.11**
	(.06)	(.06)	(.06)	(.06)
Newspaper readership				
De Morgen		-.01		.01
		(.02)		(.02)
Het Laatste Nieuws		.13***		.11**
		(.01)		(.01)
Trust in newspaper				
Quality newspapers			-.21***	-.17***
			(.04)	(.04)
Tabloids			.10**	.06+
			(.03)	(.04)
R^2	.14	.15	.16	.17

Note. +: p < 0.10; *: p < 0.05; **: p < 0.01; ***: p < 0.001

Conclusion and Discussion

In their study on co-occurrences pointing to framing differences, Greussing and Boomgaarden (2017, p. 1764) conclude that 'it remains questionable whether these co-occurrences reveal frames in the sense of abstract interpretation lenses, or rather remain on a highly issue-oriented topical level'. Similar nuances can be applied to the results of our co-occurrence study.

Nevertheless, our study clearly differentiates the two newspapers' word lists (hypothesis 1) albeit in a less explicit manner regarding routine reporting as compared to crisis reporting. In this respect our study is not quite in line with Greussing and Boomgaarden's study (2017) that mainly shows that in times of crisis tabloid and broadsheet reporting styles tend to converge. Our results are more in line with those of Beckers and Van Aelst (2019), indicating that different media tend to shift gears in times of crisis, as seen during the 2015 refugee crisis.

Beckers and Van Aelst noted that the Flemish commercial broadcaster focused more on crime and politics, contrasting with a more human-interest approach in its public counterpart's reporting. This echoes the lexical differences between the tabloid and broadsheet newspapers we looked at in this study: crime, politics and locality on the one hand, family, debate and religion on the other.

Although questions about causality cannot be answered by our second parallel study on fear of terrorism among Flemish media consumers, a number of variables hint at some resonance (hypothesis 2) between media content level and audience perception level. Readership of HLN and level of trust in quality newspapers are related with different levels of fear of terrorism.

These conclusions may point to the need for some sort of ethical evaluation, as they suggest that a quality newspaper's less sensationalistic coverage of terrorism is superior to a tabloid's simplistic representations of criminal and law and order matters. Bek (2004) comments on the assumption that the nonexistence of 'low-brow' media would completely cut off the man in the street from current events, possibly encouraging him to ultimately turn to quality media such as broadsheet newspapers to at least get some information. A further mitigating factor suggesting that 'something ought to be done' about tabloids cultivating fear of terrorism are negative correlations between fear of terrorism and psychological well-being (Asad Ali Shah et al., 2018). Such valid objections to the tabloidisation of terrorism coverage notwithstanding, terrorism is such a dangerous phenomenon that it should not be sugar-coated by the media.

Note

1. This research was supported by the FWO (Research Foundation Flanders) project 'Diversity and Information Media: New Tools for a Multifaceted Public Debate' (DIAMOND), grant number: S008817N and the BELSPO (Belgian Science Policy) project BR/165/A4/IM²MEDIATE – Image of Immigrants in Media: Thought-provoking Effects.

References

Asad Ali Shah, S., Yezhuang, T., Muhammad Shah, A., Khan Durrani, D., & Jamal Shah, S. (2018). Fear of terror and psychological well-being: The moderating role of emotional intelligence. *International Journal of Environmental Research and Public Health, 15*(11), 25–54.

Beckers, K., & Van Aelst, P. (2019). Did the European migrant crisis change news coverage of immigration? A longitudinal analysis of immigration television news and the actors speaking in it. *Mass Communication and Society, 22*(6), 733–755.

Bek, M. G. (2004). Research note: Tabloidization of news media. An analysis of television news in Turkey. *European Journal of Communication, 19*(3), 371–386.

Berbers, A. P. V., Joris, W., Boesman, J., d'Haenens, L., Koeman, J., & van Gorp, B. (2016). The news framing of the 'Syria fighters' in Flanders and the Netherlands: Victims or terrorists? *Ethnicities, 16*(6), 798–818.

Bump, P. (2017, February 6). President Trump is now speculating that the media is covering up terrorist attacks. *Washington Post.* https://www.washingtonpost.com/news/politics/wp/2017/02/06/president-trump-is-now-speculating-that-the-media-is-covering-up-terrorist-attacks/

De Albuquerque, A. (2018). Political parallelism. In *Oxford research encyclopedia of communication.* https://doi.org/10.1093/acrefore/9780190228613.013.860

De Coninck, D. (2020). Fear of terrorism and attitudes towards refugees: An empirical test of group threat theory. *Crime & Delinquency, 68*(4), 550–571. doi: 10.1177/0011128720981898

Dubois, E., & Blank, G. (2018). The echo chamber is overstated: The moderating effect of political interest and diverse media. *Information, Communication & Society, 21*(5), 729–745.

Elchardus, M. (1994). Gekaapte deugden: Over de nieuwe breuklijn en de zin van limieten [Hijacked virtues: On the new fault line and the meaning of limits]. *Samenleving en Politiek, 1*(1), 20–27.

Flaxman, S., Goel, S., & Rao, J. M. (2016). Filter bubbles, echo chambers, and online news consumption. *Public Opinion Quarterly, 80*(1), 298–320.

Gerbner, G., & Gross, L. (1976). The scary world of TV's heavy viewer. *Psychology Today, 9*(11), 41–45.

Greussing, E., & Boomgaarden, H. J. (2017). Shifting the refugee narrative? An automated frame analysis of Europe's 2015 refugee crisis. *Journal of Ethnic and Migration Studies, 43*(11), 1749–1774.

Haim, M., Graefe, A., & Brosius, H.-B. (2018). Burst of the filter bubble? *Digital Journalism, 6*(3), 330–343.

Hallin, D. C., & Mancini, P. (2004). *Comparing media systems. Three models of media and politics.* Cambridge University Press.

Herman, O., Jakubícek, M., Rychlý, P., & Kovár, V. (2019). Word sense induction using word sketches. In C. Martín-Vide, M. Purver, & S. Pollak (Eds.), *Statistical language and speech processing* (pp. 83–91). Springer Nature Switzerland AG.

Lexico (s.d.) *Collocation.* https://www.lexico.com/en/definition/collocation

Lin, D. (1998). Automatic retrieval and clustering of similar words. In *Proceedings of the 17th international conference on computational linguistics* (pp. 768–774). Association for Computational Linguistics.

Matthes, J., Schmuck, D. & von Sikorski, C. (2019). Terror, terror everywhere? How terrorism news shape support for anti-Muslim policies as a function of perceived threat severity and controllability. *Political Psychology, 40*(5), 935–951.

Nellis, A. M., & Savage, J. (2012). Does watching the news affect fear of terrorism? The importance of media exposure on terrorism fear. *Crime & Delinquency, 58*(5), 748–768.

Pariser, E. (2011). *The filter bubble: What the internet is hiding from you.* Penguin.

Pomerantsev, P., Applebaum, A. Gaston, S., Fusi, N., Peterson, Z., Quattrociocchi, W., Zollo, F., Schmidt, A. L., Peruzzi, A., Severgnini, B. de Cesco, A. F., & Casati, D. (2019). *Journalism in the age of populism and polarisation: Lessons from the migration debate in Italy.* London School of Economics and Political Science. https://www.lse.ac.uk/iga/research-and-publications/Journalism-in-an-age-of-populism-and-polarisation

Raeijmaekers, D. (2018). *Little debate: Ideological media pluralism and the transition from a pillarized to a commercialized newspaper landscape (Flanders, 1960–2014)* [Doctoral dissertation, University of Antwerp].

Rashid, S., & Olofsson, A. (2021). Worried in Sweden: The effects of terrorism abroad and news media at home on terror-related worry. *Journal of Risk Research, 24*(1), 62–77.

Slaets, A., Verhoest, P., d'Haenens, L., Minnen, J., & Glorieux, I. (2020). Fragmentation, homogenisation or segmentation? A diary study into the diversity of news consumption in a high-choice media environment. *European Journal of Communication, 36*(5), 1–17. doi: 10.1177/0267323120966841

The Economist (2016). *Globalisation and politics.* https://www.economist.com/briefing/2016/07/30/drawbridges-up

Vaccari, C., Valeriani, A., Barberá, P., Jost, J. T., Nagler, J., & Tucker, J. A. (2016). Of echo chambers and contrarian clubs: Exposure to political disagreement among German and Italian users of Twitter. *Social Media + Society, 2*(3), 1–24.

Van Gorp, B. (2005). Where is the frame? Victims and intruders in the Belgian press coverage of the asylum issue. *European Journal of Communication, 20*(4), 484–507.

Williamson, H., Fay, S., & Miles-Johnson, T. (2019). Fear of terrorism: Media exposure and subjective fear of attack. *Global Crime, 20*(1), 1–25.

Zemni, S. (2009). *Het islamdebat* [The debate on Islam]. EPO.

Zhu, R., Krever, R., & Siu Kay Choi, A. (2018). The impact of newspaper reports on fear of violent crime in Hong Kong. *Newspaper Research Journal, 39*(4), 470–480.

9

ISLAMOPHOBIA IN THE PORTUGUESE OPINION PRESS

CAMILA ARÊAS, ALFREDO BRANT, ANA FLORA MACHADO, COLIN ROBINEAU,
HELENA CRUZ VENTURA & ABDELWAHED MEKKI-BERRADA

Abstract

In the Portuguese opinion press from 2010 to 2020, the question of Islamophobia appears in two forms: in discourses containing a discriminatory content against Muslims, and in discourses discussing the political uses of the term. While the first form is present in different degrees in all newspapers under study, the second form is mostly visible in the right-wing newspaper *Observador*, which criticises the political function, especially the intimidation (self-censorship) that the notion of Islamophobia fulfils. Following these findings, this chapter intend to observe how the term 'Islamophobia' is mobilised by *Observador*'s columnists in order to legitimise what they call a 'rational critic' of Islam, with no restraints regarding 'political correctness'. Our main goal is to show how those columnists denounce the European political left and intellectuals of 'sociologising' the issue of Islamic fundamentalism and shaping a 'political correctness' that would compensate for their colonial guilt. To overcome this discursive impasse and liberate the violent speech on Islam, these journalists demand, on the one hand, the end of the 'guilt-tripping' of Europeans and, on the other, the end of Muslims' 'victimisation'.

Keywords: Islamophobia, opinion, press, Portugal, discourse analysis, right-wing press, left-wing parties

Introduction

This chapter analyses the journalistic coverage of Islam in the Portuguese opinion press over the last ten years (2010–2020). The study undertakes a quantitative and qualitative analysis of discourses, either focused on Islamophobia, or containing Islamophobic content, published by columnists and editorialists in all online traditional Portuguese newspapers (OTPN) during this period. The article aims to highlight that what we refer to as *mediated Islamophobia* is both discernible and analysable in the materiality of opinion-press journalists' discourses. Put differently, the goal is to observe how *Islamophobia*, often portrayed in the mediatised public space as a general and diffuse phenomenon, is instead constructed and reconstructed *in* and *by* the discourses employed by press columnists.

Without ignoring the controversial nature of the concept of Islamophobia (see the introduction to this book) in the context of present-day European public debate our specific goal is to observe the central role it plays in ongoing discursive disputes between various actors seeking to define it according to their respective positions, ideas and interests. By taking into account the capacity of the Islamophobia notion to signify relationships to Islam and/or Muslims centred on aversion, hatred and/or fear, thereby referencing a social reality that is both locally and globally relevant, this study seeks to show the ways in which exclusion-, violence- and discrimination-based relationships can be discerned in the materiality of media discourses. The notion must therefore be viewed as an 'object of discourse' (i.e., a product and producer of social realities) rooted in argumentative, declarative and pragmatic strategies worthy of detailed analysis.

By employing a critical semiotic approach to discourse analysis, we seek to highlight the principal themes, representations and arguments utilised by journalists and columnists in online traditional Portuguese newspapers (OTPN). We use a news media corpus that includes all Portuguese daily press publications: *Público, Diário de Notícias, Jornal de Notícias, Correio da Manhã,* and *Observador*. In total, we analysed 1,553 articles taken from newspaper websites based on keywords.[1] In keeping with the French school of discourse analysis (Charaudeau, 1992; Kerbrat-Orecchioni, 2009), we combined lexical and semantic linguistic analysis, as well as corpus-assisted discourse analysis (CADA), using the Sketch Engine software[2] (see also chapter 5 in this book). This methodological framework allows for the identification, via an initial quantitative step, of the most recurrent terms and concepts found in the news media corpus. This is followed by a qualitative analysis of how these lexical fields are joined to key arguments and theses espoused by OTPN columnists, journalists and editorialists (Venkatesh et al., 2016).

In debates around Islam in the Portuguese opinion press from 2010 to 2020, the Islamophobia issue appears in two main forms: (1) in discriminatory discourses aimed at Islam or Muslims, and (2) in discourses concerning the issue of political usage of the Islamophobia notion. While the former appears in all newspapers to varying degrees based on their editorial position, the latter is most visible in the right-wing *Observador* newspaper, whose editorialists criticise the political function supposedly served by the Islamophobia notion, particularly in terms of intimidation (self-censorship).

Based on these observations, this chapter is structured in two parts. First, we undertake an analysis of journalistic discourses containing Islamophobic (xenophobic or racist) content. Second, we explore journalistic usages and discussions related to the Islamophobia term. Our objective is to emphasise specific aspects of these two discursive levels, from which *mediated Islamophobia*, that is, Islamophobia conveyed both *in* and *by* the materiality of journalistic language, is deployed. In line with the view held by Mekki-Berrada and d'Haenens (Introduction to this book) that the Islamophobia concept is characterised by complexity and 'semantic immaturity', the aim here is to rehabilitate the notion, while putting forth provisional and operative definitions based on conclusions from this empirical linguistic study of how Islamophobia is expressed and translated within the situated context of the discursivity of the Portuguese opinion press.

This case study of Portugal is conceived as a contribution to the contemplation and questioning of mediated Islamophobia. As a result of Portugal's specific sociohistorical and political traits, areas of both convergence and dissonance with the mediated debate around Islam[3] in the French-speaking world are present. While in Portugal Islamophobia is not considered a 'public issue', nor a national phenomenon, the notion is nonetheless frequently invoked in opinion pieces regarding Islam, Muslims and/or the veil, especially in the context of the terrorist attacks that occurred in Europe over the course of the decade under study.

Islamophobic Content in Journalistic Discourse

This first part of the study describes and discusses results from the discursive analysis that was conducted regarding discriminatory discourses employed by journalists who authored opinion pieces in OTPN. The study of this news media corpus, based on four lexical-discursive fields – 'islão, islâmico, islamita, islamista, mulçulmano'; 'véu, hijab, niqab, nikab, burca, burqa'; 'jihad, djihad, jihadismo, terrorismo, terrorista'; 'islamofobia' – enables us to analyse the linguistic and discursive features specific to each of these keywords. In addition, their associations with other words (co-occurrences) within semantic networks can also be analysed. Structured as such, the study enables us to outline a brief archaeology of the ideas, arguments and representations shaping the debate around Islam in the Portuguese opinion press.

Islamophobia and Racialisation: A Question of Domination

The discursive analysis for the first lexical field ('islão, islâmico, islamita, islamista, mulçulmano') uncovered a dominant representation of Islam and Muslims rooted in the dual process of essentialisation and dichotomisation. The former entails conceiving Muslims as an imagined and homogeneous community, while the latter consists of calling upon Manichean representations of Islam and Muslims in either evaluative (good/bad) or axiological (true/false) terms. In this regard, it is worth noting the use of paired oppositional terms such as 'Europe and Islam'; 'Muslims and Christians'; 'Muslims and Western Europe'; 'the West and the East'; 'Us and the Others'; 'the international community and the Muslim community'; 'the State and the Stateless'; and 'the civilised and the 15th-century savages'.

In each of the surveyed OTPN, we observed that journalists referenced Islam or its followers in a homogeneous manner, not making any distinction as to geographical, social, political, cultural or ethnic origins, and thereby approaching the idea of an 'imagined community' (Anderson, 1991). This paradigm is criticised in a *Público* article, in which Álvaro Vasconcelos decries 'the attribution to Muslims of a unique identity associated with fanaticism, violence, and disrespect for rights, especially those of women' (Vasconcelos, 2017, our translation). Indeed, the religious group is often invoked based on the discursive strategy of collective-identity assignment, which is consistent with a process of Muslim 'racialisation' shaped in Europe by specific national sociopolitical features (colonialism, immigration, secularism or Catholicism).

From this perspective, particularly in articles addressing the terrorism issue, the employed interpretive framework for Muslims living in European countries takes the form of a dichotomous opposition between 'Muslim' and 'non-Muslim', as well as between the 'good Muslim' (moderate) and the 'bad Muslim' (extremist), always in accordance with their degree of adherence to European values. For example, *Correio da Manhã* columnists speak of a 'European community of Judeo-Christian tradition' or of a 'Western civilisation', in opposition to the 'new enemy' or 'murderers' from the Muslim community. While the former is characterised by the values of freedom and human rights, the latter is defined in terms of religious fundamentalism and extremism.

Such opinion pieces tend to present the West as in decline and/or threatened by a conquering cultural, religious or even demographic force, whose values are in opposition to both the West and its (especially Catholic) history. We therefore observe the emergence of the 'Islamist' culturalist rhetorical paradigm, which, in employing a logic similar to that of Samuel Huntington, operates against the backdrop of a 'clash of civilisations'. The founder of the *Observador* newspaper goes as far as to suggest that 'we should reread the much-vilified Samuel Huntington and his *Clash of Civilizations* to be reminded that, if in Western Christianity there is a tradition of separating what belongs to Caesar from what belongs to God, in Islam, God is Caesar … The Islamic tradition incorporates elements that contradict our way of life … which attracts so many immigrants and which the doctrines of sharia and the apostles of jihad seek to oppose' (Fernandes, 2015, our translation).

The discursive analysis for the second lexical field ('hijab, veil, niqab, burqa') serves to reinforce this 'Islamist' perception, insofar as its primary identification is rooted in its visible and tangible dimension, i.e., based on physical appearance and religious markers. The various veil types in question are frequently invoked by columnists in a way that groups them together in the form of a list. This hinders both appreciation of their respective features, as well as any consideration of their associated contextual components (material and symbolic), which could help signify how and why they are worn. In this way, the veil is signified in OTPN as a sign of 'oppression', 'submission', 'subordination' and 'abuse'. In the *Observador*, columnist Maria João Marques likens fully veiled women to 'dementors', phantasmagoric creatures who appear in the Harry Potter series.

While the qualitative nature of this depiction of Muslim women certainly varies depending on the newspapers' respective editorial stances, the issues addressed by the writers often overlap (gender equality vs. subjugation of women, or freedom of religious expression vs. public safety). Though the articles display a considerable divergence of opinions between columnists, they nonetheless present the issue in similar manners, based on three key arguments: the segregation of women, the incompatibility of the veil with European values and the public order issue. The news media coverage draws a denigrating portrait of Muslim women, as needing to be liberated from 'servitude' by European values.

The journalistic framing of the debate thus provides a culture- and security-based reading of the issue that reflects a gendered form of *stigmatisation* or *Islamophobia* directed against Muslim women, whose 'false consciousness' supposedly pushes them to 'reproduce the instruments of their own domination' (Mekki-Berrada, 2018, p. 15). By 'stigmatising', we refer to any discourse that seeks, through the violence of language, to denigrate, discredit, discriminate, inferiorise, marginalise, dehumanise, animalise, exclude and render 'invisible' the Muslim Other (Arêas, 2012, 2015). Whether directed against the religion or its followers, *Islamophobia* thus represents a linguistic expression of the domination- and power-based social relationships present in the Luso-European reality, which Islamophobic discourses in turn help reinforce and normalise.

Islamophobia and Power: A Question of Governmentality

The terms comprising the third lexical field of the study – 'jihad, jihadism, jihadist, terrorism, terrorist' – relate to politico-religious actions and forms of radical struggle carried out in the name of Islam. As to linguistic materiality, the 'ism' suffix is indicative of the connotative meaning attributed to these terms, associated to religious, ideological and political radicalism. Across the OTPN, these terms quantitatively and qualitatively represent the most significant lexical field, as reflected in both the articles' length and the number of pages comprising this section of the analysis. For the decade under study, the Portuguese news media coverage was marked, following 9/11, by the occurrence of terrorist attacks in Europe (Germany, England, Belgium, Spain, France). According to the press columnists, these events signal the arrival of a new form of terrorism – Islamist – which confronts European states with major (geo)political, cultural and security-related issues. This context is therefore the one shaping the debate around Islam in the opinion press from 2010 to 2020.

The analysis of this lexical field is in line with the previous one, insofar as jihad as a Koranic principle (like the veil, possibly) is presented as proof of the ontologically violent nature of Islam, and as the key to explaining global terrorism. The articles addressing the jihadist issue emphasise the incompatibility of Christian and Muslim civilisations. The Crusades are provided as historical evidence, with the 'clash of civilisations' theory providing the requisite intellectual basis. We note that Portuguese press columnists do not tend to make reference to the idea of a secular Europe, but rather to that of a Christian Europe defined by its relationship of otherness to the Muslim religion, or even to the Muslim civilisation. We also note the emergence of a journalistic line of argument employed by the columnists, which, based on the idea of 'civilisational superiority', degrades Muslim societies back to their supposed natural state, alternately described as 'primitive', 'animalistic', 'medieval', 'barbaric', 'tribal' or 'obscure'. The inability of Islamic societies to dissociate the religious, the social and political, the temporal and the spiritual from one another is thus affirmed.

Next, the traits and features of a Europe that is at war with Islam are outlined in numerous terrorism-focused articles, which employ a security-based interpretive framework. The portrait of a Europe adrift, torn between freedom and security, transformed by the 2015 migrant 'crisis', and disoriented by its growing Muslim population is presented. Numerous journalists list European neighbourhoods or cities they now deem to be 'ghettoised' or 'communalised' under the auspices of Islam. The titles of the *Observador* columns metonymically convey these representations: 'Jihadi Lord, may I have Britain back? Thank you', 'London and unreality', 'To die standing in Paris', 'I am, I no longer know what', 'This Europe can finish in Nice' and 'Europe as Israel'. Note the use of personal pronouns (I, we, the others), which strengthens the degree of personification of the imagined communities.

Interpreting terrorism as a diffuse and intangible phenomenon gives rise to an alarmist journalistic line of argument designed to feed into a sense of fear or 'moral panic', in turn calling for (geo)political firmness and vigilance in regard to security. European political and diplomatic bodies, as well as national immigration, security, prevention and intelligence services are the primary targets of this journalistic criticism. The integration-based models of French-speaking countries are presented as the example to follow in the struggle against fundamentalism, while Anglo-Saxon multi-culturalism is alleged to have provided the evidence of its own failure. As Mekki-Berrada (2018, p. 24) emphasises, 'Islamophobia is first and foremost a question of power and of the governmentality of Muslim Otherness.'

More broadly, analysis of the articles associated with this lexical field allows us to highlight the following: (1) discursive representations of a Europe defined by its values and its history with regard to Islam; (2) an explicit defense of the 'clash of civilisations' theory that pits Europe against Islam and advocates for the Westernisation of the 'barbarian/primitive' Muslim; (3) the portrayal of a Europe transformed and disoriented by both its growing population of Muslims and its lapsed sovereignty over certain 'lost territories'; and (4) recognition of French-speaking countries as the avant-garde in the fight against terrorism, with the French model widely presented as the example to follow.

It must be noted that the shape the debate ends up taking in the Portuguese opinion press does not result in a space for either discussion or representation of a domestic form of Islam. In general, columnists always refer to 'Islam in Portugal' and not to 'Portuguese Islam'. In the first lexical field, what notably emerges from the articles is the representation of a European Islam, as well as a community of Muslims at the European level. In the second lexical field, analysing the French public debate over laws banning the veil enables Portuguese columnists to position themselves politically and ideologically in a European debate, one with no domestic equivalent. In the third lexical field, the analogy between the jihadist phenomenon and the Iberian history of Al-Andalus and the Crusades is recurrent.

In the overall corpus, there is only a single mention of terrorism on domestic soil: the construction of the Martim Moniz mosque was the subject of controversy regarding possible risks of radicalisation. The Immigration and Borders Service is also strongly criticised. The absence of a Portuguese Islam in the opinion press can be understood as part of a currently dominant political-media discourse emphasising the uniqueness of Portugal's colonial history, especially in regard to its relationship with Islam.

Journalistic Uses of the Islamophobia Term

> Islamist cannibalism is back on the offensive ... We know well what comes next: the ritual display of generic piety and warnings of the threat of 'Islamophobic drift' ... These responses reveal much about the curious relationship we share with language today ... The new policy of words has the effect of overshadowing the ideas challenging us. This new policy of words, which abuses the unintelligence of language, cuts across political parties ... It is perhaps useful to remember that 'phobia' comes from the Greek word for 'fear' and that in this case, fear isn't exactly an absurd emotion. (Tunhas, 2017, our translation)

In this second part, the analysis focuses on the journalistic uses of and debates around the Islamophobia term. As such, it is not a lexical field, but instead a single keyword – Islamophobia – that is the focus of this part of the study. Via linguistic and discursive analysis, we analyse the way in which the term is invoked by Portuguese press columnists. How is the concept used by these journalists? With which enunciative, rhetorical, argumentative and pragmatic objectives is the *Islamophobia* term employed within the corpus? To answer these questions, the following analysis takes the form of a meta-discursive study focused on the processes of signification (reappropriation, misappropriation) guiding the usage of the *Islamophobia* keyword in the co-text of the sentences and the context of the article.

During a first reading of the articles containing the term in the Sketch Engine software[4] we were challenged by how frequently three variations of Islamophobia appeared: 'Islamophobe(s)', 'Islamophobic(s)' and 'Islamophobia[5]' (in quotation marks). The quantitative analysis of the absolute frequency (log) of these terms in the overall corpus shows the term Islamophobia appeared 67 times, Islamophobe 7 times, Islamophobic 6 times and 'Islamophobia' (in quotation marks) 21 times. From the perspective of significance (logDice), these terms are associated with verbs[6] and nouns[7], among which we note a very high significance (logDice from 11 to 13) for the 'xenophobia', 'racism' and 'intolerance' terms, which appear in all the analysed newspapers, often being employed as synonyms to help define Islamophobia. The term refers, on the one hand, to a widespread and diffuse phenomenon ('Islamophobic atmosphere', 'Islamophobic temptation') and, on the other hand, to actors, behaviours or discursive practices ('Islamophobic accusation', 'Islamophobic argument'). In both instances, Islamophobia is consistently presented as a 'growing' phenomenon. By framing Islamophobia as an issue on the basis of other notions, including 'immigration', 'multi-culturalism', 'machismo' and 'neofascism', these articles advance the argument that Islamophobia results from issues associated with Muslim integration in Europe.

This lexical mapping informs us that, across the entire press corpus under study, the notion of Islamophobia is often presented as being synonymous with *racism* and xenophobia, with these terms at times appearing between quotation marks.[8] From the quantitative analysis, we also learn that the right-wing conservative newspaper *Observador* is the publication where the Islamophobia term and its variants most frequently appear (23 articles out of a total of 47), accounting for half of the newspaper's overall output during the period under analysis. By comparison, the term appeared in *Correio da Manhã* 34 times out of 1,264 articles, in *Publico* 24 times out of 129 articles, and in *Diário de Notícias* and *Jornal de Notícias* 20 times out of 113 articles.

In the analysed corpus, *Observador* journalists were the ones who most often denounced the political usage of the Islamophobia notion, given its supposed goal of preventing or disarming any critique of Islam. The Islamophobia concept is systematically invoked by the columnists to condemn it, while legitimising what they describe as a 'rational criticism' of Islam, free from 'political correctness'. Although journalistic condemnation targeting the political function of the Islamophobia term is present across the entire corpus, only in the *Observador* does the systematic resumption of this argumentative strategy elevate it to a predominant rhetorical paradigm.

By focusing our analysis onto the journalistic uses of the Islamophobia term in the *Observador*, we seek to highlight how its columnists: (1) criticise the political function of the Islamophobia semantic class, which is supposedly invoked for the purpose of intimidation and censorship; (2) denounce the political left, as well as European intellectuals, for having both 'sociologised' the Islamic fundamentalism issue, as well as fashioned a form of 'political correctness' to make up for their colonial guilt; (3) call for an end to both Europeans' 'self-imposed guilt trip', as well as the 'victimisation' of radical Muslims; and (4) assume a first-person ('I') critique of Islam that subjectively involves both the columnist and the reader. These elements structure the subsequent analysis into two parts: the first devoted to developing the two initial points, the second bringing together the two latter points.

Critiquing *Islamophobia*'s Political Function: A Denunciation of Intellectuals, the Political Left and Television News Media

Discursive analysis of the 23 *Observador* articles containing the Islamophobia term reveals an argumentative, even rhetorical paradigm whereby political usage of the Islamophobia semantic class is denounced and equated to 'liberticide' (Mekki-Berrada, 2018). This paradigm argues that the norms surrounding 'political correctness' (aimed at preventing Islamophobic, racist or xenophobic discourse in the public space) ultimately prevent even the most legitimate and reasoned critiques of Islam from occurring. This rhetorical strategy then assumes the form of a denunciation of the political function – of labelling (anti-Muslim racism) and intimidation (self-censorship) – which, according to these columnists, is the true motivation behind usage of the Islamophobia notion. As journalist Maria João Marques illustrates: 'Criticising Islam is no longer possible. It is no longer accepted in cosmopolitan salons. It's bad form' (Marques, 2016, *Observador,* our translation).

This journalistic argument is part of a broader critique against both 'humanist and relativist ideology', as well as the 'culture of apology' supposedly promoted by intellectuals, the political left and certain European news outlets. *Observador*'s columnists accuse these actors, whom they often refer to as 'petty sociologists' (*'sociólogo de pacotilha'*), of having remained paralysed and silent in the face of the advance of Muslim extremism out of fear that the issue would easily be appropriated by the political far right. They also accuse them of 'sociologising' the issue of Islamic fundamentalism via either 'social media jargon'

(*'jargão socio-mediático'*) or a 'mediated sociologism booklet' (*'cartilha do sociolês médiatico'*) and, by doing so, shaping the discursive norms of 'political correctness', which seeks to mitigate the European left's (colonial) sense of guilt. This is illustrated in the following passage by Helena Matos in the *Observador*: 'The academic left's tactical silence has been complicit in the extremism that holds Muslims hostage and failed to prevent the French far right from indulging in the Islamic stew. Let's learn the lesson: avoid ghettos and reject the identity politics that render minorities hostage to fascists' (Matos, 2017).

The first pillar of this journalistic denunciation consists in legitimising criticism of Islam on the basis of a critique of terrorism. As illustrated by Rui Ramos in *Observador,* 'It would be unwise to continue invoking "racism" and "Islamophobia" so as to prevent any debate of jihadism' (Ramos, 2016). Not only is this an amalgamation linking Islam to the terrorism issue; it is also and above all else a rhetorical device that asserts the possibility of criticising terrorism only to legitimise, via a shift in meaning, a (broader) critique of Islam. The *Observador*'s editor-in-chief, José Manuel Fernandes, conveys this shift in meaning in the following passage:

> This brings us to a second key point: the role of Islam. In the days following the attacks, I suddenly saw that there were more people concerned about Islamophobia than about fundamentalist extremism, which was surprising. It's one thing to separate the Muslim majority from the fanatical minority, which makes perfect sense. It's another thing to pretend that no aspects of the culture, habits and political customs of Islam can be associated to these radical deviations. It would be nice if people began recognising this. (Fernandes, 2015, our translation)

It is also in this paradigm of accusing intellectuals and the left that the criticism of European media, particularly the 24-hour news channels, takes shape. Recurrent among all the studied newspapers, this indictment relies on a dual argumentative strategy: the media is criticised either for the increased visibility it provides to terrorist events, or for euphemising the Islamist nature of the attacks. In this regard, the *Observador* decries the 'double standard' in news media coverage that crimes committed based on religious motivations benefit from: 'When a Muslim is murdered, it's stated that he was killed by a white Catholic. When a Muslim kills, social or psychological, rather than religious explanations are sought' (Gonçalves, 2019). The columnist Gonçalo Portocarrero de Almada takes up this idea, pointing out that while the murder of Muslims is criticised, those of Christians are trivialised: 'What should not happen is that acts of aggression against Christians be reduced to mere "outbursts" or "accidents," while acts against members of other religions, or racial or sexual minority groups are viewed as "attacks against humanity"' (Almada, 2019). In another article, Rui Ramos criticises television news media's tendency to condemn populist or far-right parties' political appropriation of the terrorism issue: 'As if the problem were the demagogic exploitation of the attacks, not the attacks themselves, their frequency and violence … The effort put into deflecting the conversation away from the politically incorrect issue of the jihadist campaign against the West is remarkable' (Ramos, 2016).

A second argumentative technique associated with this form of journalistic denunciation consists of turning the accusation of racism against the actors, particularly those on the left, who invoke Islamophobia: 'Believing they are defending the dominated on their behalf, those who cry "racism" and "Islamophobia" appear to suffer from an ethnic or cultural superiority bias' (Ramos, 2016). In this way, the *Observador* editorialists point to a discursive impasse (created by the left) that prevents any criticism of racial, ethnic or religious minorities, which in turn ends up confining the Muslim topic to its belonging group. For example, in an article titled 'The White and Activist Left's Moral Disability', Gabriel Mithá Ribeiro criticises the identity assignment game whereby Arabs and Muslims are included in the list of 'minority groups who, according to the left, must love each other while hating the white man'. He also defends the need to 'liberate individuals from their belonging group so as to offer them the possibility of criticising others, as well as their own group' (Ribeiro, 2019).

Maria João Marques also points to the left – which she has a tendency of 'psychiatrising' by referring to the 'hysterical' left – as bearing primary responsibility for the excesses of the right:

> The primary blame lies with the hysterical progressive left that canonised political correctness as the yardstick for measuring a person's decency… Well, it was inevitable that something similar would happen on the right… On the one hand, as a reaction and, on the other, because (much to my regret) the human tendency towards stupidity is not limited to the ideological side opposed to mine … Those who warned that this Islamic stew would be calamitous were labeled Islamophobes and intolerant. And he who remains silent, consents, right? (Marques, 2014, our translation)

Note that the question posed at the end challenges the reader and accomplishes its pragmatic or performative goal (Ducrot, 1984, p. 183): the reader must respond. One must note that journalistic denunciation aimed at the political function of the Islamophobia semantic class is often based on rhetorical questions of this kind, as is the case with 'polemical negation'. This argumentative process consists in anticipating opposing discourse in order to counter it, before reaffirming the original thesis (Ducrot, 1984, p. 185). For example, at the time of the London bombings, *Observador* columnist Paulo Tunhas drew a degrading portrait of a 'ghettoised England', to then challenge the reader:

> Am I 'racist'? Of course not. If I can be permitted to express the extent of my good intentions, racism is for me the pre-eminent human sin. I am simply pointing out a fact (Ghettoised England) that should be taken into account. (Tunhas, 2017, our translation)

This passage demonstrates the extent to which the assertion of a legitimate critique of Islamic religious radicalism subjectively implicates the columnist in his own discourse, via the use of the personal pronoun 'I' (Kerbrat-Orecchioni,

2009). Relying on this assumption of 'enunciative responsibility' (Charaudeau, 1992), Paulo Tunhas invites this right-wing newspaper's target audience to do the same, i.e., to assume responsibility for uttering a critique of Islam viewed as being 'politically incorrect'.

Towards an Exit from the Discursive Impasse: The Liberalisation of Violent Speech

Formulated like that, this denunciation by Portuguese press columnists, especially in the *Observador*, presents the portrait of a Europe ensnared in the trap of 'political correctness'. To overcome this discursive impasse, the journalists in question call for an end, on the one hand, to Europeans' 'self-imposed guilt trip' and, on the other, to the 'victimisation' of radical Muslims. In short, they call both for 'violent speech' (Arêas, 2012) to be liberated, as well as for the assumption of the 'enunciative responsibility' (Rabatel & Chauvin-Vileno, 2006) of an uninhibited criticism of Islam and Muslims. From a discursive standpoint, we note that the subjective register, i.e., the use of the first person (I, we), functions as the main tool for this kind of argumentative strategy.

To this end, by narrating via a personal and almost intimate approach, columnist Maria João Marques offers an account of the historical transformation related to the establishment of 'political correctness' discursive norms:

> I must admit that I cannot stand the mantra that, paradoxically, has taken hold since 2001 saying that Islam is a religion of peace, that it has nothing to do with the terrorist attacks... You would imagine being in a theatre, watching a film where Islamists' terrible treatment of women is presented as being a complete fabrication concocted by ill-intentioned, xenophobic individuals ... I confess that I miss being able to discuss these matters as I did in the days when tolerant spirits did not unleash such ferocity against individuals pointing out the obvious problems posed by Islam... To suggest that disrespect for women is the norm for the average Muslim today is considered foolishness akin to KKK racism... But this exculpation of Islam comes at a price: we are now letting Islam off the hook so that the worst can occur. (Marques, 2016, our translation)

By employing a tone of sarcastic humour, the columnist thus shares with readers the essence of a line of thought that is no longer acceptable to express in public, but does so using a subjective register of discourse wherein her enunciative responsibility is implied. She seeks to convince the reader of the falsity of current, seemingly dominant discursive norms, and why they ought to be rejected.

This argumentative exculpatory strategy is at the core of an article in the *Observador* written by Helena Matos, the title of which makes explicit – in an ironic way – the question of enunciative responsibility: 'The others aren't the problem. We are.' The columnist criticises the linguistic precautions taken by media and left-wing political operators by asking them to accept responsibility for them: 'Our problem when it comes to terrorism is not the terrorists, it is the relativism with which we analyse their actions. The more these actions are explained using the manual of mediated sociologism (a type of Marxism gilded with abundant Christian guilt), the more we tolerate them.' According to the columnist, sociological explanations for terrorism only serve to place the blame on European countries: 'There is always some action or decision that we or our ancestors took in the present, or five hundred years ago, which explains, justifies and excuses terrorism and terrorists in our eyes' (Matos, 2015).

This same argument is reiterated in unison by the *Observador*'s various columnists. The newspaper's editor-in-chief, José Manuel Fernandes, sets the tone by reminding us that the attacks on *Charlie Hebdo* and the Bataclan 'were not our fault' and, moreover, 'the barbarians who committed them are not our people'. The writer is here alluding to the comments the intellectual Boaventura de Sousa Santos, the most famous postcolonial studies sociologist in Portugal, made in the wake of these attacks in France, where he rejected the 'clash of civilisations' thesis, referring instead to a 'clash of fanaticisms'. However, according to José Manuel Fernandes,

> What our preacher [de Sousa Santos] has done is simply … to say, as he always does, that we are the barbarians. The time has come to end this idea that the fault is always ours – ours today, ours in the era of colonisation and decolonisation, ours since the time of the Conquest of Ceuta, or the Crusades, or Julius Caesar. (Fernandes, 2015, our translation)

The issue of guilt is also addressed by the columnist Maria João Marques, who portrays Europe as immobilised by the discursive norms of 'political correctness', the fear of being accused of Islamophobia and the 'culture of apology'. Her argument is that terrorism is encouraged via the 'complicity' of those who justify it for social reasons and who tend to

'victimise' and 'excuse' the terrorists: 'European solidarity and tolerance are synonymous with impunity and therefore with the growth of terrorism.'

She thus claims to put the culprits and the victims in their place: 'The fault lies with the individuals who choose to kill and rape, and with the religion and ideology that inspires them. But they have accomplices who treat them as if they were children who are not to be punished but only taught moral lessons' (Marques, 2016).

We can thus see how the assertion of enunciative responsibility and of 'violent speech' against Islam assumes the form of a meta-discursive reflection with regard to the linguistic component and, more precisely, with regard to the discursive impasses caused by the fear of Islamophobia. In this respect, Helena Matos, in one of her columns, criticises the usage of the term 'excision' rather than 'genital mutilation': 'We're now living through a period of veritable word-purging. In fact, it makes as much sense not to employ the term "genital mutilation" to avoid offending populations originating in Africa, as it does to not use the term "homicide," but instead "crossed with a knife"' (Matos, 2017).

In summary, these analyses highlight the ways in which *Observador* columnists frame the ethical norms of 'political correctness' as a form of discursive censorship that sustains the culpability of European actors. To exit this seeming discursive impasse, they defend the liberation of violent speech and criticism as a means to overturn hegemonic discursive norms. We take from this that this journalistic denunciation is an attempt to redraw the boundaries of the 'speakable' and the 'unspeakable' (Foucault, 1969), that is, the norms of legitimate discursivity and thus the 'conditions of possibility' for critical discourse regarding Muslims.

It is important to note that, apart from the Portuguese academic Boaventura de Sousa Santos, the leftists or the intellectuals who have supposedly succumbed to a 'culture of apology' are never named and never linked to the specifically Portuguese context. Instead, the writers who support the denunciation of the political function of the *Islamophobia* semantic class appear to be making reference to a European scale, as well as to a shapeless mass of left-wing actors whose features are never made explicit. By and large, the issue of Islamophobia as a social and political reality in the Portuguese context is never addressed in the corpus under study.

Conclusion

Our study of Portuguese press opinion pieces regarding Islam over the last ten years (2010–2020) sheds light on both the lexical fields, as well as the argumentative-rhetorical strategies through which we can grasp, via the materiality of the language, words, ideas and representations conveyed by columnists, what is referred to as mediated Islamophobia. Through linguistic and discursive analysis of their columns, we conclude that the Islamophobia issue is deployed on two levels: (1) that of discourses that embody Islamophobic statements in various forms (ethnocentric, xenophobic, racist, culturalist) and to varying degrees based on the newspapers' editorial stance (right–left; progressive– conservative); and (2) that of discourses that utilise the Islamophobia term in a meta-analytical manner and in turn seek to denounce the term's political usages.

At this second level of analysis, columnists play the role of both prosecutor and lawyer when they present an indictment of 'political correctness' and a plea for a critique of Islam. These various argumentative processes create a form of journalistic rhetoric that addresses Islamophobia based on its political and discursive effects, while at the same time disregarding the 'experiential Islamophobia' lived out in everyday life situations. The *Observador*'s column-ists are then mostly operating in the meta-discourse, in the sense that they above all else denounce the *Islamophobia* concept for being a political weapon that intimidates and prevents any critique of Islam; in other words, for being a liberticidal instrument.

However, as seen in the first part of the study, many Portuguese opinion press writers, from *Correio da Manhã* to the *Observador, Público, Diário de Notícias* and *Jornal de Notícias*, were unafraid to portray Islam as a religion historically opposed to Europe's 'roots' and 'values', or as a religion that supposedly has, if not an essentially violent character, then at least an intrinsi-cally violent one. A curious paradox thus arises: the *Observador* columnists denouncing the impossibility of criticising Islam are contradicted by their own articles, as well as those of their colleagues.

Notes

1.   The study's keywords are: Islam, Islamic, Islamist, Islamite, Muslim; hijab, veil, scarf, niqab, niqab, burka, burqa; jihad, djihad, jihadism, terrorism, terrorist; islamophobia. (In Portu-guese: *islão, islâmico, islamita, islamista, mulçulmano; véu, hijab, niqab, nikab, burca, burqa; jihad, djihad, jihadismo, terrorismo, terrorista, islamofobia.*)
2.   Using algorithms, this software allowed us to quantify the frequency and significance (log-Dice) of the project's keywords, as well as their associations with other words (co-occur-rences), within semantic lexical networks. Then, based on our reading of the sentences and paragraphs in which these statistically significant term pairings appeared, we identified the main arguments and meaning processes that were invoked in a recurrent, even systematic, manner by the journalists and columnists from the OTPN under study.
3.   In the literature review, we note that the only previously undertaken social science study regarding Islamophobia in Portugal – titled 'Islamophobia and its narratives in Portugal:

Knowledge, politics, media and cyberspace' (Araújo, 2019) – undertakes a general analysis of the phenomenon, while only very briefly addressing the media aspect.
4. https://www.sketchengine.eu
5. In Portuguese: *islamofóbo(s), islamofóbico(s), islamofobia*.
6. 'claim, suggest, label, consider'.
7. 'xenophobia, racism, growth, trivialisation, ambiance, accusation, argument, negotiation, temptation, extremism, populism, terrorism, violence, habit, fear, war, anti-Semitism'.
8. On this point, it would be interesting to examine the use of *Islamophobia* in quotations marks by these columnists. We note that, while certain columnists consistently use quotation marks to either distance themselves from the term or deemphasise its connotative power, other authors view the use of quotation marks by intellectuals, the media and politicians as a red herring indicative of 'political correctness'.

References

Anderson, B. (1991). *Imagined communities. Reflections on the origin and spread of Nationalism.* Verso.
Arêas, C. (2012). Stigmatization as an argument: Between denunciation and legitimization of the burqa ban. *Signes, Discours et Sociétés n° 9, July 2012.*
Arêas, C. (2015). The mediatization of the « burqa affair » in France: Visibility strategies and inconic crisis. *Canadian Journal of Communication, 40*(1), 30–50.
Bayrakli, E., & Hafez, F. (2017). *European Islamophobia Report.* SETA Foundation, Leopold Weiss Institute.
Charaudeau, P. (1992). *Grammar of meaning and expression.* Hachette.
Cohen, S. (1972). *Folk devils and moral panics.* Mac Gibbon and Kee.
Ducrot, Oswald (1984). *Le dire et le dit.* Minuit.
Foucault, Michel (1969). *The archaeology of knowledge.* Gallimard.
Kerbrat-Orecchioni, C. (2009). *The enunciation of subjectivity language.* Armand Colin.
Mekki-Berrada, A. (Ed.) (2018). Femmes et subjectivations musulmanes [Muslim women and subjectivation]. *Anthropologie et sociétés, 42*(1), 14–33.
Rabatel, A., & Chauvin-Vileno, A. (2006). La question de la responsabilité dans l'écriture de presse [The question of responsibility in press writing]. *Semen, 22,* 5–24.
Venkatesh V., Nelson B. J., Thomas T., Wallin J. J., Podoshen J. S., Thompson C., Jezer-Morton K., Rabah J., Urbaniak K., & St. Laurent M. (2016). Exploring the language and spectacle of online hate speech in the black metal scene: Developing theoretical and methodological intersections between the social sciences and humanities. In N. Varas-Diaz & N. Scott (Eds.). *Heavy metal music and the communal experience* (pp. 127–150). Lexington Books.

News media corpus (cited columns and articles)

Almada, P. G. P. (2019, April 27). Cristianophobia: A new holocaust? *Observador.*
Fernandes, J. M. (2015, January 16). The difficult days of Professor Boaventura. *Observador.*
Gonçalves, A. (2019, March 23). Another 5 useless days. *Observador.*
Marques, M. J. (2014, August 27). Mr. jihadist, can I have Britain back? Thank you. *Observador.*

Marques, M. J. (2016, March 23). Je suis I don't even know what. *Observador*.

Marques, M. J. (2016, July 20). But do we really want this in Europe? *Observador*.

Marques, M. J. (2016, August 31). Europe of gender equality. *Observador*.

Matos, H. (2015, January 11). The problem is not the others. It's us. *Observador*.

Matos, H. (2017, May 1). Bullshit talk. *Observador*.

Ramos, R. (2016, July 15). This Europe could end in Nice. *Observador*.

Ribeiro, G. M. (2019, July 10). The moral deficiency of the white, activist left. *Observador*.

Tunhas, P. (2017, March 23). London and unreality. *Observador*.

Vasconcelos, A. (2017, July 12). Europe: The acquis of the ethical revolt. *Público*.

10

ISLAMOPHOBIA AND FAR-RIGHT PARTIES IN SPAIN: THE 'VOX' DISCOURSE ON TWITTER

ALFONSO CORRAL, CAYETANO FERNÁNDEZ & ANTONIO PRIETO-ANDRÉS

Abstract

This chapter analyses the Spanish far right's discourse on Islam, Muslims and immigration from Arab-Islamic countries. It focuses on two Vox profiles on Twitter: the party's main account, and that of its president, Santiago Abascal. The study covers three months (November 2020 to January 2021), including two events of the utmost relevance: the migration crisis caused by the arrival in the Canary Islands of hundreds of immigrants from the African coasts, and the run-up to the campaign for the election of the regional parliament of Catalonia. The main objective is to verify the existence of anti-immigration, xenophobic or Islamophobic discourses in both Vox accounts' posts. A review of 383 messages has revealed a certain wariness and revulsion of anything related to Islam, Muslims and irregular immigration.

Keywords: far-right parties, Islam, Muslims, discourse, Islamophobia, immigration, populism, Twitter

Introduction[1]

Since the 1980s, Europe has witnessed the emergence of several right-wing parties, a phenomenon described by Acha Ugarte (2018) as the 'third wave' of European extremism. This trend has become even more pronounced over the past 20 years, as in several European countries right-wing parties play a key role in government formation (Pérez Curiel, 2020). In Spain, the extreme right was not particularly prominent until the emergence of Vox in 2013. Vox's real strength became evident only after the 2018 regional election in Andalusia, the first time Vox was voted into a regional parliament (Ortiz Barquero, 2019;

Vázquez Barrio, 2021). This milestone event ended the apparent exception that Spain represented in Europe with respect to the presence of political forces with a radical right-wing orientation (Turnbull-Dugarte, 2019; Alonso & Rovira Kaltwasser, 2015).

This chapter builds on studies examining the populist discourse of Vox on social media networks (Pérez Curiel, 2020; Castro Martínez & Mo Groba, 2020; Vázquez Barrio, 2021). Specifically, it focuses on messages referencing Islam, Muslims and immigration from Arab-Islamic countries, posted on two Vox profiles on Twitter: the party's main account, and that of its president, Santiago Abascal. The analysed time period covers three months (November 2020 to January 2021; see Methods for more detail), and two events of the utmost relevance for this study: the migration crisis caused by the arrival in the Canary Islands of hundreds of immigrants from the African coasts, and the run-up to the campaign for the election of the regional parliament of Catalonia. The main objective of this research is to verify the existence of anti-immigration, xenophobic and Islamophobic discourses in both Vox Twitter accounts' posts. To this end, we carried out a quantitative content analysis of Vox's and Abascal's Twitter messages, complemented by a computer software-assisted quantitative study of the terminology, and a corpus of messages that aims to exemplify the discursive tone observed.

Far-right Populism in Spain: Vox

Vox was formed in 2013. The reasons for its gradual rise are known. In the opinion of Turnbull-Dugarte (2019), the 'glue' binding its supporters was opposition to the Catalan secessionist movement, rather than political mistrust or concerns about immigration and the economic downturn as has been the case in other European countries. Other campaign issues have included abortion, gay marriage, illegal immigration and Muslim immigration, which Vox all opposes. Olalla et al. (2019) point out that Vox's success in the 2018 Andalusia election may have been due to inordinate media attention, especially considering that the opinion polls had not predicted such positive results for Vox.

On its website, Vox (n.d.) defines itself as 'a movement born out of the extreme necessity to put Spanish institutions at the service of Spaniards, in contrast to the current model that puts Spaniards at the service of politicians'. In its political strategy for the country, it proposes '100 urgent Vox measures for Spain' in response to problems that, according to Vox, most concern Spaniards: threats to the unity of Spain, the destruction of the middle class, high taxes, border security and the curtailment of liberties. For this reason, Vox considers itself a defender of national unity and collective morality (Vox, 2014); an idiosyncrasy that Gracia (2014) synthesises as follows: no to abortion, yes to the family, yes to the unity of Spain, and no to ETA (the now defunct terrorist organisation that aimed to achieve the independence of the Basque Country).

Although Vox acknowledges itself as a centre-right, conservative, liberal and democratic party (Sanchís & Tejero, 2014), it could be labelled a far-right populist formation that prioritises the national over the foreign: it emphasises ethnic nationalism (Ferreira, 2019; Rydgren, 2017). This explains its strong Euroscepticism (Pérez Curiel, 2020), and its rejection of immigration, especially immigration from Arab-Islamic countries (Akkerman, 2018; Zúquete, 2017). Furthermore, it is categorised as populist because it promotes a clear distinction between two homogeneous and antagonistic groups, the 'pure people' and the 'corrupt elite' (Mudde, 2016). Vázquez Barrio (2021) identifies the same populism in an analysis of the discourse employed by Abascal on Twitter. According to her, the underlying issues are 'the central role of the people; anti-elitism; the consideration of the people as a homogeneous entity along with the exclusion of people from outside (immigrants) and inside (ETA supporters, secessionists, coup proponents, communists, and lefties); and the use of simplistic, aggressive language' (p. 137).

After the 2018 success in Andalusia, expectations of a Vox victory in the general election for the Spanish parliament in April 2019 were realised as Vox won 24 seats (10.3 per cent of the vote). However, the different political forces failed to reach an agreement on the formation of a government, and a new general election had to be called, which was held in November of the same year. This further benefited Vox, which consolidated its position by winning 52 seats (15.2 per cent of the vote), becoming the third strongest political force in Spain, behind the Socialist Party (PSOE) and the Popular Party (PP), which won 120 and 89 seats respectively (Castro Martínez & Mo Groba, 2020).

Since its emergence in 2006, Twitter has played a pivotal role in the expansion and development of these types of political forces (Alonso-Muñoz & Casero-Ripollés, 2018). This is what Gerbaudo (2014) has called 'Populism 2.0'. In global terms, this particular social media network has transformed significant aspects of the political ecosystem, bringing, for example, immediacy, a multiplication of classic sources (parliamentarians, leaders, parties, etc.) as well as new ones (the citizens themselves), a search for virality, bidirectional communication and a changed relationship with the media (Campos-Domínguez, 2017; Pérez Curiel, 2020). Furthermore, social networking sites allow users to circumvent the control of gatekeepers in traditional media, while reaching a larger number of people (Vidgen et al., 2021). In addition, there is a high number of anonymous users (Christopherson, 2007), a reality exploited by the extreme right to launch anti-Muslim and Islamophobic messages, among other types of claims (Awan, 2014).

Methods

For this study, out of all profiles of Vox and its members on Twitter, we decided to focus solely on the official account of the political party (@vox_es), and that of its leader, Santiago Abascal (@Santi_ABASCAL). According to the report *State of Hate: Far-Right Extremism in Europe* (Mulhall & Khan-Ruf, 2021), these were the most popular Vox-related accounts, along with those of Rocío Monasterio (deputy in the Madrid Assembly and president of Vox in the Community of Madrid, 209,000 followers on 22 February 2021), and Javier Ortega Smith (secretary general of Vox and Congress deputy, 187,000 followers). In this context, it should be noted that the @vox_es account ('Vox account' from here on) had 434,600 followers on 22 February 2021, while Abascal's account had 560,600 followers.

It was then necessary to delimit the object of the study in time. As the main purpose of the study is to establish the connection between Vox, Islam, Muslims and immigration from Arab-Islamic countries, we decided to examine a three-month period in which relevant events had occurred, such as the migration crisis in the Canary Islands, and the initial days of campaigning for the election of the Catalan regional parliament, which was held mid-February. The analysis period therefore spans three full months: November and December 2020, and January 2021.

In total, the initial corpus included 2,749 tweets (73.3 per cent from Vox's account and 26.7 per cent from Abascal's). To manage the Twitter data, we used the Twitonomy[2] application, a tool that enables a large number of tweets to be compiled in a single spreadsheet, and retrieves the following data: date, time, tweet text, links, type of message, number of likes, number of retweets and so on. At this point, an initial screening was carried out to exclude any posts that did not fit the study subject (Islam or immigration), which reduced the corpus to 523 messages (73.2 per cent from Vox and 26.8 per cent from Abascal). At this point it became clear that 19 per cent of the information published on Vox's and Abascal's accounts was related (directly or indirectly) to Islam, Muslims or Arab-Islamic immigration. A second filtering was applied to remove duplicates or retweets between the two accounts, providing a final corpus of 383 messages (80.9 per cent from the Vox account and 19.1 per cent from Abascal's). In this respect, it should be noted that we did include tweets, retweets and replies in our analysis. Contrary to Larsson's (2015) claim that retweets only serve to disseminate information posted by other users, it is reasonable to think that Vox and Abascal could rely on other people's accounts when subscribing to controversial or offensive ideas.

The research technique chosen to analyse the messages was quantitative content analysis, a common approach to the analysis of political discourse on social networking sites (Piñeiro-Naval, 2020), that focuses on statistical analysis to obtain descriptive findings on a series of variables. For Berelson (1952), content analysis is a tool for the objective, systematic and quantitative description of communicative texts. This procedure offers objective and precise data using frequency indicators, and the existing inter-relations between the evaluated variables, allowing the researcher to make sense of the occurrence and co-occurrence of concepts, terms or characteristics.

The variables used in this study represent 14 categories through which we have sought to observe, among other aspects, the tone of the discourse, iconography, thematisation, hashtag use and dependence on the mass media. IBM SPSS Statistics 25 was used to analyse the data; in addition, QSR NVivo was used to analyse the most frequent terminology found in the 383 messages that make up the research corpus, following the semantic affinity model described by Arcila Calderón et al. (2020).

Research Questions and Hypotheses

To clarify the relation between Vox's and Abascal's tweets, and discourses about Muslims and immigration from Arab-Islamic countries, we formulated the following research questions and hypotheses:

RQ1: What are the most frequent events and themes in the corpus under study?
RQ2: What terms characterise the discourse of Vox and Abascal on Twitter?
RQ3: What kind of discourse is promoted in terms of Islam and immigration in the accounts analysed?
H1: In the corpus, messages dealing with Islam, Muslims and immigration from Arab-Islamic countries are the most prominent.
H2: The discursive line on these issues is mostly negative, even going as far as to espouse violent and offensive statements in some cases.

Results

With regard to the typology of messages, of the 383 units analysed, 238 are tweets (62.1 per cent), 111 retweets (29 per cent) and 34 are replies or threads (8.9 per cent). A total of 80.7 per cent of all posts include images or videos, in line with the nature of the Twitter social network, which, due to the limited number of characters per tweet, facilitates the inclusion of graphic material that complements or highlights the messages. In addition, 41 per cent of tweets include references to press reports, or allude to the media as an anchor point for their messages. Meanwhile, with regard to the sources of information that feed the tweets, 67.4 per cent of the cases use self-referential sources; in other words, they do not rely on external sources for their commentary. Instead, the assertions come from the party itself, or from its representatives. The second most prominent source are journalists and the media (22.7 per cent). The general public appears in fourth place (2.9 per cent), and messages from other political parties are hardly used at all in a direct way (1.3 per cent). There is, therefore, hardly any room for anonymous accounts (1 per cent), and other types of accounts (4.7 per cent).

Although messages from other political parties are scarcely used as a starting point for Vox messages, these parties are referenced frequently: in 49.9 per cent of the analysed tweets, there are references to other political parties (see Table 10.1). The government coalition (PSOE and Unidas Podemos) is mentioned in 23.2 per cent of the total number of posts. If we add the separate references to these two parties (Unidas Podemos, 3.1 per cent; PSOE, 2.6 per cent), this amounts to 28.9 per cent of the total number of messages from Vox and its leader about migration and Islam. It is striking that hardly any mention is made of PP (3.1 per cent of the total), Vox's rival in the fight for its political space, or of the Catalan parties (2.3 per cent), bearing in mind that the period analysed includes a large proportion of the campaign and campaign run-up for the Catalan election. There is a significant group of 'Others' (15.4 per cent), including other groups (when PP and PSOE are mentioned in the same tweet, for example), or cases involving other national, regional or European parties.

Looking at the main themes chosen by Vox and Abascal when dealing with immigration and Islam, it is confirmed that the recurring theme is illegal immigration, present in 54.8 per cent of messages. This is followed by the links of migration and Islam with crime (21.7 per cent), and social conflict (7.6 per cent). Multi-culturalism (6 per cent) and religion (Islam, with 5.2 per cent) are treated in a more marginal manner. Finally, other topics were found in only 4.7 per cent of cases.

Table 10.1: Political party source (N and percentage of total)

Political party	N	% of the corpus
Government/Coalition	89	23.2
Other	59	15.4
PP	12	3.1
Podemos	12	3.1
PSOE	10	2.6
Catalan parties	9	2.3
Total	191	49.7

At the same time, we analysed which events are most frequently mentioned. 'Events' is understood in a broad sense, including the mention of recurring groups or situations, such as the issue of *menas* (unaccompanied migrant minors or UAMs), and scenarios related to the Spanish cities on the border with Morocco, Ceuta and Melilla. At least one of these events is mentioned in 75.7 per cent of the posts, demonstrating that these are the situations on which the Vox messages place their communicative focus.

As such, the key event for Vox is undoubtedly the arrival of *pateras* (a type of small, unseaworthy boat) to the Canary Islands from the neighbouring coasts of the African continent, which accounts for 40.5 per cent of the total number of tweets. This situation was particularly intense in November 2020. The coincidence of these events with the COVID-19 pandemic and the subsequent economic crisis, which hit tourism – the main source of income for the islands – particularly hard, formed an explosive cocktail that sparked grassroots demonstrations and criticism of the poor management of the humanitarian, health and social crisis by the authorities. This situation was used by Vox to campaign in the Canary Islands with one of its key messages, namely the fight against illegal immigration and all that it entails.

The second relevant event, due to its link to the issue of migration and Islam, is the election in Catalonia (14.4 per cent), held on 14 February 2021. It should be remembered that the period analysed covers the months of November 2020 to January 2021, and therefore encompasses part of the run up to the campaign for this election, where one of the main electoral hooks used by Vox was the issue of migration and the problems of social coexistence and crime, or loss of cultural identity caused by migration in general, and Islamic migration in particular.

Other situations or groups whose appearance is recurrent in Vox's discourse are unaccompanied migrant minors, or *menas*, accounting for 6.8 per cent of the total references, and issues specific to the autonomous cities of Ceuta and Melilla, located on the African continent, such as incursions in the form of border fence-jumping (2.3 per cent), or diplomatic relations between Spain and Morocco (1.8 per cent). Other events account for 9.9 per cent of the tweets by Vox and its leader linked to the subject matter of this study.

To finish this general analysis, we are now going to look specifically at the number of messages that directly or indirectly allude to Islam. Concretely, 23.2 per cent of all messages directly refer to Islam, while 27.9 per cent do so indirectly, making a total of 51.2 per cent. This means that, when it comes to the issue of immigration, Vox links more than half of its posts to the issue of Islam.

Finally, we analysed the tone of the discourse about immigration. A positive tone means the message emphasises the beneficial or favourable aspects of immigration; a negative tone means it emphasises the harmful, prejudicial or unfavourable elements; a neutral tone means it does not mask a political position or value judgement. A total of 94.3 per cent of the 383 messages are negative, and only 5.7 per cent are neutral. We did not find a single positive mention related to migration or Islam.

Analysis of Terminology

For this second analysis, the 100 most frequent words of five or more characters in the corpus were selected and grouped. After the elimination of stopwords, understood as words that do not contribute meaning, 31 terms were retained. They were grouped by semantic affinity, into three thematic blocks. The result can be seen in Table 10.2.

The first group of words includes terminology referring to Islam. For example, we see that terms such as 'mosques', 'multi-culturalism' and 'Morocco' are frequently repeated, or that some concepts or hashtags show Vox's opposing stance on these issues: '#StopIslamización' (stop Islamisation), 'jihadists', 'fundamentalists', 'Islamists'. The second block contains references to migration itself, although we also include allusions to groups, including unaccompanied migrant minors. Finally, there is the largest block of words, related to the negative aspects of immigration. This grouping includes the concepts or hashtags that Vox and Abascal use to reinforce their discourse presenting illegal immigration as one of Spain's major problems. That is why there are so many words here about the illegality of the arrivals ('illegal', 'borders', '#FronterasSeguras' (secure borders), 'expulsion', 'patera'), the idea of invasion ('#StopInvasionMigratoria' (stop migratory invasion), 'avalanche', 'thousands', 'arrival', 'call effect'), and the insecurity that, from Vox's perspective, this generates, together with its link to crime ('insecurity', 'detainees', 'mafia'). Ultimately, immigration is portrayed as a major problem ('crisis').

Table 10.2: Most frequent words grouped into thematic blocks (percentage of total words recorded)

Islam	%	Migrant groups	%	Immigration – negative sense	%
#StopIslamización	.18	immigrants	.48	illegal (plural)	.41
Islamists	.13	immigration	.38	illegal (singular)	.37
Morocco	.09	migration	.27	invasion	.32
multi-culturalism	.08	menas	.21	borders	.19
mosques	.08	minors	.06	mafia	.12
jihadists	.08			security	.12
fundamentalists	.06			thousands	.11
				insecurity	.11
				effect	.09
				expulsion	.08
				problem	.08
				#StopInvasiónMigratoria	.08
				detainees	.08
				call effect	.08
				arrival	.07
				patera (small boat)	.07
				crisis	.06
				avalanche	.06
				#FronterasSeguras	.06

Focus on Vox's Discourse: From #StopInvasiónMigratoria to #StopIslamización

The arrival of small boats in the Canary Islands and the election of the regional parliament of Catalonia were the two central events for Vox and Abascal in the period observed. In relation to the issue of migration, the accounts frequently used two hashtags, linked to each of these events: #StopInvasiónMigratoria (Stop Migratory Invasion) in the Canary Island crisis, and #StopIslamización (Stop Islamisation) in the Catalan election campaign. This does not imply, as we have already noted, that there was no room for other recurrent issues, such as Islamism, UAMs or jihadist terrorism, among other topics. Indeed,

Vox's hostility and enmity towards Islam and immigration from Arab-Islamic countries is illustrated in many of the messages studied. For this reason, our aim below is to show some examples of tweets and retweets that clarify the discursive tone of Vox and its political leader.

Sometimes, several of the central themes or events that we detailed in the quantitative results come together in a single message. This is the case in a Vox post (14 January 2021) that states the following: '150 Maghrebi youths stone four policemen and civil guards in the south of Gran Canaria. We don't want them roaming the streets making us unsafe, or staying in our hotels! #MenasFuera [UAMs out].' This tweet shows not only the association between UAMs and the Maghreb, but also conflict, violence and the migration crisis in the Canary Islands. Something similar happens in this retweet of a post from the account of Jorge Buxadé, a Vox MEP, who links the arrival of immigrants in Europe to two terrorist attacks: 'With nine dead bodies still warm from Islamic terrorism in France and Austria, the European Parliament is still talking about protecting the rights of these fake refugees. The situation is unbearable in Greece, Lampedusa and the Canaries. A wall' (Vox, 9 November 2020). For his part, the leader of Vox, Santiago Abascal, relies on statements by Macron and Merkel, following the same attacks in Nice and Vienna, calling for the European Union's borders to be tightened, to defend himself and his party against accusations of racism: 'We are called Europhobes and racists for demanding exactly the same thing' (Abascal, 11 November 2020). In addition, this message retweeted by Abascal (14 January 2021) and leading to an *Okdiario* headline proves his rejection of Arab-Islamic immigration by linking it to crime: 'A Moroccan woman with no official papers swindles more than €40,000 from an elderly man and a ONCE [Spanish National Organisation for the Blind] worker. But don't worry, it's going to pay our pensions.'

Such generalisations and prejudicial, offensive, hostile or adverse statements towards Islam are an ongoing feature of the 383 units analysed. It is sufficient to reiterate that in our quantitative analysis the tone was found to be negative in practically 95 per cent of the publications studied. It is, therefore, common to find statements that speak of 'cultural suicide', 'barbaric customs', 'migratory invasion', the 'dissolution of Europe' and 'suicidal policies'. On other occasions, criticism is directed at how immigration and Islam are dealt with in the autonomous cities of Ceuta and Melilla, and the relationship with Morocco is also frowned upon because of its implications for Islam and immigration in Spain. This is an example: 'The Government spends 9 million on 130 SUVs for the Moroccan police and forgets about the #EquiparacionYa [the demand for equal pay for national and regional security forces, as the latter are paid more than the former] of our agents. They arm themselves to the hilt using our money while they invade us, plunder us and we pay contributions to subsidise their *menas*' (Vox, 11 November 2020).

However, the campaign for the Catalan election revealed Vox's full animosity towards Islam. In fact, to our mind, the party's rejection of Islam became one of its main campaign slogans. For example, these three tweets posted by the Vox account link to three news items from the newspapers *El Mundo*, *La Razón* and *ABC* respectively (Figure 10.1): 'The jihadists arrested in Barcelona arrived in Spain by *patera* via Almeria and were ready to attack. The government allows potential terrorists to enter our country illegally every day. It shall be held responsible for what happens' (Vox, 11 January 2021); 'Daesh orders attacks on churches and police in Spain: the infiltration of jihadists in the *pateras* has increased the risk of attacks. Only VOX has demanded the application of National Security law in the face of the migratory invasion. The rest of the parties opposed it' (Vox, 17 January 2021); 'They introduce Islam into schools in Catalonia. But they don't let you choose Spanish as a vehicular language [as opposed to Catalan, for teaching purposes]. Let's be clear, separatism is Hispanophobia and submission to Islam' (Vox, 18 January 2021).

Figure 10.1:[3] Tweets from Vox (11, 17 and 18 January 2021)

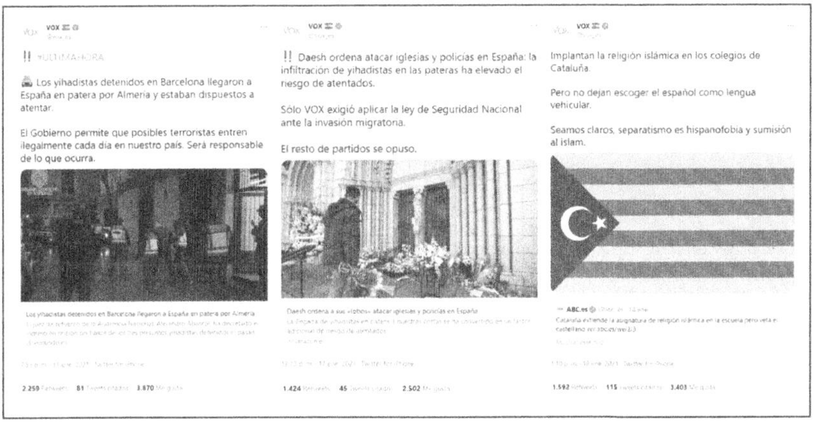

Source: Twitter

A few days later, one of Vox's candidates in the election, Antonio Gallego, wrote a message reiterating the same ideas, which was retweeted by the party's official account: 'Catalonia must not be the host country for illegal immigration. We will not allocate public money to supporting or sponsoring this. #Vox will close fundamentalist mosques, we will not teach Islam in schools and we will close centres for *menas*. That is our promise' (Vox, 22 January

2021). However, it was not until 27 January that we saw the #StopIslamización hashtag for the first time. It appeared in a retweet of a post by Ignacio Garriga, the president of Vox in Catalonia: 'They preach secularism, but they instil Islam in the classroom. We are told about pluralism, but freedom is increasingly reduced. They sing the praises of coexistence, but local people have been obliged to join forces to defend themselves. #StopIslamización We will take back Catalonia!' (Vox, 27 January 2021). This message was accompanied by a propaganda video produced by Vox, a highly accusatory and anti-Islamic piece, constructed from news headlines and images riddled with Islamic motifs and references to the 2017 attacks in Barcelona, meant to demonstrate that Islam and immigrants of Arab-Islamic origin are a problem that must be eradicated in Catalonia.

From that point on, the hashtag #StopIslamización was repeated 29 times in just two days on Vox's account and once again on Abascal's account, specifically, the retweet of Garriga's post that we have just seen. This tweet perfectly sums up the campaign strategy in Catalonia, what Vox's proposals with respect to Islam were and what role Twitter played in this regard (Figure 10.2). The image that accompanies the tweet alludes to the billboard that Vox put up in front of the mosque in Palafruguell (Girona), declaring, 'Separatism takes us to the Islamic Republic of Catalonia.' In this sense, it should be explained that Vox has modified the Catalan pro-independence flag, changing the original star for a crescent moon.

Figure 10.2:[4] Tweet from Vox (27 January 2021)

Source: Twitter

Finally, on 28 January, Twitter decided to temporarily block Vox's official account for disseminating messages inciting hatred, after several Muslim organisations established in Catalonia made complaints about its content (González, 2021). Abascal reacted to this decision by tweeting about it. In one, he stated the following: 'By the way, the tweet that triggered the censorship offers data on the violence suffered by Spaniards … in Catalonia and the Canary Islands. The tech millionaires don't want the consequences of the migratory invasion they support, along with some governments, to be made public' (Abascal, 28 January 2021).

Conclusion and Discussion

In relation to the research questions and hypotheses, it has been demonstrated throughout these pages that (1) the migration question is a key issue to which Vox devotes 20 per cent of its communication on Twitter; and that (2) in the corpus analysed, more than half of the messages deal with Islam, Muslims and immigration linked to Arab-Islamic countries, either directly or indirectly. This indicates the extent to which Vox and its leader consider Muslims in Spain as being exogenous to Spanish identity, not only traditionally, but even ideologically. In this sense, it can be affirmed that, although indirectly, illegal immigration (more specifically, immigration related to the migration crisis in the Canary Islands or the periodic fence-jumping that takes place on the border between Spain and Morocco in the autonomous cities of Ceuta and Melilla, carried out by this same migrant population) ends up being linked to Islam, given that the vast majority of its protagonists are North Africans or sub-Saharan Africans, the majority of whom are Muslims. In short, Vox and Abascal promote an alarmist approach based on the paradigm of the securitisation of Spain and Europe.

In addition, the idea that Muslim immigrants who have already made Spain their home are jeopardising traditional Spain, which is eminently Catholic and monocultural, takes centre stage for Vox. This explains its exacerbated criticism of the teaching of Islam in schools in the wake of the Catalan election campaign, of the opening of new mosques, seen as a threat to traditional Spanish values and of the increase in public insecurity and crime, which Vox blatantly links to the presence of these groups in Spanish society.

The discursive line studied is eminently negative, and at times violent or offensive. The fact that 94.3 per cent of the 383 messages are negative and only 5.7 per cent are neutral speaks volumes about the discursive position of Vox and its leader on to migration and Islam. But it is not just that Vox is opposed to these realities; the tone, if we analyse the exact words used, links migration and Islam to crime, insecurity, mafia and jihadist terrorism and fundamentalism. Furthermore, this is done, as has been shown with the tweets presented here, adopting a populist approach that contrasts 'us' and 'them'; 'the people' and 'the workers' on the one hand, and 'the elites', 'the globalists' or 'the rulers' – belonging to the other ideological extreme – on the other. These 'elites' are presented as an opponent, and even as the enemy.

We cannot confirm that Abascal is fulfilling the same role as other European populist leaders who do portray themselves as true champions of anti-Islam and anti-immigration (Alonso-Muñoz & Casero-Ripollés, 2018). It is just an impression that will have to be examined in more depth in future studies. We can confirm that the tone of the Vox account is more critical, adversarial and hostile towards Islam and immigration than Abascal's account, which has a lower profile. Consequently, future research should examine the figure of Abascal in relation to other Vox leaders such as Javier Ortega Smith, Rocío Monasterio, Jorge Buxadé and Iván Espinosa de los Monteros. At the same time, a similar analysis should be conducted of the accounts of PP and its leaders, since this party is Vox's rival in the Spanish political arena. It should be remembered that Vox's allusions to the PP were not very frequent in the time interval studied; indeed, mentions were directed more insistently at the other extreme (the left), apparently demonstrating the party's preference for winning votes by convincing voters who are closer to the right.

Notes

1.   This research was funded by the Department of Science, University and Knowledge Society, from the Government of Aragon (Spain) (Research Group S05_20D).
2.   See: https://www.twitonomy.com
3.   Translation: (A) The jihadists arrested in Barcelona arrived in Spain by *patera* via Almeria and were ready to attack. The government allows potential terrorists to enter our country illegally every day. It shall be held responsible for what happens. [Article preview] The jihadists arrested in Barcelona arrived in Spain by boat via Almeria. The National Court judge, Alejandro Abascal, has decreed the imprisonment without bail of the three alleged jihadists arrested last … (B) Daesh orders attacks on churches and police in Spain: the infiltration of jihadists in the *pateras* has increased the risk of attacks. Only VOX has demanded the application of National Security law in the face of the migratory invasion. The rest of the parties opposed it. [Article preview:] Daesh orders its 'wolves' to attack churches and police in Spain. The arrival of jihadists in dinghies on our coasts has become an additional risk factor for attacks. (C) They introduce Islam into schools in Catalonia. But they don't let you choose Spanish as a vehicular language [as opposed to Catalan, for teaching purposes].
4.   Translation: Let's be clear. Separatism takes us to the Islamic Republic of Catalonia. VOX will stop the Islamisation of Catalonia. VOX will fight multicultural policies. VOX will make local neighbourhoods safe again. #StopIslamisation.

References

Acha Ugarte, B. (2018). The far right in Western Europe: 'From the margins to the mainstream' and back? *Cuadernos Europeos de Deusto, 59*, 75–97.

Akkerman, T. (2018). Partidos de extrema derecha y políticas de inmigración en la UE [Far-right parties and immigration policies in the EU]. In J. Arango, R. Mahía, D. Moya, & E. Sánchez-Montijano (Eds.), *Inmigración y Asilo, en el Centro de la Arena Política.* Anuario CIDOB de la Inmigración 2018 (pp. 48–62). CIDOB.

Alonso, S., & Rovira Kaltwasser, C. (2015). Spain: No country for the populist radical right? *South European Society and Politics, 20*(1), 21–45.

Alonso-Muñoz, L., & Casero-Ripollés, A. (2018). Communication of European populist leaders on Twitter: Agenda setting and the 'more is less' effect. *El Profesional de la Información, 27*(6), 1193–1202.

Arcila Calderón, C., De la Vega, G., & Blanco, D. (2020). Topic modeling and characterization of hate speech against immigrants on Twitter around the emergence of a far-right party in Spain. *Social Sciences, 9*(11), 188.

Awan, I. (2014). Islamophobia and Twitter: A typology of online hate against Muslims on social media. *Policy & Internet, 6*(2), 133–150.

Berelson, B. (1952). *Content analysis in communication research.* Free Press.

Campos-Domínguez, E. (2017). Twitter y la comunicación política [Twitter and political communication]. *El Profesional de la Información, 26*(5), 785–793.

Castro Martínez, P., & Mo Groba, D. (2020). El issue de la inmigración en los votantes de VOX en las elecciones generales de noviembre de 2019 [The issue of immigration for VOX voters in the November 2019 general elections]. *RIPS: Revista de Investigaciones Políticas y Sociológicas, 19*(1), 39–58.

Christopherson, K. M. (2007). The positive and negative implications of anonymity in internet social interactions: 'On the Internet, nobody knows you're a dog'. *Computers in Human Behavior, 23*(6), 3038–3056.

Ferreira, C. (2019). Vox como representante de la derecha radical en España: Un studio sobre su ideología [Vox as a representative of the radical right in Spain: A study of its ideology]. *Revista Española de Ciencia Política, 51*, 73–98.

Gerbaudo, P. (2014). Populism 2.0. In D. Trottier & C. Fuchs (Eds.), *Social media, politics and the state: Protests, revolutions, riots, crime and policing in the age of Facebook, Twitter and YouTube* (pp. 16–67). Routledge.

González, M. (2021, January 28). Twitter bloquea la cuenta de Vox por 'incitar al odio' contra los musulmanes [Twitter blocks Vox account for 'inciting hatred' against Muslims]. *El País.* https://elpais.com/espana/2021-01-28/twitter-cierra-la-cuenta-de-vox-por-incitar-al-odio-contra-los-musulmanes.html

Gracia, A. I. (2014, January 28). Los cuatro pilares de Vox: no al aborto, la familia, la unidad de España y no a ETA [The four mainstays of Vox: No to abortion, yes to the family, yes to the unity of Spain, and no to ETA]. *El Confidencial.* https://www.elconfidencial.com/espana/2014-01-16/los-cuatro-pilares-de-vox-no-al-aborto-la-familia-la-unidad-de-espana-y-no-a-eta_76858/

Larsson, A. O. (2015). Comparing to prepare: Suggesting ways to study social media today – and tomorrow. *Social Media & Society, 1*(1), 1–2.

Mudde, C. (2016). Europe's populist surge: A long time in the making. *Foreign Affairs, 95*(6), 25–30.

Mulhall, J., & Khan-Ruf, S. (Eds.). (2021). *State of hate: Far right extremism in Europe 2021.* Hope not Hate Charitable Trust. https://www.hopenothate.org.uk/wp-content/uploads/2021/02/ESOH-LOCKED-FINAL-1.pdf

Olalla, S., Chueca, E., & Padilla, J. (2019, January 10). *Spain is no longer exceptional: Mainstream media and the far-right party Vox. Euro crisis in the press.* The London School of Economics and Political Science. https://blogs.lse.ac.uk/eurocrisispress/2019/01/10/spain-is-no-longer-exceptional-mainstream-media-and-the-far-right-party-vox/

Ortiz Barquero, P. (2019). The electoral breakthrough of the radical right in Spain: Correlates of electoral support for VOX in Andalusia (2018). *Genealogy, 3*(4), 72.

Pérez Curiel, C. (2020). Trend towards extreme right-wing populism on Twitter. An analysis of the influence on leaders, media and users. *Communication & Society, 33*(2), 175–192.

Piñeiro-Naval, V. (2020). The content analysis methodology. Uses and applications in communication research on Spanish-speaking countries. *Communication & Society, 33*(3), 1–15.

Rydgren, J. (2017). Radical right-wing parties in Europe. What's populism got to do with it? *Journal of Language and Politics, 16*(4), 485–496.

Sanchís, J. L., & Tejero, L. (2014, January 31). *Vox, la peor pesadilla del PP* [Vox, the PP's worst nightmare]. El Mundo. https://www.elmundo.es/opinion/2014/01/30/52eaa3bc268e3eff628b457c.html

Turnbull-Dugarte, S. J. (2019). Explaining the end of Spanish exceptionalism and electoral support for Vox. *Research and Politics, 6*(2), 1–8.

Vázquez Barrio, T. (2021). Populism in the 2019 general elections. Analysis of the speeches by the three right-wing candidates on Twitter. *Communication & Society, 34*(1), 123–141.

Vidgen, B., Yasseria, T., & Marettsa, H. (2021). Islamophobes are not all the same! A study of far-right actors on Twitter. *Journal of Policing, Intelligence and Counter Terrorism, 17*(1), 1–23.

Vox (n.d.). *¿Qué es Vox?* [What is Vox?]. https://www.voxespana.es/espana/que-es-vox

Vox (2014). *Manifiesto fundacional* [Founding manifest]. https://www.voxespana.es/espana/manifiesto-fundacional-vox

Vox (2018). *100 medidas para la España Viva* [100 measures for Living Spain]. https://www.voxespana.es/noticias/100-medidas-urgentes-de-vox-para-espana-20181006

Zúquete, J. P. (2017). The European extreme-right and Islam: New directions? In C. Mudde (Ed.), *The populist radical right: A reader* (pp. 103–123). Routledge.

PART IV

RESPONDING TO ISLAMOPHOBIA, EXTREMISM AND RADICALISATION

11
COPING WITH ISLAMOPHOBIA: (SOCIAL) MEDIA, A DOUBLE-EDGED SWORD[1]

ANS DE NOLF, LEEN D'HAENENS & ABDELWAHED MEKKI-BERRADA

Abstract

This chapter explores experiences of Islamophobia among Muslim youth living in Flanders. In-depth interviews with 20 Muslims aged 19 to 33 were conducted between spring 2020 and summer 2021. All interviewees self-identified as Muslims, and all had been confronted with racism or anti-Muslim sentiment in their daily lives. This study seeks to complement and deepen the existing knowledge on Muslims' experiences and coping with anti-Muslim sentiment in Flanders. Findings are meant to inspire follow-up research and serve as evidence for future policymaking.

Keywords: anti-Muslim sentiment, anti-Muslim prejudice, racism, Islamophobia, coping with anti-Muslim sentiment, young Muslim adults, Flanders, social media

Introduction

> When we say the word Islam, for most people it rings an ISIS bell, or a jihad bell or you know, a bourka bell. (Emir, 23)

About six per cent – about 400,000 people – of the Flemish population are Muslims (Hertogen, 2017; Pew Research Center, 2017a). Regularly, many of them are confronted with negative stereotypes, discrimination and even hate crimes, which are on the rise (Zempi & Awan, 2019). Furthermore, terrorist attacks in the West by Islamist terrorist groups such as Al-Qaeda or Islamic State (IS) (Soehl, 2019) and the unfunded belief that Islam is a 'backwards' religion (Mondon & Winter, 2019) have caused a growing acceptance of Islamophobic discourses, where Islam is believed to be incompatible with the West's secular, liberal and democratic values (Soehl, 2019; Mondon &

Winter, 2019), and to be the antithesis of Western values (Ljamai, 2020). This 'us and them' thinking is more prevalent in polarised societies, where the 'other' is more likely to be stigmatised, and even dehumanised, with Muslims being labelled as parasites, Trojan horses, disease or terrorists (Pavetich & Stathi, 2021; Ljamai, 2020; Koomen & Van Der Plight, 2016). This stigmatisation and dehumanisation, along with an aggressive political discourse on Muslims, creates a hostile atmosphere in which inter-group tensions and extremist thinking can become worse or more vicious if Muslims are continuously associated with threat, going as far as to morally 'legitimise' hate crime (Zempi & Awan, 2019; Pavetich & Stathi, 2021).

The unwarranted idea that Islam is inherently violent, backward and radical existed long before 9/11 (Helbling, 2014). Yet, 20 years later, the War on Terror discourse still influences the ways Muslims are portrayed in the media (Kundnani, 2014; Mineo, 2021). Media portrayals of Muslims are predominantly negative, with Islam and Muslims being unfairly included in headlines about terrorist attacks and clashes of ideologies, and in Islamophobic news pieces (Rezaei et al., 2019). While the predominantly negative portrayal in Western media befalls all Muslims, the portrayal of Muslim women is particularly harsh. Muslim women are represented as being (financially) oppressed, likely uneducated, helpless and as terrorists (Mastro, 2016). Generally, their portrayals fall into three main categories: as victims of Muslim men, as escapees from an oppressive religion or as pawns of Muslim ideology, with the veil as a token of fundamentalism, patriarchal oppression or militancy (Sinno, 2020; Kahf, 1999).

Islamophobia and its Consequences for (Young) People

The term 'Islamophobia' refers to a fear, hatred and hostility towards (perceived) Muslims, that is perpetuated by negative stereotypes and prejudices resulting in bias, discrimination, hostility, violence and the marginalisation and exclusion of Muslims from social, political and civic life (Ali et al., 2011; Lean, 2017; Zempi & Awan, 2019). The influx of refugees from predominantly Muslim countries in Europe has sparked an increase in media attention to Muslims and Islam. Muslims are prominently featured in news stories related to the War on Terror (Mertens & De Smaele, 2016; Poole & Richardson, 2006), which creates a climate of fear and threat, that partially explains the negativity bias in public opinion.

Studies from all over the world have documented Muslims' experiences with Islamophobia. In a 2009 Dutch study, Dutch Muslim teenagers reported having experienced discrimination, which indicates they were seen as dangerous, criminal, aggressive and as potential terrorists, resulting in them being closely monitored and shunned (Kamans et al., 2009). When in a minority position, most Muslims experience discrimination, prejudice and hostility because of their (perceived) religion (Aroian, 2011; Ismail, 2015; Ljamai, 2020; Shain, 2020; Soehl, 2019; Tineo et al., 2021). In the US, Muslims are the group most targeted by hate crime (Aroian, 2011). Based on Metropolitan Police figures, Shain (2020) draws the same conclusion for British Muslims, who are targeted by hate crime more often than any other religious minority in the UK.

According to the Pew Research Center (2017b), the number of assaults against Muslims in the US is at an all-time high, surpassing the 2001 peak in assaults. Even in school settings, Islamophobic incidents are on the rise, with an increase in verbal and physical attacks, such as bullying, rejection and aggression against Muslim students (Adam & Al-Mateen, 2019).

Elkomy (2019) examined how Muslim children and adolescents deal with microaggression, or 'the common, daily practice of verbal, visual, or societal/individual attitudes that convey covert discriminating acts – whether intentional or unintentional – against a person or group based on religious, ethnic, or gender affiliations' (Musa, 2019, p. 50). Although these acts occur mostly 'under the radar', they can cause significant mental and physical harm to the victims. Microaggression targeting Muslims specifically has intensified over the years under the influence of a growing Islamophobic and polarised climate (Elkomy, 2019; Musa, 2019). Microaggression, along with Islamophobic incidents, is never benign. As young Muslims are constantly exposed to it, microaggression is a problem on the societal level, with a severe impact on victims (Elkomy, 2019; Musa, 2019).

A major factor contributing to negative stereotypes about Muslims is explained by Pettigrew and colleagues' (2010) threat theory: when a minority population increases, it can become perceived as a higher threat. This threat perception generates more negative prejudice, which in turn can be manipulated by media and politicians, resulting in even more prejudice (Tineo et al., 2021; Pettigrew et al., 2010). Yet, contrary to how they are often portrayed, Muslims are not a homogeneous group, and thus it is important to note that their experiences with Islamophobia or anti-Muslim sentiment can differ depending on their racial or ethnic background (Musa, 2019; Adam & Al-Mateen, 2019).

The impact of acute and sustained exposure to discrimination, exclusion and Islamophobia on child development and mental health cannot be overlooked (Aroian, 2011; Lean, 2017). Furthermore, young Muslims' social

identity is fiercely contested by the dominant discourse through formal institutions, social relationships and the media, which can result in a social, political
and psychological fallout (Sirin & Fine, 2007). More negative consequences
of Islamophobia include poor self-concept, behavioural problems, poor academic performance, limited life aspirations, estrangement or withdrawing
from mainstream society, and stress-related illness in victims (Aroian, 2011;
Brondolo et al., 2008; Coker et al., 2009; Paradies, 2006; Rumbaut, 1994; Sirin
& Fine, 2007; Tineo et al., 2021).

   Aroian (2011) points at gender variations in reports of Islamophobic
incidents. While boys mostly report Islamophobia at school by classmates
and school staff, girls tend to report incidents of Islamophobia mostly in
non-school settings, by strangers. Boys perceive that they 'have it easier'
than girls because a hijab immediately reveals a Muslim identity, which can
provoke anti-Muslim sentiment (Aroian, 2011; Shain, 2020). Based upon Tell
MAMA's report (2019), Shain (2020: p. 2) states that 'the majority of religiously
motivated hate incidents (both at street level and online) are committed
against Muslim women, that the perpetrators are mostly white men and that
the number of incidents is rising'. Still, boys are also victims of their perceived
Muslimness, for example by having first and/or last names that function as
religious and ethnic identifiers (Aroian, 2011). This can explain why young
Muslims in particular, who are still in the process of searching where they
belong, are feeling unwelcome and unaccepted (Kamans et al., 2009).

Methods

This chapter builds on conversations with young Muslims in Flanders held by
De Nolf et al. (2021), and other studies on the role of (social) media in coping
with discrimination, contempt and Islamophobia (Eckert et al., 2018; Bacchus,
2019; Vitullo, 2021). Specifically, it focuses on the occurrence of Islamophobia
in Flanders, and how Muslim youth copes with this phenomenon, with special
attention to the role of (social) media in the face of Islamophobia. We draw on
interviews with 20 young Muslims in Flanders, conducted over a 17-month
period (April 2020 to September 2021).[2] Interviewees were asked about
their experiences with discrimination, contempt and violence in relation
to their Muslim identity, as well as coping strategies. We used a typology
of seven strategies used by young Muslims in Flanders – relativisation,
avoidance, communication, oppression, conciliation, reaction and passive
coping strategies – identified in a preliminary qualitative study by De Nolf
et al. (2021), which was based on Omlo (2015). This typology was verified

and expanded in this new round of interviews, with specific attention to the role of social media as a space where young Muslims can find support. The interviews were conducted in an open fashion, allowing the informants to speak freely about their experiences, and provide feedback on the interviews. The information obtained through interviews was supplemented with relevant research literature.

Participants

This chapter explores the experiences and coping strategies of Muslim youth and young adults (aged 19 to 33) living in Flanders. All participants were at least 18 years old, and self-identified as Muslim. Ethical approval for the multi-country study our research is part of was granted by the Research Ethics Board of Laval University.[3] Via targeted snowball sampling, using the personal network of one of the researchers and the personal networks of the participants, 20 informants were selected. Table 11.1 shows an overview of our informants.

Table 11.1: Overview of informants

Name	Age	Gender	Residence	Country of birth	Migration background	Highest educational level	Strictness of religious affiliation
Emir	23	M	Urban	Iraq	First generation	University	Strict
Meyra	22	F	Rural	Belgium	Second generation	College	Practicing
Layla	21	F	Urban	Belgium	Second generation	University	Strict
Malik	24	M	Urban	Iran	First generation	University	Practicing
Musa	24	M	Rural	Morocco	First generation	College	Practicing
Driss	24	M	Urban	Iraq	First generation	College	Not practicing
Yannick	23	M	Urban	Belgium	Second generation	College	Practicing
Berat	22	M	Urban	Belgium	Second generation	College	Practicing
Noor	19	F	Rural	Belgium	Third generation	College	Strict

Name	Age	Gender	Residence	Country of birth	Migration background	Highest educational level	Strictness of religious affiliation
Yara	19	F	Rural	Belgium	Second generation	College	Practicing
Fatma	24	F	Rural	Belgium	Second generation	College	Not practicing
Ines	26	F	Urban	Belgium	Second generation	University	Practicing
Ozan	33	M	Urban	Iraq	First generation	University	Strict
Ziara	22	F	Rural	Belgium	Second generation	University	Practicing
Adilah	24	F	Urban	Morocco	First generation	College	Practicing
Ronan	23	M	Rural	Belgium	Third generation	College	Strict
Amira	22	F	Rural	Belgium	Second generation	College	Practicing
Asim	28	M	Urban	Belgium	Second generation	High school	Practicing
Hamza	26	M	Urban	Syria	First generation	High school	Practicing

Interviews

The interviews can be described as semi-structured, in-depth interviews. They were carried out in the language preferred by the informant (English or Dutch). Informants were asked (1) if they had ever experienced negative reactions based on their (perceived) religious affiliation; (2) if so, how they dealt with those experiences; and (3) how, in their opinion, media representations might impact such experiences. The interview questions were based on the interview guide used in an ongoing, broader international research project.[4]

By opting for a semi-structured interview method, we could collect open-ended data on the experiences, feelings, thoughts and beliefs of the informants (see also Boeije, 2014). An additional benefit of this approach lies in its iterative possibilities: informants can express themselves and add topics during the interview, allowing the interviewer to adjust the interview questions when an important subject surfaces (Savin-Baden & Major, 2013).

The semi-structured in-depth interviews were recorded and transcribed with the consent of each informant. During the transcription process, the names of the informants were changed, and specific place names were omitted to ensure confidentiality.

Data Analysis

The aim of the study is to deepen our understanding of the experiences of Islamophobia of young Muslims in Flanders, with a special focus on the role of (social) media. Data analysis consisted of three steps. First, codes were assigned to the interview transcripts to perform a thematic analysis, with sensitising concepts[5] forming the 'common thread' of the research (Van den Hoonaard, 1997). When coding, we opted for a mixed coding approach. Hereby we used open codes. Then, the open codes were merged into broader categories via axial coding (Roose, 2017). Finally, through selective coding, these different categories were then linked to one another (Roose, 2017).

Results

Islamophobia in Flanders

Islamophobia, defined by de Koning (2019, p. 26, our translation) as 'the totality of prejudices, stereotypes and discrimination suffered by Muslims because of a one-sided, negative and stigmatising interpretation of their religious tradition', is anything but a myth among young Muslims in Flanders. During the interviews, every single informant mentioned having experienced Islamophobic incidents, ranging from getting side-eyed on the bus for wearing a hijab, to getting physically attacked because of their religious beliefs. From these conversations, multiple themes emerged regarding prejudices, stereotypes and discrimination.

All informants, without exception, acknowledged and testified to the existence of various prejudices and stereotypes about Muslims and Islam. For example, they feel condemned purely based on their appearance. Participants also frequently noted the gendered aspect of Islamophobia. Female informants who do not wear a veil explained this is to avoid discrimination and hostility.

I have seen it happen lots of times that women who wear a veil get called out when going to the store or just going out. (Amira, 22)

Several informants made similar statements, which they believed to be indicative of an increased Islamophobia against female Muslims. Yet, one informant made an opposite claim: Fatma felt that her younger brother experiences more Islamophobia than she does, because his 'typically Arab' appearance makes him seem 'dangerous' and 'a criminal'. Perception was another recurrent theme in the interviews: it makes no difference how devote or strictly practicing young Muslims experiencing Islamophobia *are*. What matters is how devote one is *perceived to be*. Similarly, the actual migration background of a Muslim youngster does not make any difference, yet how 'foreign' one looks matters. Some informants recounted non-Muslims making jokes when they suspected that the informant had migrated recently, irrespective of whether this assumption was true.

Interestingly, the place of residence of the young informants experiencing Islamophobia did seem to make a difference. Informants who live in rural communities experience more subtle Islamophobia, yet Islamophobia is more prevalent in their daily lives, whereas informants living in urban communities reported less Islamophobia overall, but the Islamophobia they reported was more extreme, with more physical attacks and more extreme accusations. For all informants, stigmatisation and prejudice are a reality, but the ways these phenomena manifest themselves tend to differ.

As a result of stigmas and prejudice, the informants feel unwelcome. Most of them notice discrimination based upon the assumption that *Muslims are the antithesis of Belgian culture*. They observe among Belgians a strong 'us and them' thinking: the 'us' group, Belgians, versus the 'them' group, Muslims. Informants feel like there is no place for Muslims, who are seen as *unacceptably deviating from the societal norm*, in the 'us' group: *You notice that people look at you differently* (Musa, 24).

Although each informant has encountered prejudice and negative stereotypes based on their faith, the contents of these prejudices and stereotypes are not always the same. Informants would, for example, refer to statements focusing, on the one hand, on Muslims' weaker abilities – such as *Muslims are less intelligent, not highly educated, not well integrated* and *cannot speak Dutch properly* – and, on the other, on Muslims as a threat – like *Muslims are terrorists* and *dangerous criminals*. Finally, informants also mentioned prejudices with regard to the economic status of Muslims, in statements such as *Muslims are poor, live in social housing,* and *refuse to work*.

Some informants expressed more nuanced views of the general 'us versus them' thinking, arguing that not all Muslims are viewed in the same way. They would recall that non-Muslims often see them as an *exception to the rule,* and not realise that most Muslims are 'good ones', and that it is a minority they should be angry at. Yet, on this account, other informants, like Ronan, remarked that 'even if you are a "good one", you are still viewed as one of "them"' [Muslims as opposite to Western values].

These prejudices and stereotypes are not without consequences. Discrimination and racism were frequently discussed in the context of Flanders, and in different ways.

> Racism that's…. us – we really live it. If there is one thing people can't stand, it's Muslims. (Meyra, 22)

Informants experience discrimination in different areas: in public services, employment, training, treatment in public places and in experiences with potential romantic partners and government officials. Some of the participants indicated not knowing whether this discrimination is due to their religion, their (perceived) ethnicity or to a combination of both.

Experiences of Islamophobia are quite diverse across informants. The most commonly experienced expressions of Islamophobia tend to be non-verbal, like staring and physical distancing.

> On the street … the looks that people give you are so weird because I've done nothing wrong and yet people look at you as if you've done something to them or as if you've ruined society. (Noor, 19)

Verbal and physical expressions of aggression are also described by several informants.

> The first time, I was eleven I think, and I was at a birthday party and a group of boys pushed me in a corner and kept hitting me, just because I was a Muslim. (Amira, 22)

Many informants mentioned experiencing Islamophobia in a subtle way, for example, jokes made at their expense, ranging from, 'You are not going to explode, are you?' to 'Nice bike! Where did you steal it from?', and jokes about their God or Prophet. They admitted appreciating the occasional joke, but said the way in which these jokes are told is hurting them.

> You can tell immediately whether they are joking to make fun or to hurt … and the latter happens quite often. (Ronan, 23)

This kind of subtle racism was mentioned in various interviews, and perceived as problematic. One of our informants, Ronan (aged 23), believes it would result in more radical views, straight-up racism and more physical attacks. Radicalisation and extremism were mentioned in relation to both 'sides' of Islamophobia, specifically, in relation to both the majority population and the Muslim minority. For example, Fatma (aged 24) stated that she could imagine that Muslim youth radicalises after feeling rejected and targeted by Western society time and time again. Other informants, like Ronan, indicated that non-Muslims also radicalise and become more extreme in their anti-Muslim sentiment and, as a result, Muslims do not always feel safe.

Media and Islamophobia

For young Muslims, media can function as a double-edged sword: causing and fuelling Islamophobia, yet also providing support and comfort.

> Media does both: you have these groups of other Muslim youth where you can come home, where you can tell what happened, and who are going to help you, but on the other side you also got these pages like HLN or political pages who mention the word 'Muslim' or 'allochthone' and the reactions there … are sickening. (Ronan, 23)

(Social) Media as Fuel

When asked where Islamophobia comes from, our informants pointed to hostile media as a main cause and as a locus for manifestations of Islamophobia. Interestingly, when young Muslims talk about negative portrayals in the media, traditional media like television, radio and newspapers are mentioned most often, as well as online versions of newspapers on social media platforms. All informants mentioned the negative portrayal of Muslims by Flemish news media, as well as the negative discourse around Islam on social media. For example, Amira (22) stated that, in the media, the tiny portion of Muslims who commit crimes get all the attention, which results in her feeling that she must prove herself as 'a good Muslim' every time she meets new people.

> No, the media is not neutral anyway and it's that negative image of Muslims that scares people. (Driss, 24)

However, some informants also reported a more nuanced version, according to which negative sentiments of Belgians towards Muslims result in more negative media coverage of Islam. Muslims are represented as bad or dangerous in the media, and Islam is frequently linked to terrorism. An additional 'bias' was mentioned, namely that when a terrorist attack is committed by a Muslim, the reason is found in religion, and when a non-Muslim commits an attack, the media often emphasise the individual psychological state of the terrorist.

In the in-depth interviews there was much talk of a predominantly negative stereotyping of Muslims by the media. Here, the Muslim youngsters distinguished between different types of media and motives. According to them, negative stereotyping has a stronger influence in the case of sensation-oriented and clicks-driven media because these media financially benefit from it. Informants also linked the need for sensation in certain media to the misrepresentation of Muslims on these media platforms:

> Have you ever seen a documentary providing terrorism statistics about Muslims? The number of terrorists, of extreme Muslims who want to kill or murder other people is 0.01 per cent of all Muslims in the whole world. Yet those people are represented in 80 or 90 per cent of the media coverage. So, what do you do with the 99.99 percent of Muslims who lead a normal life and have their struggles like everyone else? (Musa, 24)

Country of media production also plays a role, according to the Muslim youngsters. For example, several informants mentioned that the US media focus more on terrorism, whereas the Belgian media tend to present a generally more diverse, albeit predominantly negative image of Muslims. Media are not seen as the only cause of Islamophobia, but their role should not be overlooked, according to the informants in this study.

> I think Islamophobia partly comes from the media, from some political parties, from [non-Muslim] parents, but at the end of the day it comes from the individuals themselves, and until those individuals know what the truth is, they are surrounded by negative information, for example from the media. (Berat, 22)

(Social) Media as Comfort Zones

When asked about the positive sides of media, most informants consider social media as means to educate other people, to provide comfort when faced with Islamophobic (or other negative) incidents, and to find like-minded people. In traditional media, Muslims feel mostly under- and misrepresented, whereas on social media they find interesting educational and inspiring content made by other Muslims, portraying Muslims and Islam in a connecting way. Young Muslims also look for role models on social media. Muslim role models are rare in regular media such as television and radio, while on social media Muslim influencers do provide accurate representations of Muslims and Islam. For example, Amira thinks that social media, like YouTube, Instagram and podcasts, which all showcase very capable and interesting Muslim content creators, really have the potential to change the perspectives of other young people on Islam. This belief was shared by other informants.

Additionally, informants mentioned that social media can be used to actively advocate an alternative perspective on Muslims. For example, in case of a terrorist attack, there are posts on Islamophobia designed for Muslims to share with Koran quotes renouncing violence, to get people to see Islam through a different lens. Furthermore, some informants reported that pages on social media like Instagram can give them a boost when they need it the most. Our informants regularly mentioned Instagram pages with quotes and reels about the Muslim community making them feel like they are not alone. Interestingly, only female informants reported using such Instagram pages. Male informants tend to lean more towards Facebook. Not only influencer pages and role models on social media can provide comfort to young Muslims. In the interviews, informants indicated finding comfort with their friends on social media, like in real life, but also connecting with other like-minded individuals who have experienced the same issues, or who believe in the same things.

> On social media, you find these soulmates – who understand you, that's what I like about social media. People are also more approachable than in real life. If I would not have the support that I have now from my immediate surroundings, I would search for it on social media. (Amira, 22)

Conclusion and Discussion

The findings of this explorative investigation offer insights into the experiences of young Muslims in Flanders with respect to racism and anti-Muslim prejudice. We attempted to be as exhaustive as possible in presenting the role that (social) media can play for young Muslims in dealing with Islamophobia. Furthermore, the coding of the interviews was done consistently and iteratively, thus minimising researcher bias.

Our in-depth interviews with 20 Flemish Muslims showed that all informants have experienced anti-Muslim sentiment, albeit in different ways and at different frequencies. When looking at the occurrence of anti-Muslim senti-ment, the literature shows greater emphasis on the religious and customary aspects of Islam, such as the contents of the Koran and their interpretation, than became apparent in our findings, where the focus was more on outward appearances and the stereotypical impressions people can have of individuals who 'look' like Muslims. This may be due to the specific context of data collection, Flanders, which provides a much narrower scope than that of the international literature. Additionally, in line with the literature, gender turned out to be an important determinant of experiences with Islamophobia, as Muslim women are mostly more easily identified as 'Muslim' when wearing a headscarf. The dual role of media was discussed as young Muslims pointed to (traditional) media as a main cause of Islamophobia, and to (social) media as a site of comfort and strength.

This research is limited by the size of the sample. It focuses on the personal, subjective experiences of mainly higher educated young Muslim adults living in Western Europe. Further research will need to focus on a more diverse set of education levels, age groups, geographic origins and cultures. An intersectional approach of 'complex religion' (Wilde, 2018) to social inequality and exclusion is recommended for future research. Furthermore, social desirability must be factored in when interpreting the research results. As the informed consent form mentioned the study was about Islamophobia, it is possible that the informants' answers were coloured by prior knowledge of the research theme. To minimise this factor and to reassure the informants, it was stressed that there were no wrong answers. We also emphasised that participation in itself was very useful, to prevent informants from answering in ways they thought might benefit the research.

Seven coping strategies in the face of anti-Muslim sentiment, as formulated in previous research by De Nolf et al. (2021), were verified in this new round of interviews. In line with findings reported by De Nolf et al. (2021) and Omlo (2015), informants indicated that they mostly try to relativise their Islamophobic experiences, and encountering Islamophobia by not wearing a headscarf or other outwards signs of belief, by not talking about their beliefs in conversations and by ignoring comments on news stories about Muslims. Yet, when opting for a reactive coping strategy, or a communicative coping strategy, informants use (social) media as a remedial tool, offering a space for sharing positive posts about Islam and Muslims, and opening their world to like-minded others to confide in. Overall, (social) media provide support in coping with Islamophobia, as they facilitate reactive strategies, as well as communicative strategies such as talking to like-minded others about shared experiences.

Building on this qualitative exploratory research, quantitative, preferably longitudinal, cross-country survey research is recommended, to quantify the findings and uncover potential cause–effect relationships. The results of this and further research may serve as guidelines for anti-discrimination and anti-racism policymaking and intervention models. Positive actions likely to counter prejudice – such as facilitating contact between Muslims and non-Muslims – can be put forward in policies. This must be done in an informed and well-considered way so as not to unduly emphasise differences between cultures, which might contribute to a further culturalisation of the debate (Zemni, 2009). Any type of government intervention can help defuse anti-Muslim sentiment, but it can just as easily exacerbate it (Kundnani, 2014). Evidence-based policymaking and intervention programmes can help overcome that risk.

Notes

1. This chapter stems from a project mainly funded by the Social Sciences and Humanities Research Council (SSHRC): *Scholarly and mediatic Islamophobia: A transnational study of discourses and their impact* (Original French title *Islamophobie savante et médiatique: Étude transnationale des discours et de leur impact*; SSHRC 2019-2023, #890-2018-0016), for which Abdelwahed Mekki-Berrada is the Principal Investigator.
2. This period includes two events of special relevance for this study: the decapitation of French professor Samuel Paty, which fuelled polarisation, and the Covid-19 crisis, which dominated the news and took over the social debate.
3. Approval No. 2019-155/29-07-2019.
4. 'Islamophobia in Scholarship and the Media: A Cross-National Study of Discourses and their Impact' led by the third author, Abdelwahed Mekki-Berrada, Laval University, Quebec, Canada, and funded by the Social Sciences and Humanities Research Council of Canada (SSHRC # 890-2018-0016; 2019–2024).
5. These concepts were chosen based on our research objective, the literature and the interview transcripts.

References

Adam, B., & Al-Mateen, C. S. (2019). Hate, disillusionment, and pain: The impact of islamophobia on American Muslim youth. *Journal of the American Academy of Child & Adolescent Psychiatry, 58*(10), 50.

Ali, W., Clifton, E., Duss, M., Fang, L., Keyes, S., & Shakir, F. (2011). *Fear, Inc.: The roots of the Islamophobia network in America*. Center for American Progress. https://www.americanprogress.org/issues/religion/reports/2011/08/26/10165/fear-inc/

Aroian, K. J. (2011). Discrimination against Muslim American adolescents. *The Journal of School Nursing, 28*(3), 206–213.

Bacchus, N. (2019). Resisting Islamophobia. *American Journal of Islam and Society, 36*(4), 1–26.

Boeije, H. R. (2014). *Analysing in qualitative research.* Lemma.

Brondolo, E., Brady, N., Thompson, S., Tobin, J. N., Cassells, A., Sweeney, M., Mcfarlane, D., & Contrada, R. J. (2008). Perceived racism and negative affect: Analyses of trait and state measures of affect in a community sample. *Journal of Social and Clinical Psychology, 27*(2), 150–173. https://doi.org/10.1521/jscp.2008.27.2.150

Coker, T. R., Elliott, M. N., Kanouse, D. E., Grunbaum, J. A., Schwebel, D. C., Gilliland, M. J., Tortolero, S. R., Peskin, M. F., & Schuster, M. A. (2009). Perceived racial/ethnic discrimination among fifth-grade students and Issociation with mental health. *American Journal of Public Health, 99*(5), 878–884. https://doi.org/10.2105/ajph.2008.144329

De Koning, M. (2019). *Vijf mythes over islamofobie* [Five myths on Islamophobia].Yunus Publishing.

De Nolf, A., d'Haenens, L., & Mekki-Berrada, A. (2021). Face to face with anti-Muslim sentiment: A qualitative study into the coping mechanisms of young college and university Muslim students and graduates in Flanders. *Religions, 12*(2), 135.

Eckert, S., Wallace, S. O., Metzger-Riftkin, J., & Kolhoff, S. (2018). 'The best damn representation of Islam': Muslims, gender, social media, and Islamophobia in the United States. *CyberOrient, 12*(1), 4–30.

Elkomy, F. (2019). Microaggression in Muslim youth. *Journal of the American Academy of Child & Adolescent Psychiatry, 58*(10), 50.

Helbling, M. (Eds.). (2014). *Islamophobia in the West: Measuring and explaining individual attitudes.* Routledge.

Hertogen, J. (2017). Non-profit data. http://www.npdata.be/

Ismail, A. A. (2015). Ways of coping and religious commitment in Muslim adolescents. *Mental Health, Religion & Culture, 18*(3), 175–184.

Kahf, M. (1999). *Western representations of the Muslim woman* (illustrated edn). Amsterdam University Press.

Kamans, E., Gordijn, E. H., Oldenhuis, H., & Otten, S. (2009). What I think you see is what you get: Influence of prejudice on assimilation to negative meta-stereotypes among Dutch Moroccan teenagers. *European Journal of Social Psychology, 39*(5), 842–851. https://doi.org/10.1002/ejsp.593

Koomen, W., & Van der Pligt, J. (2016). *The psychology of radicalization and terrorism.* Routledge/ Taylor & Francis Group.

Kundnani, A. (2014). *The Muslims are coming!* Adfo Books.

Lean, N. (2017). *The Islamophobia industry: How the right manufactures hatred of Muslims* (2nd ed.). Pluto Press.

Ljamai, A. (2020). Feelings of anxiety among radical Muslim youths in the Netherlands: A psychological exploration. *Archive for the Psychology of Religion, 42*(3), 335–358.

Mastro, M. A. (2016, Spring). *The mainstream misrepresentation of Muslim women in the media.* The Cupola. https://cupola.gettysburg.edu/cgi/viewcontent.cgi?article=1012&context=islamandwomen

Mertens, S., & De Smaele, H. (Eds.). (2016). *Representations of Islam in the news: A cross-cultural analysis.* Lexington Books.

Mineo, L. (2021, September 9). *Muslim Americans reflect on the impact of 9/11.* Harvard Gazette. https://news.harvard.edu/gazette/story/2021/09/muslim-americans-reflect-on-the-impact-of-9-11/

Mondon, A., & Winter, A. (2019) Mapping and mainstreaming Islamophobia: Between the illiberal and liberal. In I. Zempi & I. Awan (Eds.), *The Routledge international handbook of Islamophobia* (pp. 58--70). Routledge.

Musa, I. (2019). Building resilience: Clinical perspectives on helping youth cope with Islamophobia. *Journal of the American Academy of Child & Adolescent Psychiatry, 58*(10), 50–51.

Omlo, J. (2015). *How migrants deal with discrimination. Radicalise, withdraw or tolerate?* Republiek Allochtonië. http://www.republiekallochtonie.nl/blog/achtergronden/hoe-migranten-omgaan-met-discriminatie-radicaliseren-terugtrekkenof-verdragen

Paradies, Y. (2006). A systematic review of empirical research on self-reported racism and health. *International Journal of Epidemiology, 35*(4), 888–901.

Pavetich, M., & Stathi, S. (2021). Meta-humanization reduces prejudice, even under high intergroup threat. *Journal of Personality and Social Psychology, 120*(3), 651–671. https://doi.org/10.1037/pspi0000259

Pettigrew, T. F., Wagner, U., & Christ, O. (2010). Population ratios and prejudice: Modelling both contact and threat effects. *Journal of Ethnic and Migration Studies, 36*(4), 635–650.

Pew Research Center (2017a). *Europe's growing Muslim population.* https://www.pewforum.org/2017/11/29/europes-growing-muslim-population/

Pew Research Center (2017b). *Assaults against Muslims in U.S. surpass 2001 level.* https://www.pewresearch.org/fact-tank/2017/11/15/assaults-against-muslims-in-u-s-surpass-2001-level/

Poole, E., & Richardson, J. E. (2006). *Muslims and the news media.* Bloomsbury Academic.

Rezaei, S., Kobari, K., & Salami, A. (2019). The portrayal of Islam and Muslims in Western media: A critical discourse analysis. *Cultura, 16*(1), 53–73.

Roose, H. (2017). *Methodology of social science: An introduction.* Amsterdam University Press.

Rumbaut, R. G. (1994). The crucible within: Ethnic identity, self-esteem, and segmented assimilation among children of immigrants. *International Migration Review, 28*(4), 748.

Savin-Baden, M., & Major, C. H. (2013). *Qualitative research: The essential guide to theory and practice.* Routledge.

Shain, F. (2020). Navigating the unequal education space in post-9/11 England: British Muslim girls talk about their educational aspirations and future expectations. *Educational Philosophy and Theory, 53*(3), 270–287.

Sinno, N. (2020). Caught in the crosshairs. *Journal of Middle East Women's Studies, 16*(1), 1–18.

Sirin, S. R., & Fine, M. (2007). Hyphenated selves: Muslim American youth negotiating identities on the fault lines of global conflict. *Applied Developmental Science, 11*(3), 151–163.

Soehl, T. (2019). Mode of difference and resource for resilience: How religion shapes experiences of discrimination of the second generation in France. *International Migration Review, 54*(3), 796–819.

Tell MAMA (2019). *Annual report 2018: Normalising hatred.* Faith Matters. https://tellmamauk.org/wp-content/uploads/2019/09/Tell%20MAMA%20Annual%20Report%202018%20_%20Normalising%20Hate.pdf

Tineo, P., Bonumwezi, J. L., & Lowe, S. R. (2021). Discrimination and posttraumatic growth among Muslim American youth: Mediation via posttraumatic stress disorder symptoms. *Journal of Trauma & Dissociation, 22*(2), 188–201.

Van den Hoonaard, W. C. (1997). *Working with sensitizing concepts: Analytical field research.* Sage.

Vitullo, A. (2021). The online intersection among Islamophobia, populism, and hate speech: An Italian perspective. *Journal of Religion, Media and Digital Culture, 10*(1), 95–114.

Wilde, M. J. (2018). Complex religion: Intersections of religion and inequality. *Social Inclusion, 6*(2), 83–86.

Zemni, S. (2009). *Het Islamdebat* [The Islam debate]. EPO.

Zempi, I., & Awan, I. (2019). *The Routledge international handbook of Islamophobia.* Routledge.

12

SAFE SPACES AND SENSITIVE ISSUES: TOWARDS AN EMIC UNDERSTANDING OF RADICALISATION

ALEXANDER VAN LEUVEN & ANN TRAPPERS

Abstract

Radicalism and related concepts are predominantly conceived from an outsider or etic perspective. Research concerning these concepts reveals unexpected socio-political intentions that are being covertly maintained. Therefore, it is hard to satisfy the needs that policies on the matter overtly claim to target. This chapter envisages further contributions to policy work on the matter, by gathering insider or emic perspectives of youth targeted by these policies – which is long overdue. We explore both *institutional alienation* as a constructive concept, and *safe spaces* as a method, to gather emic perspectives on what radicalism and the discourse on radicalism mean to the people targeted by these policies. To that end we review an ethnography from a safe space programme conducted by the Brussels non-profit organisation Foyer. We find that emic voices are highly effective in pinpointing what exactly causes the problematised behaviour. Involving all stakeholders will enable us to develop more constructive polies.

Keywords: safe spaces, grievances, institutional alienation, emic youth voices, Islamophobia

Context

Much effort has been invested in Belgium in so-called radicalisation or deradicalisation policies since 2013. Belgium is a federal state, and most policy domains are complexly dispersed over several government levels. (De)radicalisation policies are no exception. Theoretically, security is a federal-level competence – pertaining to institutions such as a formally unified police force and three different intelligence services – and prevention is a regional-level competence, although in practice this division is not very clear. For instance, the federal ministry of security funds local prevention practices, and the Flemish region struggles with a highly securitised approach to prevention, which is not a separate policy domain, as it is intertwined with many forms of social policy (Fadil & de Koning, 2019).

In any case, compared to neighbouring countries, Belgium has a locally focalised deradicalisation approach, based on the idea that municipalities are best connected to the social partners who develop practice within the framework of said policies (Jaminé & Fadil, 2019a; Somers, 2016; Van Leuven, 2017).

This chapter focuses on the prevention sphere of (de)radicalisation policies, although, as mentioned, prevention is inextricably intertwined with safety and security policies. In the literature this relation is called *securitisation*. Belgian Muslims are considered a potential security risk, and the security policies on radicalisation, collectively named Plan R, are in fact a final version of the security policies on mosques, named Plan M (Jaminé & Fadil, 2019a). The latter monitors domestic Islamic practices and incidentally related foreign influences, acting on the etic premise that being Muslim must be moderated in Belgium. As seen in Chapter 4 of this book, this relates to the position of Muslims in Belgian society. Muslims' incidental social needs are to a certain extent responded to as a matter of prevention of radicalisation, and this is also how socio-preventive actors can secure their core practices (Jaminé & Fadil, 2019a).

Securitisation manifests itself in the stigmatisation of Muslims, as shown by Thomas Frissen (2019), who describes how violent Daesh jihadis make use of the unstable position of Muslims in the West to gain support and terrain. Their mediatised acts of terror are primarily intended to fuel a culturalised analysis of their motives and subsequent securitised policies targeting local Muslims.

Furthermore, Islamophobia, as elaborated in the introduction of this book, is a major cause of radicalism and extremism in Belgium. Consequently, Muslims would radicalise because they are involuntarily associated with a violent ideology or an ideology that is not consistent with the Belgian rule of law, rather than because they would adhere to such an ideology a priori. Ideology is ultimately used as an a posteriori rationalisation (Schmid, 2013) of acts of political violence.

In these circumstances it is worth considering abandoning the concept of radicalisation, and instead focusing on *institutional alienation* as a link between Islamophobia, unresolvable social grievances and radicalism. This should offer a more constructive frame of reference to approach the phenomenon, involving those who might be considered key stakeholders: youth who protest or cease to abide by the democratic rule of law in Belgium.

Institutional Alienation

Institutional alienation is a concept that remains to be explored in the context of Belgium's radicalisation prevention efforts. It has always been difficult to critically approach the meaning of the term 'radicalisation'. Terrorism scholar Rik Coolsaet (2016) argues that radicalisation has essentially become a catch-all term that covers a range of behaviours, from veiling, over acting out grievances, to using violence. Furthermore, in the ample research that involves youth workers (Van Bouchaute et al., 2018; Debruyne, 2015), including one unique participatory study (Claes et al., 2020), and one that actually involves youth voices (Figoureux, 2021), this vagueness is overshadowed by pejorativity. As such, the use of the concept radicalisation has proven to be harmful (Fadil & de Koning, 2019), and mostly[1] serving an exclusionary (Fadil & de Koning, 2019) and a terrorist political agenda (Frissen, 2019).

Alienation is recognised as one of many causes for terrorism in Belgium (Schmid, 2013). More specifically, in this chapter the concept of alienation is highlighted as a key focus for the prevention of radicalisation. This path had already been followed for some time in the Netherlands, with alienation identified as a dominant cause by Buijs, Demant and Hamdy (2006), when researching youth moving to Syria's civil war. Subsequently, political scientist Amy-Jane Gielen (2008) examined radicalisation as a process based on the ups and downs of identity development, moving away from explanations of radicalism that involve returning to one's roots based on compelling ideas from recruiters (Van Leuven, 2017). Gielen's work resonated well with professionals who work with so-called radicalising individuals (Jaminé & Fadil, 2019b; Van Leuven, 2017).

In this section we advance an exploration of institutional alienation as a central concept. The basic idea is that institutional alienation is what could potentially make individuals disengage from society, and then re-engage with groups outside of it. Whereas the paths of radicalisation are very individual and impossible to predict (Coolsaet, 2016; Schmid, 2013), it should be more feasible to base interventions on an individual's level of alienation from social institutions as indicated by the relatively exceptional unresolvedness of their grievances, assuming that social institutions provide protection from grievances, support in resilience and care after harm. This will be elaborated in what follows.

Origins

Alienation is the process of acquiring a sense of detachment from the society one is part of. Institutional alienation is alienation from social institutions. Why is this concept of alienation important to our research? Theoretically, social institutions – including family, school, work, leisure organisations, social assistance and care facilities, police, justice and media – are expected to socialise and support individuals. These are decisive institutions when it comes to alienation, as explained in what follows.

The concept of alienation has been investigated by the post-war Frankfurter Schule, in its contributions to critical theory (Jaeggi, 2014), together with the concepts of *(mono)cultural dominance* in society, and *instrumentality*. The latter favours gain and goals to social norms. These phenomena are very reminiscent of the critique of radicalisation. The first one can be seen in the problematisation of Muslim identity and/or its expressions, which is an exact adaptation of premises of the Flemish far right (Blommaert & Martens, 1999).

Nevertheless, the concept of alienation has lost its centrality in critical theory, because it was considered to presuppose that there is a given and fixed, normal or natural position in society for every human being. The concept is therefore too essentialist for critical thinking. Furthermore, being alien(ated) quickly became seen as a personal pathological situation. Recently, Rahel Jaeggi (2014) has explored the reinstallation of the concept, while allowing for an appreciation of the societal role in alienation. Building on the work of Karl Marx, she argues that there is a socially shared responsibility for individuals' actions, because these actions are shaped by society.

This confronts us with an old epistemological conundrum of the social sciences, that of the fundamental anthropological question of *institutionalisation* (Zijderveld, 1974). Do we see humanity as shaped by its institutions, without any room for individual agency? Or do we see humans as able to reshape these institutions as we go along? Or does the answer lie somewhere in the middle, or even elsewhere? Whatever the answers are, and to what extent society – comprised of institutions – shapes behaviour, that extent will have to be accounted for. When individuals are socialised into social institutions, then the process of socialisation cannot be left out of the equation.

Jaeggi (2014, p. 245) argues that the degree of alienation determines whether it is possible to achieve self-determination and self-realisation, and defines alienation as follows: 'Someone is alienated … if she cannot react to her own given [socialised] conditions.' From this she moves on to the question of how we should make this process apparent to its participants. In the next sections we will investigate if the method of *safe spaces* can make this process apparent and as such support resilience to alienation.

Application

Before looking at practices in the next section, and applying the theoretical framework of institutional alienation, we acknowledge that the concept of alienation has always been relevant in radicalisation prevention. It might even be considered the elephant in the room.

The novelty of our perspective on radicalisation becomes evident when we look at the work of Loïc Wacquant (2008). When doing ethnographic field work in the ill-famed Chicago ghetto, Wacquant disregarded conventional ideas about the ghetto. He argued that the ghettoised neighbourhoods had imploded, because the ghetto is a product of racial segregation that concerned a complete set of social institutions, like schools and medical centres, for all the ghettoised neighbourhoods. Wacquant then describes a *broken social contact,* where individuals consider themselves relieved of rights and responsibilities, because the government has stopped delivering the services they are required to provide. He points at the disappearance of these institutions, or the *implosion* of the ghetto, and the rendering of an *anti-ghetto,*[2] to explain why youth resort to violence as an alternative for institutionalisation. Ultimately, this results in the idea of a ghetto as a dangerous neighbourhood, which is more commonplace than the notion of an anti-ghetto. Roughly speaking, people join gangs in absence of institutions. Bearing in mind Rahel Jaeggi's (2014) arguments, it becomes clear that people need social structure for their self-realisation.

Wacquant's work was not exclusive to Chicago. He also did research in the Parisian banlieues, with similar findings on *advanced marginality* (Wacquant, 2008). In the first decade of this century, a similar situation occurred in Brussels, where the Molem gang and drug and car traffickers provided an alternative future for youngsters who realised their futures would be different because of their '"Islamic" appearance'. At a later age, many of these youngsters would attempt to return to society through the institute of marriage (Van Leuven, 2013).

But even before Wacquant's (2008) comparative sociological study came out, a 2006 report for the Dutch government (Buijs et al., 2006), which would in turn influence Belgian practices, suggested youth perceived a breach of trust by the government. According to the report, based on interviews with young salafi Muslims, this perception of a breach of trust is a first step towards radicalism and extremism. This is the basic idea behind the 'process' thinking within the catch-all approach to radicalisation. As such, what appears to be a swift process, could be detected earlier on. Of course, in these earlier stages, things could evolve in many directions, of which extreme violence becomes just one, quantitatively negligible, option. Once again, this catch-all conceptualisation of radicalisation becomes problematic.

Another example of alienation-inspired policy is that of the city of Mechelen (Van Leuven, 2017), which was, from its inception on, based on theories about social alienation and mutual individual and governmental responsibilities. It does not focus on risk factors specific to individuals, but rather looks for protective factors, and, as such, assesses to what extent individuals are embedded in social institutions, as well as the number of these embedding institutions. While this approach gained much appraisal from beyond the city walls, the city itself indicates having a difficult time with online media as an institution. It is very hard for social professionals to assess whether the specific activities of an individual on social media are threatening alienation or supporting socialisation.

To overcome this challenge, Mechelen has been looking at safe spaces as a method to gain more insights in the online dynamics of the media institute. Yet, it does not provide a conceptualisation of safe spaces. However, a safe space is considered a social intervention that provides a space where youth can express grievances, without fear of moral, social or punitive consequences. Hence, in practice the safe space provides or refers to an educational intervention, where coping strategies are taught or alternatives are offered (in case of harmful language).

The case of Brussels's experience with safe spaces is elaborated as an ethnography in the next section, as a way of exploring Rahel Jaeggi's (2014) claim that alienation challenges us to make apparent to subjects that there are (still) ways to (re)gain control of their own path.

Safe Spaces

Introduction

Foyer is a not-for-profit organisation based in the Brussels municipality of Molenbeek. It has been active for more than 50 years in immigrant integration and empowerment. A significant part of Foyer's activities target youth: there are two youth work teams (one French-speaking and one Dutch-speaking) that structurally collaborate, and Foyer also organises a wide range of workshops on topics such as diversity and migration, aimed at various age groups. In 2019, 1,199 young people took part in one of these workshops.

Following the 2015 and 2016 terror attacks in France and Belgium, Foyer decided to include workshops aimed at the prevention of religious radicalisation in its range of activities. To tailor the workshops as much as possible to the needs and interests of the target audience, the team started by carrying out small-scale field research among young people in Molenbeek.

Molenbeek is a densely populated Brussels municipality, with 26,810 inhabitants/km^2 in the neighbourhood known as Historical Molenbeek. It has few green spaces (public parks or private gardens). Molenbeek has a high unemployment rate, and the number of unemployed inhabitants without a secondary school diploma exceeds the regional average. It is also the Brussels municipality with the highest number of inhabitants of North African origin (Brussels Institute for Statistics and Analysis, and Brussels-Capital Health and Social Observatory, 2016).

Method

Our main aim was to gain insight into the issues that young inhabitants of Molenbeek and their families experienced as most pressing or most relevant at the time of our research (June–September 2018). We organised three two-hour 'dialogue sessions' with 13 young people (six female and seven male) from Molenbeek. The average age was 16, and all were of immigrant and Muslim background. We used the four-phase dialogue method pioneered by *Stichting Nederland in Dialoog* (Plokhooij, 2020), which Foyer has used since 2007 in its project Brussels in Dialogue.

The dialogue method requires the right circumstances for the conversation to take place, i.e., a safe and welcoming environment. In this case, the sessions took place in an environment in which young people could feel comfortable (a youth club), and two trusted youth workers were also present. Not all participants knew one another, but they all knew at least one of the youth workers.

Wanting to avoid a narrow focus on Molenbeek as a problem area, we selected as theme for the first session 'Your hopes and dreams for your ideal neighbourhood'. The dialogue facilitator did not introduce the topic of violent extremism in this session; it was expected to come up spontaneously, which turned out to be the case. The opening question was simply: 'What does it mean to be a youngster in Molenbeek today?'

In the second session, the themes of violent extremism and religious radicalisation were introduced indirectly by recapitulating what participants had said in the previous session regarding Molenbeek's bad reputation in the media. During the third session, the question was asked what could be done concretely to improve the situation in Molenbeek, including the prevention of religious radicalisation among youth.

Findings

A prominent recurrent theme in the young people's dreams for an ideal neighbourhood was the presence of better-quality schools, with teachers who could relate to the reality of youth in Molenbeek. According to participants, seeing others, including older siblings, drop out of school or remain unemployed increases one's risk of following in those footsteps. In the words of the participants [translated from French]:

> Those who drop out usually realise that the secondary school degree they would eventually obtain will not be good enough to land them a job.
> Their level of French, let alone Dutch or English, is simply too poor for them to ever obtain a higher education degree.
> Many kids who try to study hard get discouraged when they see one of their elder brothers, for instance, sitting in front of his PlayStation® all day.

According to participants, religious radicalisation was one of the possible responses to the sense of frustration or alienation that several young people in Molenbeek experience as a result of their socio-economic situation. Other responses might be turning to drugs or petty crime. Participants all knew childhood friends who had taken one of these paths. In each of the cases, they had lost touch with this former friend. Even if they might still greet one another on the street, they now clearly belonged to different groups. Participants thought of religious radicalism as one of several countercultures that frustrated young people might turn to.

> It's usually the kids who have run out of options and are looking for a way out.
> Once you no longer feel part of society, you will seek out people who think like you and eventually you will start dressing and behaving like them.
> These people [recruiters] become someone's family, you know.
> These ideas promise ready-made solutions to all that is going wrong in their lives.

One of the youth workers pointed out that radicalised kids, or kids involved in drug dealing, are a minority, and that they are very difficult to reach out to:

'The only thing we can do is try to prevent them from becoming role models, by making sure the kids have positive alternatives.'

The ideas voiced by these young people tie in with a large and growing body of literature on the prevention of radicalisation and violent extremism that considers the search for an identity an important enabling factor in the radicalisation process (see also Stephens et al., 2019).

Another factor emerging from the existing research on religious radicalisation is the role of media. Our young participants also brought this up spontaneously, especially in the second dialogue session.

None of the participants believed that even extensive use of social media and the Internet in general were a direct cause of the spread of religious radicalisation. Although they recognised that the Internet helped radicalised people connect to like-minded individuals and spread information, they thought of it primarily as a means to an end.

> Young people have always tried to create a world of their own in which parents have no place.
> If you are not really looking for these things [i.e., messages of violent extremism], then you will use social media in a harmless way, to share silly things that make you and your friends laugh. Or, you know, look: we've just bought new shoes and we're walking them to the nearest underground station.

However, while participants did not point the finger at the media as a direct cause of radicalisation, they did consider it a cause of confusion. 'We don't really trust the media,' the consensus seemed to be. Everyday sources of information on current affairs were invariably social media, including YouTube channels. Even if all participants said that they had never supported ISIS, several did believe in one or more conspiracy theories.

> You really have to watch 'Le Lama Fâché' [a YouTube channel that has, among other things, propagated conspiracy theories]. That channel shows some really great stuff!

Only two participants occasionally watched news broadcasts on 'classic' mainstream media, television – with their parents. Participants said that they were confused primarily by the amount of information they received every day, some of it conflicting, and that the confusion made them unsure as to what they should believe. Here the reporting on Molenbeek in the wake of the 2015–2016 terrorist attacks had a clear impact: seeing what they considered a one-sided or distorted image of their municipality made them even more distrustful towards the media and towards journalists.

Since social media use is so prominent in young people's lives, and given their lack of trust in the media in general, we decided to focus on media and information in the workshop that we wanted to develop to contribute to the prevention of religious radicalisation.

The final dialogue session brought up the question of what could be done to create the ideal neighbourhood, including the prevention or countering of religious radicalisation. It soon became clear that participants believed that a top-down approach to the prevention of radicalisation would be ineffective or even counterproductive. One of the important aspects was the way in which young people use language: what is said is one thing; what is meant can be another.

> Many teachers and social workers don't understand our language: what we really mean when we say certain things.
> It's true that it almost becomes a game for certain kids. They know exactly which buttons to push and everyone goes bananas.

When asked for examples of buttons to push, participants mentioned that some youngsters make provocative statements such as 'Gay people deserve to die', in front of their teachers, as a form of rebellion, to stand out and look cool, rather than because they fully agree with the statement.

Even in painful situations, they find comfort in humour. According to participants, it helps to laugh at the 'lies', and it helps to laugh at the 'liars'. This, of course, adds fuel to the fire, and ends up reinforcing tensions that also affected previous generations, and used to be called 'societal vulnerability' in times when societal responsibility was more accounted for. These days, problems are coined as 'radicalisation', which adds gravely to the grievances of youth. Participants agreed that the best thing for them would be to become actively involved in their neighbourhood themselves:

> In fact, we are the ones who should self-organise to create the neighbour-hood we want.

During the sessions, participants repeatedly displayed a negative attitude to counter-messaging. This attitude was based on personal experiences with initiatives to counter and prevent violent extremism, as well as on images and clips from a counter-messaging campaign that they had seen. In many cases, the message was delivered by what they considered the wrong type of messenger, such as a teacher with whom they did not get along well, or an imam who did not appeal to them. At other times it was the message itself they found unconvincing.

> [As a person at risk of radicalisation] you're not going to like counter-messaging, when what you want is precisely something that helps you set yourself apart from society.

As one youth worker put it:

> Parents, teachers, or imams cannot debunk these ideas, because they have the power; they are the power that these kids are up against.

Consequently, he said, when talking to youngsters about their experiences related to religious radicalisation:

> people they cannot identify with should be kept out of the room, that's the way it is.

Workshops

This brings us to the concept of safe spaces, which had worked well for the dialogue sessions, and that we wanted to recreate in the workshops: we wanted to develop the type of setting that would allow for a discussion on a number of sensitive subjects, including young people's personal experiences with religious radicalisation. Such a safe space should consist of peers and adults whom the young people can trust and identify with. It is also important that this safeness is made explicit: at the beginning of a session, the facilitator should make clear that what is discussed during the workshop will stay there, and that the activity is not about giving the right answers.

The Foyer team developed two workshops on critical media awareness. 'How Real is the Virtual?', aimed at younger children (9–12 years old), and 'Media in Times of Fake News', aimed at teenagers (12+). Both workshops had largely the same content, but activities were adapted to the age group in question. Materials and methods used were videos, quizzes, interactive computer applications and group discussion facilitated by Foyer staff. The main aim was to let participants experience first-hand how manipulation works. During the workshops, participants were asked to manipulate 'neutral' videos by modifying sound, speed, lighting etc., and set to work with the ingredients of a conspiracy theory to develop their very own conspiracy theory. The overall tone of the activities was kept 'light' and playful, while the workshops would still provide in-depth information on fake news, propaganda and the like.

Pilot materials were assessed with the help of a few carefully selected experts. During the piloting phase of the workshops, we evaluated the sessions via evaluation forms for participants and teachers and through participant observation (9 hours).

During the piloting phase we found that, just like the youngsters in our dialogue sessions, many pupils who took part in the workshops believed in conspiracy theories. Yet, this did not automatically mean that they were not open to critical reflection. The workshops did function as a safe space in which participants did not feel judged by authority figures when making certain statements. They were happy to be able to discuss subjects such as radicalism, but also topics such as bullying or peer pressure, within the safe setting.

Teachers, likewise, noticed that some of the pupils would react quite differently and talk much more freely than in class:

> When the students arrived, they were quite tense. Yet I could see them relax as the workshop progressed, and by the end they were at ease and even enjoying themselves.

Still, the critical stance advocated in the workshops, particularly the one for teenagers, clearly created a sense of discomfort in some participants, who would show resistance to the message, and sometimes refuse to participate. Participants showing discomfort turned out to be already dedicated to particular ideologies to a considerable extent.

In his study *Le Jihadisme français* (2020), Hugo Micheron, one of the experts Foyer invited in the workshop development process to evaluate the material, introduces Kévin, a young man who had converted to Islam in secondary school under the influence of his brother, and who had been eager to join IS, to escape the contradiction between the rules of his faith and the many temptations of the Western world. Micheron quotes Kévin, who points out: 'Over there, you are pushed to practise. To say your prayers. Sometimes it's too much, but at least it's clear' (Kévin, quoted in Micheron, 2020, p. 39).

This clarity is an important reason why extremism appeals to some youngsters. It divides the world into neat categories, and, to quote one of the participants in the dialogue sessions, it promises 'ready-made solutions' to complex challenges.

Discussion

Much has been said and written about the role that safe spaces and non-judgmental dialogue play in the prevention of radicalisation. Our preliminary research and experiences with workshops reinforce the importance of both interlinked notions. They also show that safe spaces provided for people to express their identity should be blank canvases, so that participants can express any part of their identity they wish.

When working with young people from a setting like Molenbeek, it is worthwhile to approach them as 'urban' youth, rather than consistently viewing them through the lens of Islam. Too often participants, boys in particular, felt that people would approach them as youth 'at risk of radicalisation'. This is also what a youth worker present at the dialogue sessions indicated:

> The more you address youngsters as potential jihadists, the more they will distrust whatever it is you have to say. Simply treat them as kids growing up in an urban environment and have them build connections with others based on this shared identity.

Socio-political Implications

In this chapter we have addressed the problematic concept of radicalisation in government policies. Our selection of critical literature has shown that, in de-radicalisation policy, the focus lies on securitisation and stigmatisation. Securitisation refers to the reactionary reflex that focalises on an out-of-control situation and scrutinises all other situations as potentially out of control. It is a biopolitical response to geopolitical actions of terrorists. Stigmatisation refers to the disproportionate focus on Muslims in this reactive work.

Furthermore, we have explored a more constructive approach to prevention policies. We have elaborated the concept of institutional alienation as a more fruitful theoretical alternative to support interventions in the context of prevention policies – more fruitful because the concept of alienation makes us more aware of societal responsibilities when it comes to prevention. The socio-political context has the power to make or break opportunities for individuals, which are primarily intended to create a space where any individual can develop their potential in relation to society. The concrete workings of safe space interventions are part of socialisation processes and the support provided by institutions.

If institutions fail to support individuals, and individuals hence fail in self-realisation, alienation occurs from institutions and the society they are part of. At that point, both society and the individual have failed, and a cognitive opening ensues in the mind of the individual to seek supportive alternative institutions outside of society. Building on the work of Rahel Jaeggi (2014) and Anton Zijderveld (1974), we accept Jaeggi's conclusion that exploring how individuals can be enabled to make use of institutions should be a priority, bearing in mind that this has been unusually difficult for these individuals.

For that we turn to the educational method of organising safe spaces. These serve as a kind of emergency field institution, where it is safe for individuals to express grievances built up in absence of supportive institutions. Even if these expressions 'merely' require an educational response, that response should be made possible. There are many forms of safe spaces, and they can differ as to what the internal rules are. In absence of an established overview of safe spaces, we focused on an ethnography of a programme in Brussels run by the non-profit organisation Foyer.

It seems that the concept of alienation can provide insights in young people's grievances and whether these people find the support needed to address their grievances. Young people want to be acknowledged as individuals, and fear their future in society and the paths their teachers envision are a lie. Teachers, who are the main antagonists in a social institution that is very dominant in youth's lives, fail to understand who their pupils are and where they come from, or where they are determined to end up.

The dialogue sessions in the Foyer safe spaces show that listening to youth voices is worth doing, and that the practice can prevent us from imposing perverse policies that attribute to enlarging the problem, rather than diminishing it. Furthermore, the concept of institutional alienation reveals emic perspectives of youth, in which they see their futures as compromised. As such, it is a promising approach for future contributions to constructive, do-no-harm policies, founded on a theoretical framework that, on the one hand, creates an outlook on protecting individuals from becoming susceptible to recruitment into extremist groups, and, on the other, allows for social interventions like safe spaces that address grievances and provide a way of coping.

Notes

1. It should not be overlooked that many practitioners manage to do good work even under these circumstances, by *negotiating their practice* (Jaminé & Fadil, 2019a). In the field they continue to provide good services in terms of social assistance, while making sure they meet targets to be reported on in terms of radicalisation.
2. The anti-ghetto is to be well understood as the *opposite of a ghetto*, and not as a movement opposing a *ghetto*.

References

Blommaert, J., & Martens, A. (1999). *Van blok tot bouwsteen: een visie voor een nieuw lokaal migrantenbeleid* [From block to building block: A vision for a new local migrant policy]. EPO.

Brussels Institute for Statistics and Analysis and Brussels-Capital Health and Social Observatory. (2016). *Zoom op de gemeenten: Sint-Jans-Molenbeek* [Perspective Brussels: Molenbeek]. https://bisa.brussels/publicaties/zoom-op-de-gemeenten

Buijs, F., Demant, F., & Hamdy, A. (2006). *Strijders van eigen bodem: Radicale en democratische moslims in Nederland* [Homegrown warriors: Radical and democratic Muslims in the Netherlands]. Amsterdam University Press.

Claes, E., Flachet, T., Moustatine, A., & De Backer, M. (2020). *Radicalisering: Donkere spiegel van een kwetsbare samenleving* [Radicalisation: Dark mirror of a vulnerable society]. Academia Press.

Coolsaet, R. (2016). *All radicalisation is local: The genesis and drawbacks of an elusive concept* (Egmont paper, 84). http://www.egmontinstitute.be/content/uploads/2016/05/ep84.pdf?type=pdf

Debruyne, P. (2015). *Jeugdwerk en radicalisme: Dromen van een andere wereld (Opinie)* [Youth work and radicalism: Dreams of a different world. (Opinion piece)]. https://sociaal.net/opinie/jeugdwerk-en-radicalisme/

Fadil, N., & de Koning, M. (2019). Turning 'radicalization' into science: Ambivalent translations into the Dutch (speaking) academic field. In N. Fadil, M. de Koning, & F. Ragazzi (Eds.), *Radicalisation in Belgium and the Netherlands: Critical perspectives on violence and security* (1st ed., pp. 53–80). I. B. Tauris.

Figoureux, M. (2021). *'Stranger Danger!' Mapping the (counter-)framing, perception of, and response strategies to migration and radicalisation in Belgium* [Doctoral dissertation, KU Leuven].

Frissen, T. (2019). *(Hard)wired for terror: Unravelling the mediatized roots and routes of 'radicalization'* [Doctoral dissertation, KU Leuven].

Gielen, A.-J. (2008). *Radicalisering en identiteit: radicale rechtse en moslimjongeren vergeleken* [Radicalisation and identity: Radical right-wing and Muslim youth compared]. Amsterdam University Press.

Jaeggi, R. (2014). *Alienation.* Columbia University Press.

Jaminé, S., & Fadil, N. (2019a). (De-)radicalisation as a negotiated practice: An ethnographic case study in Flanders. In N. Fadil, M. de Koning, & F. Ragazzi (Eds.), *Radicalisation in Belgium and the Netherlands: Critical perspectives on violence and security* (1st ed., pp. 169–193). I. B. Tauris.

Jaminé, S., & Fadil, N., (2019b). *Tussen preventie en veiligheid. De Belgische aanpak in de strijd tegen radicalisering* [Between prevention and security. The Belgian approach in the fight against radicalisation]. http://www.belspo.be/belspo/brain-be/projects/FinalReports/FAR_Fin-Rep_nl.pdf

Micheron, H. (2020). *Le jihadisme francais: Quartiers, Syrie, prisons* [French jihadism: Neighbour-hoods, Syria, prisons]. Gallimard.

Plokhooij, O. (2020). *The Netherlands in dialogue: A structural approach to dialogue across society.* https://leerwegdialoog.nl/2020/04/15/the-netherlands-in-dialogue-a-structural-approach-to-dialogue-across-society/

Schmid, A. P. (2013). Radicalisation, de-radicalisation, counter-radicalisation: A conceptual discussion and literature review. *ICCT Research Paper, 4*(2), 1–91. https://doi.org/10.19165/2013.1.02

Somers, B. (2016). *Samen leven: Een hoopvolle strategie tegen IS* [Living together: A hopeful strategy against IS]. Houtekiet.

Stephens, W., Sieckelinck, S., & Boutellier, H. (2021). Preventing violent extremism: A review of the literature. *Studies in Conflict and Terrorism, 44*(4), 346–361. https://doi.org/10.1080/1057610X.2018.1543144

Van Bouchaute, B., Van Hove, T., Görgöz, R., Debaene, R., & Kerger, D. (2018). *Deradicalisering als uitdaging voor het jeugdwelzijnswerk. PWO 2016-2017: 'Preventie van radicalisering via positieve identiteitsontwikkeling in jeugdwelzijnswerk' (Syntheserapport)* [Deradicalisation as a challenge to youth welfare work. Fund for Applied Scientific Research 2016–2017: 'Prevention of Radicalisation through positive Identity Development in Youth Welfare Work. Synthesis Report]. Artevelde University College.

Van Leuven, A. (2013). *Brussels' alleged no-go zone: Anthropological perspectives on marginality and criminality in Brussels' Canal Zone* [MSc. Dissertation, KU Leuven].

Van Leuven, A. (2017). Radicaliseringsbeleid als blijvende en actieve strijd om het vertrouwen. De Mechelse integrale aanpak in radicaliseringsprocessen: Een antropologische kijk [Radicalisation policy as sustainable and active strife for trust. The City of Mechelen's integrated approach to processes of radicalisation: An anthropological perspective]. In M. De Waele, H. Moors, A. Garssen, & J. Noppe (Eds.), *Aanpak van gewelddadige radicalisering* [Approaching violent radicalisation] (1st ed., pp. 91–108). Maklu.

Wacquant, L. (2008). *Urban outcasts: A comparative sociology of advanced marginality.* Polity Press.

Zijderveld, A. (1974). *Institutionalisering: Een studie over het methodologisch dilemma der sociale wetenschappen* [Institutionalisation: A study on the methodological dilemma of the social sciences]. Boom.

13

'WAIT, WHAT?! ISLAMOPHOBIA EXISTS IN NEWFOUNDLAND AND LABRADOR?': THEORISING POLITE DISMISSAL OF ANTI-ISLAMOPHOBIA PUBLIC ENGAGEMENT

SOBIA SHAHEEN SHAIKH & JENNIFER A. SELBY

Abstract

This chapter theorises the polite dismissal of a university-sponsored public engagement project on Islamophobia in the Canadian province of Newfoundland and Labrador (NL), Canada. We draw from our experience working on this anti-racism project to map in particular the colonial resistance of provincial government officials. We use our correspondence with the NL provincial government, the Newfoundland and Labrador House of Assembly records (2000–2020), and autoethnographic data to analyse our experience of advocating for anti-Islamophobia. We theorise polite disengagement as an example of white settler logics. We also outline shifts in our definition and in the reception of anti-racism at the provincial level. We conclude by discussing new ways Islamophobia and anti-Muslim racism are being squeezed out, even if through an anti-racist provincial forum.

Keywords: Islamophobia, anti-Muslim racism, Canada, Newfoundland and Labrador, advocacy, university public engagement

Introduction

This chapter explores the polite dismissive responses we encountered amidst our advocacy work through an anti-racist project that aimed to address Islamophobia in the Canadian province of Newfoundland and Labrador (NL). This project, 'Addressing Islamophobia in NL', was a direct response to increasing anti-Muslim extremism we witnessed and experienced across

Canada and globally.[1] This now four-year collaborative, community-engaged project's main objectives were to improve localised knowledge and develop strategies to respond to Islamophobia, anti-Muslim racism and other social relations of racism in the province. While the project received both broad support and hostile refutation,[2] we focus here on the project's polite dismissal by some of our partners, the public, the media and officials from the provincial government from 2017 to 2021. The project had three phases: an initial period of public consultations in 2017, a second segment centred on our community-engaged conference in 2018 and a third phase, beginning with the launch of our report and recommendations in 2019 until the present. We characterise these polite dismissals as a gentle 'squeezing out' of anti-racism work (Ahmed, 2012). Drawing primarily on autoethnographic and discourse analysis of our own public engagement project, we argue that the denial of the existence of Islamophobia and anti-Muslim racism in the province is embedded through the logics of white settler colonialism apparent in Canadian and sub-state NL nationalisms.

The first half of this chapter begins with an overview of the origins and parameters of the 'Addressing Islamophobia in NL' community project, our methodology, and how we conceptualised Islamophobia and anti-Muslim racism. We then theorise polite disengagement as an example of white settler logics expressed in various ways throughout the history of the project, expressed through a denial of the existence of Islamophobia and racism in the province. In both sections, we outline shifts in our definition and in the reception of anti-racism at the provincial level. We conclude by discussing new ways Islamophobia and anti-Muslim racism are being squeezed out, even if through an anti-racist provincial forum.

The Addressing Islamophobia in NL Community-University Project

Like many Canadians, we were stunned by the assassination of six men at the Islamic Cultural Centre of Québec City, Québec, on 29 January 2017, the worst overtly Islamophobic attack in Canadian history. Although the attack happened in the province of Québec, several shows of support for the St John's, NL Muslim community were organised, including a human shield around a local mosque (Tobin, 2017). Community members in St John's also gathered for an impromptu meeting and, over the next 30 days, the Anti-Racism Coalition of NL (ARC–NL) came into being. ARC–NL members encouraged us to undertake consultations on Islamophobia in the province and local community (held in 2017).

We reached out to social services and community, university and advocacy organisations based in St John's. Forty people from 27 organisations and groups attended two two-hour meetings, and we also consulted with others unable to attend in person.[3] After the consultations, we undertook a year-long community-engaged conference planning process, culminating in a two-day community-facilitated conference in September 2018. We worked with a team of students, individuals from local community organisations, the ARC–NL and the National Council of Canadian Muslims (NCCM). The NCCM is a national civil liberties and advocacy organisation and a national leader in anti-Islamophobia training; we chose to liaise with them for local-programming support. Our primary goal was to build local capacity on anti-racism and Islamophobia using a 'train-the-trainer' model that we adapted to the specific ethnocultural and historical context of NL.[4] In addition to our two-day conference, we organised a film series and participated in (and led) a number of other vigils and solidarity events on-campus and in the community.[5] Much of our anti-Islamophobia and anti-racist advocacy culminated in building strong relationships with social justice and anti-racist organisations, particularly in response to national and international events.[6]

Following the conference, we wrote and disseminated a community report that included three provincial-focused recommendations to the government to address Islamophobia and racism in NL (Shaikh & Selby, 2019), beginning the formal lobbying stage of our project. The three main recommendations to the provincial government were that the Government of NL (1) develop an anti-racism/anti-Islamophobia action plan; (2) fund the Human Rights Commission of NL and the Anti-Racism Coalition of NL to monitor and report on the prevalence and effects of incidents of racist, Islamophobic and other forms of cultural and religious discrimination; and (3) promote anti-racism and anti-Islamophobia in all sectors through public education, collaborative community discussions and government policy, in all sectors in which the provincial government have jurisdiction (Shaikh & Selby, 2019).

Most recently, a solidarity vigil event at the Al Noor Mosque in St John's in June 2021 offered a poignant reminder of the years-long squeezing out of anti-Islamophobia work. We assisted in mourning the unspeakable tragedy in London, Ontario, where four members of the Afzaal family were murdered while out for an evening stroll together, to express solidarity with Muslim communities across Canada, and to demand local action on Islamophobia in the province. Among the dozen speakers was the provincial Minister of the Department of Immigration, Population Growth and Skills, Minister Gerry

Byrne. At that stage, we had engaged (and critiqued) Minister Byrne for more than four years.[7] In our short address, we referenced our 2019 project report released to the public in September 2019 (Shaikh & Selby, 2019). Supporters in the crowd yelled out, 'Shame!' One of the painted cardboard posters held up in the air at the event, aimed directly at this Minister and his office, asked, 'Why was the Addressing Islamophobia Report ignored?' In his short address, which followed ours, the Minister did not acknowledge the anti-Islamophobia and anti-racist advocacy of our team or community partners (including the project's provincial policy recommendations). Instead, after sharing his condolences with the Muslim community, he re-announced the provincial government's plans to launch a task force on anti-racism, which had been soft-launched a few weeks earlier (Government of NL, 2021). Inexplicably, the Minister spent considerable time in his speech thanking the police chief and force for its work. We understood this chilly encounter as consistent with the provincial government's overall dismissal of, and resistance to, anti-Islamophobia advocacy.

Key Terms: Islamophobia and Anti-Muslim Racism

Over the course of this project, our understanding of these terms has shifted in two ways. While we used the word 'Islamophobia' in the title of this community engagement project, we grappled with the implications of this term, both as a discourse-in-practice, and in relation to the long-standing academic and activist debates. Since our 2017 consultations, our use of the term 'Islamophobia' has shifted in two ways. First, we now understand Islamophobia as not just the discrimination of Muslims, but also the discrimination of those who are assumed to be Muslim. We now better recognise how other forms of anti-Muslimness are tied to the historical maintenance of white and colonial dominance that often go deeper than just plain fear and hate. For these reasons, we see the fear and hatred of Muslims (real or perceived) as a consequence of historic and systemic anti-Muslim racism. Second, in the early stages of our project, we used the words 'irrational fear and/or hatred of Islam and Muslims' in relation to 'phobia' and quickly discarded the word 'irrational' for similar reasons. The 'phobia' suffix was rightly critiqued for its ableism, sanism[8] and individualism. Nevertheless, like the term 'xenophobia', Islamophobia continues to have currency and salience in public discourses about anti-Muslim racism, prejudice and discrimination.

Anti-Muslimness is embedded within interlocking relations of oppression. For this reason, we now favour conceptualising anti-Muslimness as anti-Muslim racism (Love, 2017; Beydoun, 2019). We understand Islamophobia as *one* particular, historical articulation of anti-Muslimness, tied to histories of, and resistance to, colonialism, imperialism, Orientalism and racialised othering. Nevertheless, we recognise that much of the discourse about anti-Muslimness has centred on the term Islamophobia. Over the course of the project, we have sought to more clearly depict its association with overlapping and interlocking relations of racism and other intersectional discrimination.

To better consider the intersections of racism and Islamophobia, we have found Ghassan Hage's (2017) provocation in *Is Racism an environmental threat?* helpful. Hage's primary question, which relates racism to broader ecological devastation, usefully centres Islamophobia in a broader spectrum of interlocking relations of racism and other forms of oppression. Islamophobia, he says, is a 'lethal performativity of racism', itself an ever-growing targeting of a variety of racialised people, including those who are identified as Muslim, Indigenous, Black, Asian, Arab, Latinx, Roma, Jew, Sikh and/or migrant, both by the state – that is, the police, child welfare, border control – and by racists. Hage dismisses as erroneous the argument that Islamophobia cannot be conceptualised as racism because Muslims are not a race. He argues instead for remaining focused on the harm of racists. To better understand how whiteness informs anti-Muslimness, we therefore aim to disturb colonial culture while examining Indigenous–settler–migrant relations and anti-Black racism (see Patel, 2016; Mugabo, 2016). With these shifts in mind, we have come to define Islamophobia as operating with 'colonialism, anti-Semitism, religious and cultural discrimination, and other forms of intersectional oppression' (Shaikh & Selby, 2019, p. 4).

Methodology

To consider the polite dismissal of our university-based anti-racist advocacy work, we undertook a self-reflective analysis of our experience of engaging the public and provincial government ministers. We draw on critical analysis of key project correspondence, consultation and meeting notes, records of our media engagements and through Twitter and Facebook, which has been called 'autoethnography'.[9] Autoethnography relies on a mix of the methods of autobiography and ethnography, particularly detailed memory-work and note-taking about significant events that impacted us as public-facing scholars and researchers (Chang, 2008). We also draw on our various discussions and contacts made mainly between 2017 and present as part of our ongoing project. These discussions occurred in community consultations, community-engaged planning sessions, post-conference public engagement sessions, education and advocacy sessions. We also analysed three formal letters from the provincial government that we received in response to our requests for engagement. Lastly, to contextualise the political landscape of anti-racist work in NL, we searched the digitised *Hansard*, the official transcript of the proceedings of the NL House of Assembly, for issues of racism and Islamophobia from 1970 to 2020, to capture a 50-year post-Confederation period.

'Wait, what? Racism exists in NL?'

Our professional and personal experiences over more than a decade in NL suggest that there is a deep discomfort and disconnect in acknowledging that racism, racial discrimination and, in particular, Islamophobia exist in the province.[10] The rhetoric that the province is uniquely tolerant compared to the rest of Canada rests on a folkloric (and stereotypical) characterisation of Newfoundlanders and Labradorians as simple, largely unskilled labourers and fisherpeople who are exceptionally friendly. This mythos is captured in the popular 2017 Broadway musical, *Come from Away*. The award-winning musical recounts the kindness of residents in the town of Gander (population 11,500), who generously hosted many of the 7,000 passengers from 38 planes diverted to the town amidst the terrorist attacks of September 11, 2001. This 9/11 narrative of 'welcome' is especially significant in the context of our public engagement work on Islamophobia and anti-Muslim racism in the province. Islamophobia in this context sharply contrasts with the violence experienced by many Muslims and perceived-as-Muslim individuals post-9/11. In contrast, in the musical, Newfoundlanders and Labradorians are depicted as having responded with extreme generosity, supporting the travellers when few restaurants and accommodations were available.

Challenging this imaginary of welcome as foundational to the provincial culture sometimes provoked a large range of responses, all pointing to the uniqueness of NL culture, ethnicity and identity, and how these factors work to shield against hate. Some people who saw themselves as 'true Newfoundlanders', as compared to those perpetually seen as newcomers in spite of how long or for how many generations they have lived here, felt that racism exists but only because of demographics and lack of exposure to people with cultural and racial differences. Others became embarrassed or worried and wanted to be reassured that it is not really 'that bad'. And still others became hostile, not unlike other Canadians, when their ideas about NL as a kind and benevolent space were unsettled. To further consider this polite dismissal, in this section we consider three sites: responses from the public and the media work, the formal reception of our critique by three provincial ministers (through letter correspondence with them) and in broader governmental discussions in the provincial House of Assembly.

Media and Public Dismissals

We have heard people ask: 'Wait, what? Racism exists in NL?' Others have stressed, 'Maybe Islamophobia exists… but it's not *that* bad here.' While most of those who responded this way have been white, we also heard similar kinds of responses from racialised, migrant, Indigenous and self-identified Muslim people.[11] Such responses, in the form of a question, was what we heard in both our initial consultations with our community collaborators and those we engaged through our public outreach, as well as from a handful of journalists and from members of the public we engaged through the media. For example, an hour-long call-in CBC radio show in which we participated in September 2018 contributed to this rhetoric (CBC Radio, 2018). Despite our careful and multiple conversations with the show's producer prior to the show, live on the radio, the programme host framed the discussion by posing the question, 'Does racism exist in NL?' Posed this way, racism was framed in a problematically narrow and binary way. Potentially harmful in ways we did not intend, the question set up the discussion whereby some folks argued on live radio that racism did *not* exist in their experience and in their communities.

In public engagement like the above-mentioned call-in show, when it comes to questions of racial discrimination in NL, respondents tended to frame their understanding of the topic through three broad imaginaries that relate to the historical specificities of the province: the tension between Protestants and Catholics (see Korneski, 2016); urban and rural class divides (the 'baymen' who live 'past the overpass on the Trans-Canada Highway' in rural spaces along the Atlantic coast, and 'townies' who live in the City of St John's); and references to the secularisation of the province's Christian-based public education system in the 1990s (Higgins, 2011). Historians have shown how by the 19th century, three hundred years into European colonisation, everyday tensions between British and Irish settlers centred on denominational control of the education system (Rollmann, 1999). Some we engaged equated longstanding tension and discrimination between Protestants and Catholics as comparable to Islamophobia. Forms of colonial violence towards Indigenous people – past and present – did not emerge in these conversations, nor did the specificities of anti-Black, anti-Asian, anti-Latinx or anti-Muslim racism.

In the project's formal consultations, this perception extended into how many of our white, Christian interlocutors engaged with the concept of Islamophobia: that they understood it as discrimination based on religious practice and worse in larger Canadian cities. This latter claim was granted more credibility when expressed by racialised and religious-minority folks. Other attendees disagreed and offered counter-examples to suggest that both individualised and systemic racism and Islamophobia were indeed concerns. As more participants shared stories, more felt comfortable sharing their experiences. At the close of this first consultation, a consensus emerged: NL service providers and community advocates wanted to learn more about Islamophobia in spite of their initial belief that it was not really a big problem in NL.

Notably, between the first and second consultation at the end of October 2017, the question about whether or not racism or Islamophobia existed in NL was, in part, resolved by Islamophobic and anti-immigrant posters found on our campus (CBC News, 2017). Among other anti-migrant slurs, the posters described 'the Islamophobic Domination of the West'. University administrators acted swiftly to denounce the posters; campus enforcement was instructed to remove them (Emera, 2017). The culprits were never publicly identified.

Also in this same period, in October 2017, executive members of the MANAL testified before the Federal Heritage Committee in the House of Commons as part of the hearings related to Motion 103 on systemic racism and religious discrimination in Canada. Debates in Canada more largely centered on how addressing Islamophobia could impede free speech. In their intervention, MANAL executives opened their report by painting a largely positive narrative (MANAL, 2017) also referencing the *Come from Away* musical and a human shield solidarity event 3 February 2017, following the January 2017 Québec City massacre. Still, while MANAL chose to begin their submission with positive narratives about Newfoundlanders, they did not shy away from naming Islamophobia and offered a number of recommendations. This tone is in stark contrast with the media coverage that followed, most notably in a *Maclean's* article, the subtitle of which read: 'To 3,000 Muslims on the island, the province is an example to the world of how to get along' (Campbell, 2017). The article again focused on the seductive welcoming narrative of NL, rather than Islamophobia (Campbell, 2017). The *Come from Away* narrative has done work to shield critique of Islamophobia and other forms of racism in NL.

Provincial Governmental Dismissals: Letter Correspondence

Reticence to name and address Islamophobia and racism was seen most sharply throughout our advocacy with representatives of the provincial government. In the three letters we received from three different Ministers from May 2017 (from Minister Byrne, in response to our invitation to him and the Office of Multiculturalism to our community consultations), March 2018 (from Minister Davis, responding to a letter we wrote to him following his media engagement on immigrant retention in NL solely in economic terms) and October 2019 (from Minister Mitchelmore, responding to a formal meeting and our lobbying efforts around the provincial recommendations we crafted in our 2019 report), there was little recognition that Islamophobia and racism were of concern to the provincial government.

Our initial formal engagement in May 2017 with the provincial government was to invite the Minister as well as the Director of the Office of Immigration and Multiculturalism to our consultations (and later, to the conference). In his letter of response, Minister Byrne declined to participate in the Addressing Islamophobia in NL project, stating that the project 'does not fall within the mandate of the Office of Immigration and Multiculturalism', which is focused on 'supporting immigration' (G. Byrne, personal correspondence, May 17, 2017). Minister Byrne *did* list a number of efforts to support multiculturalism, inclusion, welcoming communities and cultural competency. He also recommended that we reach out to 'Newfoundland and Labrador Human Rights Commission, an arms-length agency of the Government of Newfoundland and Labrador' (G. Byrne, personal correspondence, May 17, 2017), which we did, successfully.[12]

The then-Minister's reliance on a rhetoric about multi-culturalism in Canada was predictable. Unwilling to acknowledge racism, Byrne noted that his office would 'actively acknowledge and promote cultural holidays and events' and 'increase the number and broaden the reach of Multiculturalism Week events throughout the province'. Put differently, racialised differences are contained into an annual Multiculturalism Week that does not threaten the status quo. In this move, the provincial government effectively subsumed cultural and ethnic difference through the lens of multi-culturalism, while turning a blind eye to institutionalised and deeply embedded racism.

The second letter received – dated 28 March 2019 from the Honorable Bernard Davis, Minister of Advanced Education, Skills and Labour – acknowledged the existence of racism and Islamophobia, but echoed similar erasures.

Minister Davis's letter was a response to our own letter from 28 February 2019, in which we challenged his public statements that linked the need to retain immigrants based solely on the premise of the province's economy, without considering questions of racism or cultural reception. It was not enough to focus on the labour market and jobs when thinking about immigrant retention. We asked that he and the province would take everyday Islamophobia and racism in the province seriously, in particular in relation to the well-being of migrants, and invited him to meet with us.

In response to our request to meet with him, Minister Davis wrote that he and his colleagues would 'continue to speak out, unequivocally, against hate and in support of diversity' (B. Davis, personal correspondence, March 28, 2019). For this Minister, and others, their speaking out against hate was solely in offering condolences in reference to terrorist attacks in Québec and in Christchurch, New Zealand. Despite the fact that there had been notable and public examples of racism and Islamophobia in the province, there was very little evidence of any government official speaking out against incidents of hate in *this province* (see Cooke, 2020; Emera, 2017; Dixit, 2019; Mullings et al., 2018; Tobin, 2019; Whiffen, 2021). In his letter, Minister Davis again outlined the government's active efforts 'to acknowledge and celebrate diverse cultural, religious, and national holidays', and other multi-cultural and diversity initiatives, including a diversity calendar (see Haque, 2012 for critiques of multi-culturalism).

The third letter, from Minister Christopher Mitchelmore, was in response to our meeting with him and his team on 18 September 2019, a few days prior to the public release of our recommendations. At this meeting, Shaikh, Selby, and Sulaimon Giwa (a MUNL professor and participant in the Address-ing Islamophobia conference) outlined our rationale and requested that Mitchelmore's department take action on two recommendations. In his formal response to our meeting in letter form, Mitchelmore acknowledged the importance of the project and promised that his office would review the recommendations of our community report as part of 'ongoing policy efforts to promote inclusion, respect and dignity' in the province, taking into account those of 'intersecting cultural, religious, racialised and other backgrounds' (C. Mitchelmore, personal correspondence, October 2, 2019). However, despite this acknowledgement of the issues, the minister did not propose any work or collaborative action and advised us instead to 'pursue engagement' with the private sector and labour unions. We are, of course, undertaking this work in a volunteer capacity.

Provincial Governmental Dismissals: In the House of Assembly (1970–2020)

This polite dismissal was echoed by other provincial-level politicians in the House of Assembly. To better contextualise the minimisation of racism by the provincial government, we examined discussion of racism and Islamophobia in the *Hansard*. Our search of the *Hansard* from 1970 to 2020 used the key words 'racism', 'racist', 'discrimination', 'racial discrimination' and 'Islamophobia', and found 34 records.[13] 'Islamophobia' came up in terms of a human shield three times related to this solidarity event, and twice in relation to our Addressing Islamophobia Report.[14] Most of the references to racism were in relation to the yearly UN Day for Elimination of Racial Discrimination (21 per cent). Three significant exchanges were found using the key term 'racism': in 2012, in relation to former New Democratic Party (NDP) leader, Lorraine Michael; and in 2019, in relation to two events, the first from the former Liberal Party member Perry Trimper's recorded comments about Innu people playing the 'race card' (Brake, 2019). The second 2019 moment were calls that then Liberal Minister of Fisheries and Land Resources Gerry Byrne was alleging NDP MHA Jim Dinn of supporting anti-Indigenous racist comments in a 2018 salmon fisheries advisory council meeting (McCabe, 2019).

The 2012 incident with former leader Michael is perhaps the most telling in relation to our claim that the question of whether racism exists in NL hinders meaningful dialogue about racism. Then-NDP Leader Lorraine Michael characterised then-PC Minister of Justice Felix Collins's rant about a CBC report about freedom-to-information legislation in which he made derogatory comments about developing nations as 'systemically racist' (CBC News, 2012). MHA Michael was forced to apologise twice for calling the Minister of Justice's language 'racist' in the House. Although Michael was not sanctioned for contempt of the House, on her charge of racism, the then-Speaker said: 'The language was so intemperate and distasteful – and the charge of racism is so serious and injurious to this House and all its Members – that I feel it cannot go unchallenged.'

That the use of the word 'racist' was considered so inflammatory is noteworthy. However, MHA Michael was not only criticised because of using unparliamentary language in the House, but because of her comments to the media restating her view that racism existed in NL. The severity with which allegations of racism were met is notable. Michael's statements about 'systemic racism', which suggested to the House that all people in NL could be seen as other than welcoming, tolerant and kind, fuelled outrage by members of the House.

A New Dismissal of Anti-Muslim Racism through Anti-Racism Framing

In the final stages of writing this chapter, in December 2021, the Minister of Immigration, Skills and Labour's office reached out to us by email for the first time. Along with three other ministries,[15] with one week's notice, we were invited to speak for 20 minutes on behalf of the Addressing Islamophobia in NL Project to the newly created Ministerial Committee on Anti-Racism. While we were pleased that this committee had been noticed by the provincial government (this was the first recommendation of our 2019 report), we were struck by the lack of collaboration with anti-racist organisations across the province who have been leading this work, including the Addressing Islamophobia in NL team. The hurriedness of their approach effectively silences anti-racist voices in the province, as it relies on outdated understandings of consultation. Other than the 20 minutes allotted, there has been no acknowledgement of the anti-racist work done by members of the project, including our formal community partner, ARC–NL, which has been a significant voice on issues of racism. In addition, practical challenges surfaced: the invitation came with little notice in the last week of university classes in the fall semester, and our community-based collaborative model does not allow for short turn-around.

We remain concerned that this process will echo a larger provincial project from May 2021, the Premier's Economic Recovery Team (PERT) report, known as *The Big Reset*. The report aimed to introduce 'transformational change' for the province, in order to introduce a 'better, leaner government' to reset the province's problematic fiscal situation. One of its key recommendations was to increase immigration, part of an active project to attract and retain more immigrants.[16] We were heartened to see that the PERT report (on immigration) noted that, for 'the social and economic wellbeing of the province', the provincial government should implement an anti-racism strategy that focuses on 'workplaces, schools and service providers' (PERT, 2021, p. 182). Despite this gain, the PERT report misattributed this report as the work of the 'Anti-Racism Coalition of Newfoundland and Labrador'. It also failed to cite the 2019 Addressing Islamophobia report. This misattribution, coupled with the erasure of the work we have done on anti-Muslim racism and Islamophobia, was a further sidelining of our work on addressing anti-Muslim racism. Furthermore, the inclusion of anti-racism action in an austerity report that aimed to make significant cuts to the government's budget seemed implausible. Anti-racist and anti-Islamophobia work, as we envisioned in our 2019 recommendations, requires not just lip-service, but real resources to ensure its success across all departments. It seems that it is now more difficult to ignore public conversations about racism; perhaps not being seen to address racism in meaningful ways is now more costly than in 2017, particularly with the challenges that the province faces in attracting and retaining immigrants. The challenge is to do so meaningfully and in ways that integrate all forms of racism, including anti-Muslim racism.

Conclusions

Still, the name of this public reaching out – the Ministerial Committee on Anti-Racism – maintains a kernel of hope for change: that for the first time the word 'anti-racist' has appeared in provincial-led correspondence, that a wider engagement of ministries might signify more systemic change, that our expertise is being called upon for the first time. While seemingly small, these steps are significant. Arguably, and hopefully, with this new government-led conversation on the horizon, we are now poised to enter a fourth stage in this public engagement where we can see how/whether our intervention for the provincial committee on anti-racism will appear in concrete ways the province leads going forward.

However, the persistent idea that racism and Islamophobia are barely present in the province and that Newfoundlanders and Labradorians are welcoming and generous do not allow for difficult and needed conversations about racism and Islamophobia, and more importantly, do little to eradicate rising hate. As Giwa (2018) noted in his call for a greater anti-racist response in NL, a predominantly white population may see friendliness in everyday relations, without seeing how it acts in racially self-interested ways that reinforce systemic racial discrimination. Furthermore, as our more recent engagements with the provincial government have shown, we need to be mindful of *how* government-led anti-racist initiatives are conceptualised and brought forward. Anti-racist initiatives that do not take into account the historically and contextually localised forms of racism are doomed to be no more than window dressing. As Patel (2016), Hage (2017) and Mugabo (2016) remind us, anti-Muslimness is embedded within interlocking relations of oppression, and must be read simultaneously with ongoing and embedded histories of colonial violence against Indigenous, Black and migrant peoples across the globe. Anti-racism and anti-Islamophobia initiatives must thus be collaboratively built alongside those who actively resist colonialism, imperialism, Orientalism and racialised othering.

Notes

1. Our project was formally funded from 2017–2020 by Memorial University of Newfound-land's Office of Public Engagement, by the Vice-President Academic's office, with student research assistant support through the university's Undergraduate Career Experience Programme (MUCEP), and with in-kind donations provided by the National Council of Canadian Muslims. The project is ongoing but no longer receives university funding. We both work as university professors at Memorial University of Newfoundland and Labrador (MUNL) and, as such, are also indirect employees of provincial and federal governments. We have equally co-authored this chapter.

2. More overt forms of racist dismissal have come in many forms during our community engagement: during our media work, we fielded angry and Islamophobic questions and comments from call-in show guests and, sometimes, hosts and journalists. For example, at one of our first live radio interviews in March 2018 where we were invited to discuss our project, the host read us Islamophobic and angry tweets from his twitter feed. Unbe-knownst to us, he had posted a tweet about news from a Muslim-majority country that had sentenced a woman with corporal punishment for an act of adultery. Clearly not the focus of our interview, he summarised the news and asked us to comment on it, live. We also received four different anonymous requests to obtain our project correspondence and data through our university's Information Access and Privacy Office. While as employees of a publicly funded university we understand the importance of requests for accountability through the *Access to Information and Protection of Privacy Act* (2015), we are disheartened at the frequency of these requests, which also meant additional labour for our project team and departments. Lastly, we have received hateful and racist messages on our project's social media, through regular mail, and on voicemail at our offices.

3. Though we initially conceptualised this project primarily for service providers who worked with Muslim community members, our consultations included students, labour activists, ARC–NL partners, university staff and Muslim community members.

4. NL is often understood as an immigrant-scarce province, with a Christian-majority and -practicing population, and with approximately 2 per cent visible minorities (Baker et al., 2015; Statistics Canada, 2017).

5. In addition to lobbying our provincial government, we have engaged in anti-Islamophobia advocacy and education with several of our partners, including the Muslim Association of NL (MANAL), NCCM and ARC–NL. For example, we lobbied the City of St John's mayor, councillors and staff to commemorate 29 January as a Day of Remembrance and Action Against Islamophobia, and to create a new anti-racist position on the city's Inclusion Committee. We also co-organised and participated in responses to white supremacist at-tacks on places of worship such as those in Québec, Canada (in 2017), Pittsburgh, USA (in 2018) and Christchurch, New Zealand (2019).

6. We were engaged by the NCCM, local Muslim groups and other anti-Islamophobia activ-ists across the country, when several Faculty of Medicine students at MUNL formally complained about the Islamophobic, racist and transphobic social media posts of a self-identified 'Islamophobe' medical resident (Cooke, 2020). Also, after discovering an act of vandalism at a new mosque being constructed in Conception Bay South, NL (a town close to St John's), we consulted with the Ahmadiyya Muslim Jama'at Canada as they determined their responses (Whiffen, 2021). Notably, there was little local, public or governmental outcry about this violence.

7.   This was formerly the Department of Advanced Education, Skills and Labour, where the Office of Immigration and Multiculturalism is housed.

8.   For a fuller discussion of sanism, see Poole and Ward (2013).

9.   Our project Twitter account is https://twitter.com/addressingnl; the Anti-Racism Coalition of NL's Facebook page is https://www.facebook.com/groups/1557601017591390.

10.   In 2017, when the project began, there was little acknowledgement of racism. Polling data from 2018 suggest 13 per cent of Newfoundlanders and Labradorians have experienced racial discrimination (and 9 per cent from 2013 to 2018) (Mcneish, 2018; Giwa, 2018; Mullings et al., 2018; Wilkins-Laflamme, 2018).

11.   We recognise that there are multiple and understandable reasons for racialised and Muslim communities to rhetorically minimise the existence of racism and Islamophobia.

12.   The director of the NL Human Rights Commission participated actively in our consultations and ended up co-facilitating two sessions at our September 2018 conference: one on workplace accommodation and another on human rights legislation in Canada.

13.   As a point of comparison, we looked up 'gas prices' in the same 50-year period; 64 records emerged.

14.   Following our search in 2020, there have been more references to racism in the *Hansard*. In June 2021, following the terrorist attack on the Afzaal family in London, Ontario, NDP MHA Jim Dinn called the attack 'an act of terrorism' and Liberal MHA Gerry Byrne called it 'an attack of cowardice and evil' (as cited in CBC, 2021).

15.   The other ministries are Indigenous Affairs and Reconciliation, Education and Justice and Public Safety.

16.   On the 'The Way Forward' website, under the 'Attract and Retain More Immigrants' (https://www.gov.nl.ca/thewayforward/action/attract-and-retain-more-immigrants/), the government identifies that there has been 'significant progress,' including increases in attracting immigrants, entrepreneurial initiatives, labour integration initiatives, and multicultural-welcoming initiatives (see also https://www.gov.nl.ca/immigration/files/Im-migrationInitiatives201920web.pdf).

References

Ahmed, S. (2012). *On being included: Racism and diversity in institutional life*. Duke University Press.

Baker, J., Price, J., & Walsh, K. (2015). Unwelcoming communities: Youth observations of racism in St. John's, Newfoundland and Labrador, Canada. *Journal of Youth Studies, 19*(1), 103–116. https://doi.org/10.1080/13676261.2015.1052048

Beydoun, K. A. (2019). *American Islamophobia. Understanding the roots and rise of fear*. University of California Press.

Brake, J. (2019, September 16). *Premier meeting with Innu leadership over MHA's racist remarks*. APTN National News. https://www.aptnnews.ca/national-news/premier-meeting-with-innu-leadership-over-mhas-racist-remarks/

Campbell, M. (2017, November 2). *How Newfoundlanders are taking a remarkable stand against Islamophobia*. Maclean's. https://www.macleans.ca/society/how-newfoundlanders-are-taking-a-stand-against-islamophobia/

CBC News (2012, June 20). *Michael apologizes for 'racism' comment*. https://www.cbc.ca/news/canada/newfoundland-labrador/michael-apologizes-for-racism-comment-1.1164582

CBC News (2017, October 8). *MUN condemns Islamophobic posters appearing on campus.* https://www.cbc.ca/news/canada/newfoundland-labrador/mun-condemns-islamaphobic-posters-1.4345916

CBC News (2021, April 10). *Despite years of anti-Muslim incidents, N.L. government slow to respond, says anti-racism group.* https://www.cbc.ca/news/canada/newfoundland-labrador/arc-nl-addressing-racism-after-london-attack-1.6059015

CBC Radio (2018, September 20). 'Cross-Talk' on 'Racism and Discriminations in NL'. https://podcast-a.akamaihd.net/mp3/podcasts/crosstalk-J1pZYJq8-20180920.mp3

Chang, H. (2008). *Autoethnography as method.* Left Coast Press.

Cooke, R. (2020, June 17). Doctor facing racism complaints no longer licensed to practice medicine in N.L. *CBC News.* https://www.cbc.ca/news/canada/newfoundland-labrador/zachary-kuehner-licence-deactivated-1.5613933

Dixit, P. (2019, February 26). Racist attacks make me feel like a guest in the place I've long called home. *CBC News.* https://www.cbc.ca/news/canada/newfoundland-labrador/pov-more-than-skin-deep-prajwala-dixit-1.5029959

Emera, M. (2017, October 19). Islamophobic posters found at Memorial University. *The Charlatan.* https://charlatan.ca/2017/10/islamophobic-posters-found-at-memorial-university/

Giwa, S. (2018, April 18). Newfoundland needs immigrants and anti-racism action now. *The Conversation.* https://theconversation.com/newfoundland-needs-immigrants-and-anti-racism-action-now-94712

Government of Newfoundland and Labrador (Government of NL), (n.d.) Office of Immigration and Multiculturalism. https://www.gov.nl.ca/ipgs/department/branches/workforce/immigration/

Government of Newfoundland and Labrador (Government of NL), (2021, July 7). 'Ministerial Committee on Anti-Racism Sets Path for Action'. Press Release. Office of Immigration, Population Growth and Skills, https://www.gov.nl.ca/releases/2021/ipgs/0707n06/

Hage, G. (2017). *Is racism an environmental threat?* John Wiley & Sons.

Haque, E. (2012). *Multiculturalism within a bilingual framework: Language, race, and belonging in Canada.* University of Toronto Press.

Higgins, J. (2011). *The collapse of denominational education.* Heritage Newfoundland & Labrador. http://www.heritage.nf.ca/articles/society/collapsedenominationaleducation.php

House of Assembly – NL – Hansard (n.d.). The Government of Newfoundland and Labrador. https://www.assembly.nl.ca/houseBusiness/Hansard/

House of Assembly – NL – Hansard (2012, June 19). The Government of Newfoundland and Labrador. https://www.assembly.nl.ca/houseBusiness/Hansard/ga47session1/12-06-19.htm

Korneski, K. (2016). *Conflicted colony: Critical episodes in nineteenth-century Newfoundland and Labrador* (10th ed.). McGill-Queen's Press – MQUP.

Love, E. (2017). *Islamophobia and Racism in America.* NYU Press.

MANAL (Muslim Association of Newfoundland and Labrador) (2017). *Testimony of the Muslim Association of Newfoundland and Labrador for M103.* House of Commons Committee on Canadian Heritage. https://www.manal.ca/sites/default/files/MANAL%20Testimony_23_10_2017.pdf

McCabe, M. (2019, November 7). *Gerry Byrne hurls accusations of racism, poaching to critics in legislature.* CBC News. https://www.cbc.ca/news/canada/newfoundland-labrador/byrne-accusations-legislature-1.5352183

Mcneish, S. (2018, March 22). *Poll says: Newfoundlanders and Labradorians suffering racial discrimination.* Saltwire Press. https://www.saltwire.com/newfoundland-labrador/news/poll-says-newfoundlanders-and-labradorians-suffering-racial-discrimination-195715/

Mugabo, D. (2016). On rocks and hard places: A reflection on antiblackness in organizing against Islamophobia. *Critical Ethnic Studies,* 2(2), 15–183. doi:10.5749/jcritehnstud.2.2.0159.

Mullings, D. V., Adjei, P. B., Derraugh, L. A., & Taho, L (2018). *Attracting and retaining professionals in Labrador*. The Harris Centre, Memorial University. https://www.mun.ca/harriscentre/ PopulationProject/Professionals_in_Lab_Report.pdf

Office of Immigration and Multiculturalism. (2019, April 11). *The way forward on immigration in Newfoundland and Labrador*. The Government of Newfoundland and Labrador Canada. https://www.gov.nl.ca/immigration/welcome-to-newfoundland-and-labrador-immigration/ the-way-forward-on-immigration-in-newfoundland-and-labrador/

Office of Immigration and Multiculturalism. (2021, February 5). *Mandate*. The Government of Newfoundland and Labrador. https://www.gov.nl.ca/immigration/mandate/

Patel, S. (2016). Complicating the tale of 'Two Indians': Mapping 'South Asian' complicity in white settler colonialism along the axis of caste and anti-Blackness. *Theory & Event*, 19(4). https://www.muse.jhu.edu/article/633278

Poole, J., & Ward, J. (2013). Breaking open the bone: Storying, sanism and mad grief. In B. A. LeFrançois, R. J. Menzies, & G. Reaum (Eds.), *Mad matters: A critical reader in Canadian mad studies* (pp. 94–104). Canadian Scholars Press.

Premier's Economic Recovery Team (PERT) (2021). *The big reset: The report of the premier's economic recovery team*. https://thebigresetnl.ca/wp-content/uploads/2021/05/PERT-FullReport.pdf

Rollmann, H. (1999). *Religion in Newfoundland and Labrador*. Heritage Newfoundland & Labrador. https://www.heritage.nf.ca/articles/society/religion.php

Shaikh, S. S., & Selby, J. A. (2019). *Addressing Islamophobia in NL: Community report*. Memorial University. https://www.mun.ca/relstudies/more/AddressingIslamophobia/AI_Report_Recommendations_FINAL.pdf

Statistics Canada (2017, February 8). *Focus on geography series, 2016 census*. https://www12. statcan.gc.ca/census-recensement/2016/as-sa/fogs-spg/Facts-pr-eng.cfm?Lang=Eng&GK =PR&GC=10&TOPIC=7

Tobin, S. (2017, February 3). Canada has spoken, no to hate: Hundreds support human shield for N.L. Muslim community. *CBC News*. https://www.cbc.ca/news/canada/newfoundland-labrador/human-shield-mosque-newfoundland-1.3965124

Tobin, S. (2019, February 18). *CBC News*. https://www.cbc.ca/news/canada/newfoundland-labrador/hasan-hai-racist-facebook-comments-1.5023426

Whiffen, G. (2021, February 2). Minors cause an estimated $15K worth of damage to new mosque in Newfoundland. Saltwire. https://www.saltwire.com/nova-scotia/news/minors-cause-an-estimated-15k-worth-of-damage-to-new-mosque-in-newfoundland-548130/

Wilkins-Laflamme, S. (2018). Islamophobia in Canada: Measuring the realities of negative attitudes toward Muslims and religious discrimination. *Canadian Review of Sociology*, 55(1), 86–110. https://doi.org/10.1111/cars.12180

14

MUSLIM COMMUNITIES AND THE COVID-19 PANDEMIC: THE COMPLEX FACES OF PROTECTION

SALAM EL-MAJZOUB, ANABELLE VANIER-CLÉMENT & CÉCILE ROUSSEAU

Abstract

In the face of a collective crisis such as the COVID-19 pandemic, community and spiritual resources can play an essential role in making sense of adversity, promoting solidarity and offering consolation and support to the most vulnerable. However, in such contexts, priorities are often established based on the needs and demands of the majority, and may replicate or amplify prejudices and exclusion processes. In the province of Québec, Canada, where the Muslim communities represent a minority, religious Muslim leaders have faced many challenges in asserting the protective character of religion, and in offering spiritual and social support to the Muslim community. This chapter describes the issues encountered by the Muslim community of Québec during the pandemic, and the strategies implemented across Canada to respond. Based on observations and field notes taken during interventions aimed at bringing together communities and Montréal public health services, it shows how mobilisation during the pandemic was based on pre-existing alliances, but also how the crisis context made it possible to overcome certain divisions and to create or consolidate bridges with the majority and local and national institutions. The impact of such processes on minority–majority relations is discussed.

Keywords: COVID-19 pandemic, Muslim communities, Montréal, public health

The Muslim Community's Grassroots Efforts During the COVID-19 Pandemic

The COVID-19 pandemic started in Canada in the spring of 2020, and led governments to make urgent decisions to limit virus transmission in an ever-changing crisis with initially limited knowledge. While necessary given the novelty and dangerous effects of the virus, strict confinement measures had detrimental effects on mental health (Laforest et al., 2020). Some spoke of a second wave of mental health needs following waves of virus transmission. Although 'everyone is in the same boat' was a rallying message at first, it became clear that everyone was in the same storm, but not the same boat. The psychological and physical impacts of viral transmission disproportionately affected minority groups who were already experiencing social disadvantage, or were overrepresented among essential workers (Cleveland et al., 2020). Minorities' multiple vulnerabilities in housing, employment, socio-economic status, migratory status and linguistic capacities impacted their understanding of public health measures and their ability to apply them (INESS, 2020).

This chapter discusses issues faced by the Muslim community of Canada during the pandemic, and the manners in which the community organised itself – at a grassroots level and in collaboration with regional public health units and other key actors – to get through the crisis and protect itself and the population at large from the virus. We will use the example of the Québec province, particularly of the Montréal area, to illustrate these local processes.

Based on field notes, observations and interviews with key actors, we will show how a collaboration between Muslim leaders and Montréal public health services during different waves of the pandemic partially countered divisiveness, and bridged between institution and community. Facilitating factors and barriers will be highlighted, as well as the impact of such processes on social polarisation and minority–majority relations.

Finally, we will argue that, although painful, stressful and a source of inequities, the crisis and associated adversity highlighted the Muslim community's strengths and resources, and its important contribution to mainstream society.

Muslims in Canada do not form a homogeneous community. They represent 3.2 per cent of the country's population (Statistics Canada, 2011a), mainly live in the urban centres of Ontario, Québec and Alberta, and are mostly professionals selected by the immigration services for their potential economic and social contribution (Statistics Canada, 2011b). Although the community is highly heterogeneous in terms of social, ethnic and racial composition, and is comprised of different spiritual trends and traditions, its members share a common faith, and because of that, face similar forms of prejudice. In this chapter, the expression 'Muslim community' will be used to refer to all of the country's heterogeneous Muslim communities.

On 12 March 2020, at the dawn of the first lockdown of the pandemic, the Muslim Medical Association of Canada (MMAC) and the Canadian Council of Imams (CCI) got together to form the Canadian Muslim Covid-19 Task Force (CMCTF), to protect Canadian Muslims against COVID through tailored information. The MMAC is a non-profit organisation representing Muslim physicians in Canada, while the CCI is a collective leadership of imams across Canada. At this point, social gatherings were proven to be linked to viral transmission, and houses of worship including mosques to be sites of spread (Hernandez et al., 2020). Although Canadian Muslims, like other minority groups, were at high risk of COVID-19 infection and its outcomes, early public messages overlooked multiple layers of minorities' vulnerabilities, and offered little to no tailored information about distancing measures for specific groups. The gap in public health communication had to be filled, and this is what the CMCTF aimed to accomplish. To increase its scope and outreach, it expanded to include 30 Canadian Muslim non-governmental and community organisations.

It did not take long for the CMCTF to be considered an expert of Muslim community health, centralising multi-language resources, translating and adapting public health messages for Canadian Muslims, and providing recommendations for mosques to operate safely. On 12 March, before it became a public health measure, the CMCTF called for the suspension of large congregational prayers nationally, including Friday prayers (Canadian Council of Imams, & Muslim Medical Association of Canada, 2020a). Friday prayer at the mosque is an obligatory worship for Muslim men in most Islamic traditions. Canadian religious scholars advising against it (or against the yearly pilgrimage) had to draw a rationale based on sacred texts and prophetic traditions, and provide a sound Islamic legal decree. Religious scholars did so by showing that the sanctity of life in Islam takes precedence over religious obligations, and by giving the example of public health measures in the early years of Islam, when Friday prayers at the mosque were cancelled and travel restrictions imposed in times of natural disaster or pandemics (Canadian Council of Imams, & Muslim Medical Association of Canada, 2020b). The CMCTF compiled resources in 14 languages, and answers to frequently asked questions (FAQs) from the community, that were used by hospitals in Ontario. It developed nine mosque and community guidelines, and disseminated them to more than 500 mosques nationally using various

means of communication and media platforms, allowing them to reach out
to many community members (R. Mohammed, personal communication,
October 18, 2021).

The CMCTF initiatives also included tackling vaccine hesitancy in the
Muslim community, developing guidelines on how to safely observe Ramadan
and Eid and facilitating the creation of temporary vaccination clinics in
mosques. To tackle vaccine hesitancy, the CMCTF provided recommendations and Islamic ruling on the vaccines' ingredients, answered commonly
asked questions through a FAQ document and held 11 virtual townhalls
headlined by a religious authority, a physician and a community advocate
(Canadian Muslim Covid-19 Task Force, 2020). Townhalls were offered
in English, French, Arabic, Bengali, Urdu, and Somali (Canadian Muslim
Covid-19 Task Force, 2021). One of the townhalls was given to religious
leaders to explore their own concerns and empower them to answer their
communities' preoccupations about the vaccines. Guidelines to practice a
safe 2021 Ramadan under strict lockdown were developed following regional
health measures and reviewed by seven regional public health units. The
CMCTF's collaboration with public health units also facilitated the creation
of temporary vaccination clinics in mosques to ensure vaccination uptake
was not delayed due to fasting. Echoed by imams in mosques nationally, the
CMCTF message focused on Muslims' strengths and resilience, and on the
positive aspects of celebrating Ramadan within one's family bubble (reinforcing family ties and focusing worship on personal development). It also gave
meaning to these challenging and isolating times. As the pandemic continued,
the CMCTF partnered with mental health community organisations to
assess community needs and address them through a virtual workshop series
on recovery after a pandemic. By 1 September 2021, the tools and resources
were used in more than 80 mosques, the registered online events had been
viewed more than 1,100 times, posts on Facebook had reached more than
740,000 accounts and the Task Force's initiatives had featured 133 times in
the press (Helal et al., 2021).

Negotiations and Collaboration with Regional Public Health: The Case of Québec

From the beginning of the pandemic on, collaborative discussions between
public health authorities and spiritual Muslim leaders have been taking place
in the province of Québec.

Meetings with Public Health Services during the First Wave of the Pandemic

During the first wave, in the spring of 2020, and in anticipation of the holy month of Ramadan, Montréal public health services reached out to a transcultural psychiatry team to plan and mediate a meeting with Montréal's Muslim community. The goal of this meeting was to reinforce respect for physical distancing measures to protect the Muslim community and the general population. As a mental health team based in Montréal's diverse Parc-Extension borough and with an expertise in inter-community relations and social polarisation, the transcultural team often mediates between majority and minority groups in divisive situations (Rousseau, Savard, et al., 2021). During the strict confinement of the spring of 2020, congregations of any sort were forbidden, and the provincial governmental weekly press conferences acknowledged the majority's celebrations (Easter), but not Ramadan that was approaching for Muslims. Ramadan is a month of fasting from dawn to sunset, of charity and increased worship. Inviting isolated community members to break the fast with one's family and visiting other families when breaking the fast are seen as acts of worship. Nightly prayers take place in congregation. Considering the centrality of the month of Ramadan in Muslims' life and the challenges of practicing it during a world pandemic, a meeting with Montréal public health services seemed particularly appropriate.

A devout and active member of Montréal's Muslim community who is also part of the transcultural team invited religious leaders of both Sunni and Shiite mosques from various boroughs of the Montréal area, to the meeting, and acted as a co-host. Two virtual meetings took place in April 2020 – one in French and one in English – in which the transcultural team would try to facilitate inter-cultural dialogue and co-create solutions with the Montréal regional public health unit, drawing on the resilience and strengths of the Muslim community.

At the first meeting, the 14 attending Muslim leaders expressed their communities' concerns and needs at a time of heightened global crisis. They took turns explaining the central role of mosques for worship and for answering social and community needs. Indeed, mosques offer vulnerable individuals access to food, and guidance to resources and social services. Imams mediate family conflicts, officiate divorces, marriages and funerals, and often provide individual support and counselling. With the closure of places of worship, imams felt they could not be as easily reached by the most vulnerable who stopped having access to the mosque and who may have difficulties attending virtual religious services. Leaders also worried they would not be allowed to open mosques during Ramadan to provide food boxes and meals to break the fast. Public health representatives listened to the leaders' concerns and demands, and shared their own preoccupations regarding the physical presence of community members in mosques in a pandemic context (El-Majzoub et al., 2021).

The meeting hosts' priority was to listen to, and validate the leaders' experiences and points of views, and to maintain the power dynamics as horizontal as possible. Both visibly Muslim *and* part of the institution, the Muslim co-host code-switched between minority and majority cultures, using respectful phrasing and spiritual terms when addressing religious authorities and elders. Each religious leader was given unlimited time to discuss their concerns. The transcultural team acted as a mediator and facilitator, acknowledging each participant's multiple positionings within their identity, professional role, family, religion, culture, etc.

Having validated participants' concerns and needs opened the door to a common understanding of the situation, and to searching together for solutions that would satisfy all parties. Public health actors understood the challenges experienced by religious communities, and religious leaders grasped the difficulties faced by institutions when trying to uphold public health principles with equity at the local and provincial levels. Mosques and imams' frontline role is validated, as well as the fact that the spiritual support they offer is often more accessible and more adapted to community needs. The transcultural team and public health services jointly advocated for individual psychosocial services and spiritual counselling, arguing they were essential during heightened stress and global crisis. The transcultural team suggested religious leaders submit to the regional public health unit the rationale for and safety of the activities they wished to carry so that public health services can do a risk–benefit analysis and evaluate the feasibility of each demand. In addition, the transcultural team asked public health services to frame its answers in three categories: what is possible, what is a 'maybe' and what is not possible. For instance, permission was given to mosques to provide food boxes and cook meals for distribution to break the fast, if mosques used the same sanitary protocols as food banks and other community organisations. It was also recommended that mosques inform local police in advance of food distribution, to avoid misunderstandings and neighbourhood denunciations.

This initial contact and collaboration between Muslim leaders, Montréal public health services and the transcultural team fostered trust and created an alliance between religious leaders of the minority and professionals mainly part of the majority and representing the institutions. It took place at a crucial time, that is, during the acute phase of the pandemic, with its load of uncertainty, restrictions and anxiety.

This positive experience allowed for further collaboration in subsequent waves and led to the formalisation of the transcultural team's mediation work with the creation of the CoVivre programme.

The Muslim Discussion Table in Montreal

Almost a year later, in the winter of 2021, at the height of the second wave when the province of Québec was in lockdown and under curfew, as the vaccination campaign against COVID-19 was starting and the holy month of Ramadan approaching, it seemed necessary to continue the concertation work with Muslim leaders. Montréal public health services and the CoVivre programme came together and, in collaboration with the CMCTF, initiated a virtual discussion table to continue the dialogue with Muslim leaders. This second pandemic Ramadan was going to be even more challenging than the first, since it would take place under a lockdown *and* a curfew, since people were experiencing public health measures' fatigue and since the hopes for a return to normal had been deceived. Guidance was needed on how to safely practice Ramadan without losing out on the sense of comfort, meaning and connectedness central to this holy month. Although mass vaccination brought hope to many people for a return to a 'new normal', the information campaign on vaccines was not adapted to minorities' needs. Muslims were not more hesitant, but, like other groups (including the majority), they needed adapted material and access to be reassured about the safety and efficacy of the new vaccines (Rousseau, Monnais, et al., 2021; Rousseau, Monnais, et al., 2021). Although the CMCTF had developed health material tailored to Canadian Muslims' needs, this material was mainly in English and had not reached Québec's French-speaking Muslims who represent most Muslims in the province.

The Muslim discussion table was built on the previous collaborative experience between Montréal public health services, the transcultural team (now CoVivre) and the Muslim leaders, adding the CMCTF's experience and expertise in Canadian-Muslim-adapted health initiatives.

The discussion table had several important impacts, one of which was the decision to offer Muslim leaders culturally adapted information on how to safely practice Ramadan and Eid, and on COVID-19 vaccines (CMCTF's multi-lingual material, CMCTF's FAQs on vaccines translated into French by CoVivre). The Muslim discussion table also allowed for the exchange and sharing of culturally adapted practices already successful in other countries or cities, such as pop-up vaccination clinics in mosques in London, UK, and in Toronto and Ottawa, Canada (Lee-Shanock, 2021; Nazeer, 2021; Sherwood, 2021; Trinh, 2021). Facilitated by CoVivre, Montréal public health services, and Muslim doctors, more than a dozen pop-up clinics were active in Montréal and Québec City during the spring and summer of 2021. Feedback stated that having the option to get vaccinated at the local mosque was a determining factor for many Muslims to get their shot, and was perceived as a gesture of reaching out from the majority's institutions towards minority communities.

Culturally and community-adapted initiatives such as pop-up vaccination clinics in mosques represent an example of a collaborative integrated majority–minority health initiative. On the pop-up clinic's first day, the mosque's imam and a health institution representative gave a press briefing together, an initiative rarely seen in contemporary Québec. Muslims and non-Muslims were greeted and welcomed by the mosque's imam upon entrance. Individuals coming to get their vaccine received their vaccine from health workers from the majority in a space belonging to a religious minority, a symbolically meaningful experience in and of itself.

Finally, one of the table's outcomes has been to create a regular communication channel (every three weeks) between Muslim leaders and the Montréal public health institution at a time of unprecedented crisis. This channel worked in both directions: top-down with Montréal public health services explaining epidemiological data, sanitary measures and vaccination to the leaders, and bottom-up with Muslim leaders voicing their communities' preoccupations and needs to public health representatives to be transferred to the appropriate health authority. Despite these unequal roles (secular institution–religious community; majority–minority), efforts were made during the meetings to keep power dynamics as horizontal as possible.

Facilitating factors to the Muslim discussion table included: (1) the pre-existing alliances between Muslim table organisers and Muslim leaders; (2) the co-hosting of the first two meetings by someone at the junction of Muslim communities and majority's institutions; (3) the solidarity and empathy expressed to leaders following Islamophobic crimes in the spring of 2021 (shootings against a mosque in Eastern Montréal; terrorist killing of four members of a Muslim family in London, Ontario).

Challenges encountered included retaining the initial number of religious leaders at the table and working within the limits of regional public health services' power. While attendance to the first two meetings was high (15–25 Muslim leaders), it later diminished. A combination of factors could have contributed: leaders' initial motivation, possible loss of interest when the host change with consequent reduction in trust, possibly leaders' perception that they would not get much from the meetings, insufficient communication and reminders in between meetings, the CMCTF's being less recognised in Québec and some English-speaking leaders may have not developed a solid relation to the host because they were hearing everything through an interpreter. The limits of not having decision-makers from the provincial level at the discussion table were also at stake. For instance, when the unequal impact of sanitary measures on Muslim communities and the majority (cinemas were opening, but not places of worship although offering services considered 'essential' by religious communities) was discussed, Montréal public health services could not do much besides showing understanding and carrying the leaders' messages as best as possible.

Despite these limitations, the Montréal Muslim discussion table has been strengthening the collaboration between several Muslim religious leaders, Montréal public health services and other health actors. Even if it has decreased over time, the leaders' participation could be re-activated and widened in the case of future crises or emergencies.

Discussion

As we move through further stages of the COVID-19 sanitary crisis, it is important to look back and analyse what this crisis has revealed in terms of community mobilisation capacity. From within its minority position in Québec and Canada, the Muslim community was able to mobilise resources and use strategies to protect itself from the virus and its effects, in a wider context of latent and direct Islamophobia. Understanding these community-adaptive strategies and coping mechanisms is important so they can be mobilised again or maintained to the benefit of the Muslim community or to inspire other minorities.

A Sanitary Crisis in Times of Polarisation: Avoiding Stigma and Scapegoating in a Context of Latent and Direct Islamophobia

Early in the first wave, to protect their community from the virus but also from more stigma, scapegoating and Islamophobic acts, Muslim leaders mobilised and encouraged their communities to be exemplary pandemic citizens, i.e., to respect governmental sanitary measures, and, later, to get vaccinated.

Although the pandemic initially had the potential of bringing the multitude of communities together to fight a common enemy (the virus) that did not discriminate, and after a first movement towards social cohesion, the crisis led to the emergence of conspiracy theories building on prejudices about Others, and attributing the blame to traditional villains, most often Jews and Asians (Bieber, 2020). Jewish orthodox communities in Montréal were blamed in the first wave for bringing the virus from their sister community in New York and portrayed as not following public health measures. People in orthodox neighbourhoods experienced stigma, inter-community tension and denunciations to the police (Schwartz, 2020). Having had their share of negative media attention in the past, Muslim communities in Québec feared that a mosque or a gathering of Muslims could be blamed for an outbreak, which added itself to their fear of getting sick from COVID-19 and losing loved ones.

It is important to remember that in the name of secularism, state neutrality or security, restrictive policies have been enacted through the years in Québec, spanning the debate around the niqab (face covering veil), the Québec Charter of Values, and most recently Bill 21 prohibiting religious symbols for judges and teachers. Public discourse around identity and the debates surrounding the limits of multi-culturalism, pluralism and inter-culturalism have exacerbated inter-community tension and social polarisation (Hassan et al., 2019; Kirmayer, 2019). In this climate of intolerance, concurrent with an increase in far-right groups' activities, Canada witnessed its most deadly domestic terrorist attack when Alexandre Bissonnette killed six men at the Islamic Center of Quebec City in January 2017 (Perry & Scrivens, 2018). These restrictive policies in Québec should be seen in the context of the province's own history with the Church and with its own majority–minority dynamics in the wider Canadian context (Zine, 2012). Historically, Québec has been a French-speaking province in Canada with an English-speaking minority and has asserted its distinctive identity partially through legislating its own immigration and linguistic policies. The French-Canadian or 'Québécois' identity represents a minority in Canada and a linguistic minority in North America, which means it perceives itself as vulnerable to assimilation by other cultures. In addition, French-Canadians have suffered from the Church's past oppressive and dominant control over many aspects of their lives, leaving them with a still bitter memory of organised religion, which is in turn projected negatively onto most religions (Geddes, 2009). The debate in Québec around religious symbols such as the Muslim veil is also inspired by French nationalism, secularism debates in France, and nourished by the polarisation between 'Québécois' nationalists and Anglophone federalists.

Québec's nationalist politics have long interfered, if not clashed, with Canada's federalist and multi-culturalist politics. Canada is viewed internationally as a nation welcoming and valuing collective differences. The 1971 policy on multi-culturalism, born from the need for skilled immigrants to join the workforce, contributed to the country's development and identity (Wood & Gilbert, 2005). Globalisation and the abolishment of immigrant quotas from Europe led to fast demographic changes and an increase in the presence of visible minorities, threatening the vulnerability of majority groups, and brewing intolerance (Perry & Scrivens, 2018). The tragic events of September 11, 2001 acted as a turning point for tensions worldwide with the portrayal of minorities as radical and divisive. Anti-religion and anti-immigrant sentiments grew nationally in Canada, and Muslims, among other minorities, reported more discrimination and hate crimes (Graves, 2015). Policies on national security further cemented the image of Muslims as a potential threat.

Coming back to the pandemic in Québec, the Muslim community's rapid mobilisation to play an exemplary role in support of governmental measures was mainly motivated by the need to protect the most vulnerable from COVID-19, but also by the fear of an increase in anti-Muslim sentiment and scapegoating if there were to be blamed for an outbreak.

Rallying around the Leadership of Trusted Muslim Health and Religious Experts, and Taking Advantage of these Experts' Community-Adapted Initiatives

An effective strategy adopted by the Muslim community in Canada and in Québec has been to rally around the leadership of its own medical and religious experts who offered benevolent direction and adapted support in confusing times and created the CMCTF. Community members trusted CMCTF experts because they knew they had their best physical and spiritual interests at heart. They trusted their imams, from whom they seek spiritual counselling weekly, and who were themselves taking the pandemic seriously, following and encouraging people to respect public health measures and get vaccinated.

The CMCTF used its community networks to inform Muslims nationally on how to adapt religious practices and services to respect public health measures and protect the most vulnerable from COVID-19. Their work encouraged religious leaders to promote adherence to public health measures and vaccination, even when these measures were affecting worship. Their messaging switched the focus from individual sacrifice for the greater good during the pandemic, to frame it as opportunities for spiritual growth in challenging times. They encouraged Muslims to be role models and to preach by example following the religious precepts of sanctity of life, as many imams did when they got the vaccine and advertised it.

These challenging times were used to show the strength and resourceful-ness of the Muslim community. The intersectoral collaboration between faith-based health associations, and religious and community organisations through the CMCTF's work allowed for early identification of issues in the community and for the development of culturally appropriate complementary interventions to nourish policy and public health. The CMCTF's success highlights the importance of establishing alliances with communities and of empowering communities' experiential, spiritual and professional expertise.

Voicing Community Needs and Priorities to Majority Institutions, and Negotiating Spaces of Discussion about what is "Essential"

During the first wave, meetings between Muslim leaders, Montréal public health services, and the transcultural team, and later during the discussion table meetings, religious leaders voiced their communities' needs and priorities, and opened spaces for dialogue about how what is not 'essential' to some people or communities can be 'essential' to others. The leaders communicated that to religious Muslims, mosques and religious organisations are essential for their spiritual, social and psychological needs, even more so during a crisis such as a pandemic. When trying to gauge what is 'essential' in people's lives, the needs of the majority often come before those of the minorities. In a secular society like Québec, religion and religious organisations are often perceived negatively by the general population, which deems religious needs as 'non-essential'. Religion can nevertheless play a capital role in helping people make sense of a collective crisis like the pandemic, in promoting collective resiliency and solidarity, and in finding culturally and spiritually appropriate support (Koenig, 2009). In fact, recent surveys have shown that religious people have sought comfort in their faith during the pandemic, and this has helped them cope with the uncertainty of the crisis (Gecewicz, 2020; Pirutinsky et al., 2020).

While Muslims were experiencing increased feelings of alienation coming from the lack of acknowledgement of their religious and spiritual needs in mainstream discussions of what was 'essential', they were not the only religious minority in Québec to feel forgotten by the institutions. Many religious people in Québec, regardless of denomination, perceived social inequities when golf courses or public gardens opened but places of worship did not. In such context, religious communities can perceive certain permissions given by the government as inequitable and showing the existence of a double standard, thus exacerbating feelings of neglect, alienation and isolation from the secular majority. On the other hand, when institutions perceived as serving the general population actively listen to the concerns and demands of religious minority groups, minority–majority tensions are reduced, and trust and collaboration between communities and institutions increase.

During the meetings between the leaders and Montréal public health services, the centrality of Muslims' needs was validated and supported by advocating for some changes in what were considered 'essential' services, and by giving more flexibility to the community all the while maintaining the required health and sanitary standards. This process of adaptation and change from the institution remained slow, as regional public health institutions have limited political decision-making power and were themselves navigating an ever-changing crisis requiring fast response, decisiveness and precaution. However, if governments or institutions impose measures unilaterally and show little flexibility in adapting to community needs, maintaining community leaders' support in encouraging the respect of governmental measures can become challenging, especially as the pandemic endangers their work and survival.

Transforming Mainstream Perceptions and Minority-Majority Relations by Seizing the Opportunity Brought by the Shift in Polarisation and the Collaboration with Majority Institutions

With its context of uncertainty and crisis, the COVID-19 pandemic led to social polarisation around public health measures and vaccination, which allowed Québec Muslims to experience less scrutiny and to ally with other groups around public health measures. Although a consensus existed around governmental measures at the beginning of the pandemic, divisiveness around these measures eventually increased, fuelled by social media and the presence of online echo chambers reverberating and cementing extreme opinions (Jiang et al., 2021). Mainstream media witnessed an increase in moral imperatives around public health measures, creating a discourse of blame and demonisation of those not following the rules diligently. Two groups were born: pro-mask versus anti-mask, pro-distancing versus anti-distancing, pro-vaccine versus 'anti-vax' (Lang et al., 2021). Even if some of these positions are aligned with political affiliations and can be found in more right-wing communities, this is not always the case, and oversimplification stops potential dialogue around existing ambivalences with some governmental measures (Arabaghatta Basavaraj et al., 2021; Jiang et al., 2020). With this shift of social polarisation towards governmental health measures, interactions between the majority and the Muslim minority became less focused on identity and more on the ability to apply and adhere to governmental measures to help society in its fight against COVID-19.

Collaborating with institutions of the majority in the context of the pandemic also helped change mainstream perceptions of Muslims and transform minority–majority relations. Meeting with Muslim leaders allowed public health representatives to witness the community's heterogeneity, understand that many Muslims considered religious services as 'essential' especially in a time of crisis, appreciate the community leaders' willingness and motivation to contribute to the collective effort to protect the population. All of these realisations contributed to decreasing cultural biases and building trust. Efforts were made to make meetings collaborative and dialogic, to avoid hierarchy and debate and to encourage active listening and the co-creation of solutions. For Muslim leaders, being listened to and considered collaborators by secular institutions was a powerful message of acceptance and inclusion. Seeing hate crimes affecting their community acknowledged also sent the leaders a strong message of solidarity and concern for their community's safety and well-being.

Furthermore, the collaborative work with Montréal public health services and CoVivre, and the use of CMCTF's adapted information on vaccines and on how to safely practice Ramadan, allowed Muslims to act in accordance both with their religious beliefs *and* with the governmental sanitary measures. This respect for two sets of rules may have contributed to reconciling both their identity of Muslim and Québecois and allowed trust building with the non-Muslim majority by participating actively to the larger common societal goal of overcoming the COVID-19 pandemic.

Despite these considerable advances in minority–majority relations, systemic racism remains real and still is a sensitive topic in Québec politics. Many anti-Muslim incidents have shaken the sense of security of Muslim communities in the past two years: break-ins and vandalisation of mosques in Montréal, shots fired at a Montréal mosque and the hate-motivated killing of a Muslim family in London, Ontario. Acknowledging these tragedies threatening Canadian Muslims and affecting them in the core of who they are is crucial in a collaborative process as it sends the message that the community's safety and well-being is central to the process. As pre-pandemic and pandemic experiences of Canadian and 'Québécois' Muslims continue to affect their trust in institutions and whether they feel these institutions represent them, opportunities to collaborate can help repair part of the mistrust and of the feeling of alienation.

Limitations

The COVID-19 pandemic happened at a time when conversations about health inequities were starting to emerge, with more efforts by institutions to include equity, inclusion and diversity agendas, which acted as catalysts to increase collaboration between these institutions and marginalised minority communities. Although this climate did catalyse collaborations between public health services and the Muslim community of Montréal, the impact of such interventions is difficult to measure. To this date, the Québec government and public health services to do not register ethnocultural or religious affiliation when measuring COVID-19 viral transmission's impacts. While the rationale behind the absence of demographic information is to avoid blame, it deprives communities of their own data and does not allow for more targeted interventions. Qualitatively, the collaborative interventions between Muslim leaders, Montréal public health services, the transcultural team/CoVivre and the CMCTF were appreciated by the religious leaders who participated: they felt empowered and advocated in favour of public health measures in their religious organisation and congregation.

Conclusion

To protect itself both from COVID-19 and from stigma, the Muslim community in Canada mobilised itself in spiritually and culturally appropriate ways through the CMCTF, strengthened public health messaging and opened its mosques for vaccination, all of which confirmed its positioning as a model community. Early in the first wave of the pandemic, discussions and collaboration were established between Montréal public health services and Muslim leaders, with a transcultural team (later CoVivre) acting as mediator. The collaboration was later officialised during subsequent waves, to form the Muslim discussion table. The dialogic approach between Muslim leaders and Montréal public health services allowed the former to voice their concerns and specific needs, and to co-create culturally adapted solutions with the institutions. It also allowed Montréal public health services to realise the specific difficulties faced by communities and the strengths, expertise and resilience they hold. Imams were enthusiastic about initiatives like pop-up vaccination clinics in mosques, as they saw the potential to increase Muslims' trust towards the vaccine. They also thought it could help build bridges with non-Muslims in the neighbourhood since it would send a message of openness, solidarity and collaboration to the general population.

The collaborative initiatives between the Muslim community, Montréal public health services and other community actors highlighted the Muslim community's mobilisation capacity to work in alliance with secular organisations when the well-being of the community is put forward. Muslim leaders are motivated to share their perceptions and concerns, to be heard, to co-conceive innovative solutions and to be empowered with appropriate resources. As has been shown in other international crises such as the Ebola crisis, bottom-up initiatives can be more impactful when dialogue between actors is horizontal and when the community does not feel instrumentalised to further public health services' agenda (Wilkinson et al., 2017). This is done by reciprocating, listening to the concerns of the community, passing its concerns to decision-makers and showing that the community's and the whole population's well-being is a central concern. The shift of focus in social polarisation from a majority–minority polarisation to a polarisation between followers and non-followers of governmental measures, allowed for a minority–majority alignment towards the common goal of protecting the population from the virus, and thus for a form of minority–majority reconciliation. The collaboration between Muslim leaders and institutions of the majority helped reduce the leaders' feeling of being second-class citizens, and allowed the institutions to experience Muslim communities more positively. It also permitted both Muslim leaders and institutions to notice and acknowledge the similarities they share, hopefully reducing negative perceptions on both sides and opening the door to more collaborative and integrated minority–majority initiatives and to a better 'living together'.

References

Arabaghatta Basavaraj, K., Saikia, P., Varughese, A., Semetko, H. A., & Kumar, A. (2021). The COVID-19-social identity-digital media nexus in India: Polarization and blame. *Political Psychology*. doi: 10.1111/pops.12774

Bieber, F. (2020). Global nationalism in times of the COVID-19 pandemic. *Nationalities Papers*, 50(1), 13–25. doi: 10.1017/nps.2020.35

Canadian Council of Imams, & Muslim Medical Association of Canada. (2020a, March 12). *Joint Statement 1*. https://www.cmcovidtf.com/post/joint-statement-1-cci-and-mmac

Canadian Council of Imams, & Muslim Medical Association of Canada. (2020b, March 16). *Joint Statement 2*. https://www.cmcovidtf.com/post/joint-statement-2-rationale

Canadian Muslim Covid-19 Task Force. (2020, March 25). *COVID-19 vaccine FAQs*. https://www.cmcovidtf.com/faq

Canadian Muslim Covid-19 Task Force. (2021). *CMCTF townhalls on COVID-19 vaccines*. Retrieved from https://www.cmcovidtf.com/events

Cleveland, J., Hanley, J., Jaimes, A., & Wolofsky, T. (2020). *Impacts de la crise de la COVID-19 sur les « communautés culturelles » montréalaises. Enquête sur les facteurs socioculturels et structurels affectant les groupes vulnérables* [Impact of the COVID-19 crisis on cultural communities in Montréal. A survey on socio-cultural and structural factors affecting vulnerable groups]. Institut Universitaire SHERPA. https://sherpa-recherche.com/we-content/uploads/impact_covid19_communautes_culturelles.pdf

El-Majzoub, S., Narasiah, L., Adrien, A., Kaiser, D., & Rousseau, C. (2021). Negotiating safety and wellbeing: The collaboration between faith-based communities and public health during the COVID-19 pandemic. *Journal of Religion and Health, 60*(6), 4564–4578.

Gecewicz, C. (2020, April 30). *Few Americans say their house of worship is open, but a quarter say their faith has grown amid pandemic.* Pew Research Center. https://www.pewresearch.org/fact-tank/2020/04/30/few-americans-say-their-house-of-worship-is-open-but-a-quarter-say-their-religious-faith-has-grown-amid-pandemic/

Geddes, J. (2009, April 28). What Canadians think of Sikhs, Jews, Christians, Muslims. *Macleans, 4*, 20–24. https://www.macleans.ca/news/canada/what-canadians-think-of-sikhs-jews-christians-muslims/

Graves, F. (2015). *The EKOS poll: Are Canadians getting more racist?* iPolitics.

Hassan, G., Mekki-Berrada, A., Rousseau, C., Lyonnais-Lafond, G., Jamil, U., & Cleveland, J. (2019). Impact of the Charter of Quebec Values on psychological well-being of francophone university students. *Transcultural Psychiatry, 56*(6), 1139–1154.

Helal, S., Fadel, S., Refaat, M., Mohammed, R., & Khan, H. K. (2021, October 7). *The development of an interdisciplinary task force to address the needs of Canadian Muslim communities during the Covid-19 pandemic* [Poster presentation]. Public Health 2021 Santé Publique, Virtual, Canada. https://www.cpha.ca/sites/default/files/uploads/conferences/2021/ph21-program.pdf

Hernandez, M., Scarr, S., & Sharma, M. (2020, March 20). *The Korean clusters: How coronavirus cases exploded in South Korea churches and hospitals.* Reuters Graphics. https://graphics.reuters.com/CHINA-HEALTH-SOUTHKOREA-CLUSTERS/0100B5G33SB/index.html

Institut National d'excellence en santé et services sociaux (INESSS). (2020). *COVID-19 et les approches favorisant l'observance des mesures de précaution et de protection auprès des personnes en situation de vulnérabilité* [COVID-19 and approaches promoting the observance of precautionary and protective measures for people in vulnerable situations]. Institut national d'excellence en santé et en services sociaux. https://www.inesss.qc.ca/en/covid-19/services-sociaux/approches-favorisant-lobservance-des-mesures-de-precaution-et-protection-aupres-des-personnes-en-situation-de-vulnerabilite.html

Jiang, J., Chen, E., Lerman, K., & Ferrara, E. (2020). Political polarization drives online conversations about COVID-19 in the United States. *Human Behavior and Emerging Technologies, 2*, 200-211. doi: 10.1002/hbe2.202

Jiang, J., Ren, X., & Ferrara, E. (2021). Social media polarization and echo chambers: A case study of COVID-19. arXiv preprint arXiv:2103.10979

Kirmayer, L. J. (2019). The politics of diversity: Pluralism, multiculturalism and mental health. *Transcultural Psychiatry, 56*(6), 1119–1138.

Koenig, H. G. (2009). Research on religion, spirituality, and mental health: A review. *Canadian Journal of Psychiatry, 54*(5), 283–291.

Laforest, J., Roberge, M., & Maurice, P. (2020). *Réponse rapide: COVID-19 et répercussions psychosociales* [Quick response: COVID-19 and psychosocial repercussions]. Institut national de santé publique du Québec. https://www.inspq.qc.ca/sites/default/files/covid/3018-repercussions-psychosociales-covid19.pdf

Lang, J., Erickson, W. W., & Jing-Schmidt, Z. (2021). # MaskOn!# MaskOff! Digital polarization of mask-wearing in the United States during COVID-19. *PLoS One, 16*(4), e0250817 %@ 0251932-0256203.

Lee-Shanock, P. (2021, April 12). *How community advocates in COVID-19 hotspots are working to get the vaccine message out.* CBC News. https://www.cbc.ca/news/canada/toronto/community-advocates-take-lead-on-vaccinations-in-covid-hotspots-1.5983399

Nazeer, T. (2021, February 8). In the UK, Muslims find comfort in receiving vaccines at mosques. *Al Jazeera.* https://www.aljazeera.com/news/2021/2/8/in-the-uk-muslims-feel-comforted-receiving-vaccines-at-mosques

Perry, B., & Scrivens, R. (2018). A climate for hate? An exploration of the right-wing extremist landscape in Canada. *Critical Criminology, 26*(2), 169–187. doi: 10.1007/s10612-018-9394-y

Pirutinsky, S., Cherniak, A. D., & Rosmarin, D. H. (2020). COVID-19, Mental health, and religious coping among American orthodox Jews. *Journal of Religion and Health, 59*(5), 2288–2301.

Rousseau, C., Monnais, L., Tousignant, N., Mekki-Berrada, A., Mekki-Berrada, W., Gagneur, A., Gosselin, V., Santavicca, T., Ngov, C., Guenat, C., Schinazi, J., & Bolduc, E. (2021). *Understanding vaccine hesitancy and supporting vaccine decision-making: Practical guide for professionals in contact with the public in the context of COVID-19 in Quebec. A CoVivre publication.* SHERPA University Institute – Fonds de recherche du Québec Société et Culture. https://sherpa-recherche.com/wp-content/uploads/2021/06/EN_Guide_CoVivre_Court_26-juillet-2021.pdf

Rousseau, C., Monnais, L., Tousignant, N., Mekki-Berrada, A., Mekki-Berrada, W., Santavica, T., Ngov, C., Guenat, C., & Bolduc, E. (2021). *Understanding vaccine hesitance among ethnocultural communities in the context of the COVID-19 pandemic – Integral Version. A CoVivre publication.* https://sherpa-recherche.com/wp-content/uploads/2021/07/EN_Guide_CoVivre_Long_26-juillet-2021.pdf

Rousseau, C., Savard, C., Bonnel, A., Horne, R., Machouf, A., & Rivest, M.-H. (2021). Clinical intervention to address violent radicalization: The Quebec model. In K. Bhui & D. Bhugra (Eds.), *Terrorism, violent radicalization and mental health* (pp. 153–168). Oxford University Press.

Schwartz, F. (2020, April 20). Coronavirus sparks rise in anti-Semitic sentiment, researchers say. *The Wall Street Journal.*

Sherwood, H. (2021, February 7). *Hundreds get Covid vaccine at East London mosque's pop-up clinic.* The Guardian. https://www.theguardian.com/society/2021/feb/07/hundreds-covid-vaccine-east-london-mosque-pop-up-clinic

Statistics Canada. (2011a). *Immigration and ethnocultural diversity in Canada.* (Catalogue no. 99-010-X2011001). https://www12.statcan.gc.ca/nhs-enm/2011/as-sa/99-010-x/99-010-x2011001-eng.cfm#a2

Statistics Canada (2011b). Data table: Religion (108), immigrant status and period of immigration (11), age groups (10) and sex (3) for the population in private households of Canada, Provinces, Territories, Census Metropolitan Areas and Census Agglomerations. *2011 National Household Survey.* (Catalogue no: 99-010-X2011032). https://www12.statcan.gc.ca/nhs-enm/2011/

Trinh, J. (2021, April 16). Vaccine remains out of reach for many in COVID-19 'hot spot'. *CBC.* https://www.cbc.ca/news/canada/ottawa/barrier-vaccine-access-ottawa-hot-spot-k1t-emerald-woods-1.5986853

Wilkinson, A., Parker, M., Martineau, F., & Leach, M. (2017). Engaging 'communities': Anthropological insights from the West African Ebola epidemic. *Philosophical Transactions of the Royal Society of London B: Biological Sciences, 372*(1721). doi: 10.1098/rstb.2016.0305

Wood, P. K., & Gilbert, L. (2005). Multiculturalism in Canada: Accidental discourse, alternative vision, urban practice. *International Journal of Urban and Regional Research, 29*(3), 679–691.

Zine, J. (2012). *Islam in the Hinterlands: Muslim cultural politics in Canada.* UBC Press.

15

FROM MEDIA AND PSEUDO-SCHOLARLY ISLAMOPHOBIA IN POST 9/11 MORAL PANIC TO 'META-SOLIDARITY'[1]

ABDELWAHED MEKKI-BERRADA & LEEN D'HAENENS

> To go fast you have to walk alone,
> to go far you have to walk with the Others.
> (African proverb. *Pour aller vite il faut marcher seul,*
> *pour aller loin il faut marcher avec les Autres.*)

For the political philosopher Giorgio Agamben (2003, 2014), the 'securitisation' of immigration is conceived of as a process by which social issues are transformed into security-based issues. This process of immigration securitisation involves identifying threats (real or imagined) and debating exceptional measures to address them. The migrant is conceived of here as a threat to national security (terrorism, crime), economic security (unemployment) and cultural security (a threat to identity, the fear of no longer existing as a culture or a nation). Following (or along with) Blacks, the Chinese and the Jews, it is now the Muslims' turn as *a generic representation of the foreigner* to be elevated to the status of an existential threat. There of course exist certain groups who employ a nearly unimaginable form of threatening violence while claiming to be Islamic. But via which epistemological, cognitive and discursive processes did we arrive at the conclusion that, given these fringe violent groups, about 1.9 billion Muslims supposedly represent an equal existential threat? Faced with an anomising present and an uncertain collective future, is this perhaps the result of collective anxiety?

Collective Anxiety and Anxiogenic Otherness

Anthropologist and philosopher René Girard wrote in 2005: 'The more troubled a community, the more it tends to unload its anguish onto scapegoats' (2005, p. 166, our translation). Dating as far back as 1972, in his renowned book 'Violence and the sacred' (*La violence et le sacré*) Girard revived within the social sciences the notion of the 'scapegoat', providing it with a renewed social and political impetus. The scapegoat then is the sacrificial victim banished to the sidelines, or even to death, to atone for social ills (Geisser, 2003), to channel destructive violence outside oneself and to help restore intrapsychic, social and cosmogonic order; such are the primary anthropological rationales for sacrifice (Mekki-Berrada, 2019).

In the same vein, Sigmund Freud wrote that human beings carry within them a 'life drive' and a 'destructive drive' (referred in his earlier works as a 'death drive'). If not directed at an object outside oneself, this destructiveness would necessarily turn against oneself (Freud, 1920/1981). In the present day, the external object is represented by the anxiety-provoking otherness *par excellence*, the one associated with Islam, with Muslims in general, and with Muslim women in particular. As specified by anthropologist Gilles Bibeau, this 'cultural anxiety' renders individuals receptive to conspiracy theories such as the 'Great Replacement' theory. This exaggerated, unjustified fear is prized by the far right and other European and Canadian supremacists, who view immigration in general and Muslim immigration specifically as phagocytic and occurring with the complicity of Western progressive scholars and politicians. In his ethnohistorical work (2017), Bibeau also points to the Andalusian and Christian origins of this anxiety-inducing Western myth, capable of provoking both moral panics and a besieged mentality. The conspiracy theory construes the Muslim Other into a generalised existential threat. To alleviate this collective anxiety, Bibeau calls for developing a 'plural form of universalism … which links diverse cultures in a universal that is common to us all … [a] mixed universalism … which we must promote … amid the diversity of identities [and which relates to] the presence of that certain something that links us all as human beings' (Bibeau, 2017, p. 189, our translation).

The cultural anxiety, highlighted by Bibeau, is in dynamic interaction with the discursive and political construction of threatening Muslim otherness. In the case of this synergistic process, it is a question of protecting oneself collectively from the threatening and anxiety-provoking Other by transforming them into both a scapegoat and a sacrificial victim. It is a matter of excluding this Other and, at best, stigmatising and discriminating against them. At worst, it encompasses physically eliminating the Other, as young, extreme right-wing adults did in

Québec City in 2017, in Christchurch in 2019 and in London, Ontario, in 2021, much as violent extremists aligning themselves with a violent radical reading of Islam themselves know how to do. One, much like the other, derives from destructive and exclusivist rationales seeking atonement for the collective anxieties and social sufferings experienced by the respective groups to which they identify: Islamist radicalisation and Islamophobic radicalisation share the same structure and rationale, albeit the respective enemy to 'purify or destroy' (Semelin 2005) is different. The anxiety-provoking otherness par excellence is, however, today globally associated with Islam and Muslims. This anxious relationship to the Muslim Other explains, at least in part, the essentialisation and stigmatisation of Islam (Baubérot, 2012, 2014), as much as it does so for Islamophobic behaviour, as well as for the aversion to Muslims (Geisser, 2003).

Radical Islamism, specifically the violent radical Islamism that tends to view as Islamophobic those who dare to criticise it, seems to contribute to this collective anxiety, which in turn results in an aversion to Islam and Muslims. One may, however, wonder whether or not, to explain the Islamist origins of Islamophobia in this form of a simple unidirectional cause-and-effect relationship would seem to neglect both Islamophobia's historical depth, as well as its complexity and multi-dimensionality, and thus to reduce Islamophobic radicalisation to simply the consequence of radical Islamism.[2] Such reductionism contributes to invisibilising, underestimating and trivialising Islamophobic radicalisation (Iner, 2019, p. 80), as well as to forgetting that Islamophobia also represents a form of extremism (Pratt, 2019).[3] Neo-orientalist Gilles Kepel goes even further, regarding Islamophobia as an extremist Islamist strategy to the extent that: '[The notion of] Islamophobia plays an essential role, given its objective is to victimise a population, and thereby bind it, based on this victimisation, to a community the Islamist movement seeks to control' (2017, n.p., our translation). Muslims are thus reduced, by neo-orientalists such as Kepel, to passive and manipulable beings indulging in victimisation, while the notion of Islamophobia is in turn reduced to a dominating and liberticidal invention in the hands of radical Islamists. This conspiratorial hypothesis, dear to neo-orientalists, paints progressive researchers critical of it as 'Islamo-leftists' (*islamo-gauchistes*) that is to say 'charlatans' in the service of Salafist ultraconservatism. This new charlatans' 'deception' consists of using Islamophobia as a smokescreen to conceal their project of destroying the Republic and invading Europe, 'the soft belly of the West'. Islamophobia, continues the neo-orientalist, is a 'royal ignorance that paralyses minds while playing into ISIS's hands' (Kepel, 2016a, n.p., our translation).[4]

In situations where Muslim communities are minoritised, the notion of Islamophobia is thereby often reduced to representing a 'utilitarian' conceptual simplism, which in turn renders it into a 'sham' (*imposture*, Kepel, 2016b), a form of 'ideological intoxication' (d'Iribarne, 2019, our translation), a 'weapon of mass intimidation' (Bruckner, 2017, our translation), or 'one of those words without bearing that thoroughly misleads' (Gauchet, 2017, n.p., our translation). To these influential academics and essayists, favoured by the media, the notion of Islamophobia supposedly prohibits any criticism of Islam, its founding texts for Muslims. While as previously noted the notion of Islamophobia is at times employed by Islamist extremists to silence any criticism of Islam and Muslims, such a liberticidal use of the Islamophobia notion is contrary to the freedom of expression upon which democracy is founded. While certain radical-literalist Muslims are fond of this fallacious utilisation of the Islamophobia notion, should the notion be reduced to this marginal and perverse usage? To reject the notion of Islamophobia by viewing it as an intoxication, an intimidation, an imposture and a misguidance, is this not revealing of intellectual laziness? Is this not a symptom of denying Islamophobia's social reality, in the same way that widespread denial of misogyny and racism exists in the far-right ideologies? Is this not a subtle invitation, under a pseudo-scholarly guise, to cease examining the discriminating *social reality* to which the Islamophobia *notion* refers, and thereby an invitation to limit freedom of expression and investigation to instead advance neo-orientalist discourses of truth (*discours de verité*) that favour uncritical ready-made modes of thinking? Is this not too simple an answer to the complex issue and reality of Islamophobic radicalisation? This multi-voiced book has sought to explore certain facets of this complexity.

The Complexity and Semantic Undecidability of a Notion

Islamophobia remains a controversial notion, with its inherent complexity generating both issues and tensions. The 'Islamophobia' term is itself very new, only appearing for the first time in a French-language dictionary (Le Robert) in the year 2000 (*Islamophobie*; Hajjat & Mohamed, 2016), and even more recently, in 2017, being adopted by the Office québécois de la langue française (2017). Islamophobia, which reflects 'that mixture of fear and hostility [which] has persisted to the present day, both among scholars and the general public' (Saïd, 2003, p. 371, our translation), is therefore a recent notion. It first appears in the French language at the turn of the 20th century in French colonial ethnology, then reappears in the 1980s in response to European fears regarding the Khomeini revolution, before being integrated during the 1990s into the English language via the Runnymede Trust Report

(1997), and then propelled into institutions and the media following the September 11 tragedy (Asal, 2014; Sayyid, 2014). A basic, widely employed definition is the one proposed by the Runnymede Trust (2017) for which Islamophobia represents 'hatred and hostility towards Islam and Muslims' (Kalin, 2011, p. 8). This translates in the experience of public life into forms of discrimination and exclusion that limit the most basic human rights, as well as political, economic, social and cultural freedoms (Runnymede, 2017, p. 12). A basic definition, important, but limited and requiring further exploration and refinement because, as a social reality, Islamophobia is a highly complex and multi-dimensional issue:

> In practice, understanding Islamophobia requires a wide, multidiscipli-
> nary approach. Islamophobia consists of political, cultural and economic
> dimensions and without integration of all these dimensions one cannot
> understand the phenomenon of Islamophobia, whether it is a reality or a
> figment of the imagination, whether it exists to what extent, and whether
> it is visible or invisible. (Ameli & Merali, 2019, p. 46)

The semantic undecidability of the 'Islamophobia' word, its continually in suspense (*sens continuellement en suspens,* Ricoeur, 1969) and 'incomplete' meaning (*signification incomplète,* Derrida, 1972, p. 250), as well as the controversy surrounding the notion can be explained in several ways, including:

1) Islamophobia is perceived as necessarily being a liberticidal notion intended to prohibit any criticism of Islam and Muslims (although this liberticidal tendency exists, it is the sole preserve of a radicalised minority claiming to be Muslim) (Mekki-Berrada, 2018, 2019; Sayyid, 2014).

2) With the 'phobia' suffix, Islamophobia assumes the form of a clinical term, which references a conflict that is intrapsychic in nature (and yet Islamophobia is a notion that seeks to identify and consider a given social reality, as well as socio-political conflicts (Lean, 2019; Mekki-Berrada, 2018, 2019; van der Noll & Dekker, 2016)).

3) The Islamophobia notion is supposedly insignificant because it fails to reference any socio-political reality (thus denying the Islamophobic reality in the same way as the existence of certain forms of racism or misogyny is denied – Césari, 2011; Sayyid, 2014).

4) It is much harder to adequately define (theorise) the notion than to identify (describe) its manifestations in terms of the empirical and sociopolitical reality to which it makes reference (e.g., exclusion, discrimination, micro-aggressions, violence, stigmatisation) (Bullock, 2017; Carr, 2016; Césari, 2011; Kaya, 2015a, 2015b; Sayyid, 2014, 2018).

With regard to the 'phobia' suffix, which references a form of psychopathology as defined by the DSM-V (American Psychiatric Association, 2013), Islamo-phobia is associated with an irrational fear, with Islam here representing the phobogenic object. While phobias may indeed represent a clinical category, phobias per se are presently quite treatable via psychotherapeutic techniques (primarily cognitive-behavioral therapy), sometimes in combination with anxiolytics (American Psychiatric Association, 2013). Thus, were it a simple phobia in the clinical sense of the term, psychology, psychoanalysis and psychiatry would already have been able to address Islamophobia! Certainly, there is a certain fear associated with Islam. It is perhaps a legitimate fear given that many terrorist attacks are committed in the name of Islam by a small minority of Muslim extremists. However, Islamophobia is neither a fear nor an irrational attitude: it has a rational foundation that enables it in part by virtue of its anchorage in the contemporary West's deeply rooted neo-orientalism. In this neo-orientalist model, Islam and Muslims are viewed, as highlighted by the political scientist Vincent Geisser (2003), as 'a threat to democratic values' and 'an enemy of modernity', with Muslims representing archetypes of this anti-modernity. What's more, Muslims are viewed, consciously or not, as anti-subjects. Per the Franco-Martinican psychiatrist and anthropologist Franz Fanon (1952, 1957/2001), who is at the origin of a new paradigm that contributed to the emergence of ethnopsychiatry and transcultural psychiatry, Muslims, like Blacks and other racialised groups, are situated in a 'zone of non-being' (*zone de non-être*). To consider Islam to be a 'zone of non-being' and Muslims to be non-subjects and, via essentialisation, as inevitable enemies of modernity and democracy, this point of view, biased many times over, does not in itself perhaps represent a physical form of violence. It is nonetheless a devastating cognitive and psychological form of violence, which can easily lead to physical and terrorising violence, as demonstrated by the Islamophobic killings in Christchurch, Québec, London and Oslo, among other expressions of Islamophobic violent radicalisation that have led to the mass killings of Muslims simply because they were Muslims. Such a process that creates a moral panic and leads from cognitive and psychological violence to mass violence has been clearly demonstrated by the historian Jacques Semelin in his seminal work entitled *Purifier et détruire* [To purify and destroy] (2005).

The Moral Panic of Media and Pseudo-Scholarly Islamophobia

Beyond the notion's semantic immaturity, Islamophobia is also often viewed in the social sciences as a 'moral panic' (Abu-Lughod, 2013; Sakellariou 2019; Cohen, 2002) – specifically, one that tends to be aroused in the West by the spectre of the Muslim-existential threat (Sayyid, 2014). There are also essayists and social science 'experts' whose works are 'a direct symptom of the existence, in academic circles, of a "scholarly Islamophobia," which distills hostile language under the guise of science' (Bibeau, 2017, p. 41; Saïd, 2003, p. 371, our translation). This scholarly, or rather pseudo-scholarly, Islamophobia (*islamophobie pseudo-savante*, Mekki-Berrada, 2019) is sustained by experts still deeply imbued with a primitive 18th- and 19th-century form of orientalism (Saïd, 2003), which is in the present day conveyed in the media as well as in European, North American and Asian extreme right-wing spaces (Saïd, 2003; Sayyid, 2018).

Islam has always been subject to aversion, from the polytheistic tribe of the Quraysh, in which the prophet Muhammad was born in about 570 AD, to Crusaders from the 12th century onwards, with their papal ambition to reunify a Europe scattered across a plethora of kingdoms. These Crusaders mobilised thousands more under an Islamophobic and genocidal credo (Hentsch, 1988), a strategy still employed in the present day, consisting of unifying the political interior by contriving a common external enemy (e.g., Muslims, refugees). It is, however, especially with the *Reconquista*, particularly under the repressive guidance of the very catholic Ferdinand of Aragon and Isabella of Castile in the 15th century, that the Islamophobic radicalisation went as far as forced apostasy in the form of the obliged departure and killing of thousands of Muslims and Jews whose crime consisted of displaying their religiosity. Scholarly orientalism, which first appeared at about this time, would take off in earnest three centuries later with Napoleon's Expedition to Egypt (1798–1801), serving as a pseudoscientific and ideological prelude to the legitimation of European colonialism (Kumar, 2012; Saïd, 2003). These are two strong historical and political moments (the *Reconquista* and the Egyptian Campaign) that are deeply embedded in the present-day Western cognitive space. Orientalist thought, inspired by these two key moments in Western history, shaped the West's most enduring anti-Islamic and anti-Muslim prejudices. While, on the one hand, the Orient is imaginary (*Orient imaginaire*, Hentsch 1988), a creation of the West and a vast mental realm that characterises everything that is not Western (Saïd, 2003) and, on the other hand, Orientalism has as its primary mission to 'study' the Orient, scholarly Islamophobia (*islamophobie savante*, Mekki-Berrada, 2019) is a version of Orientalism incapable of considering Islam without contempt or denigration. This version is equally resistant to any deep anthropological understanding of Islam's internal logic and *system of meaning* (Geertz, 1968/1992), or of the *discursive tradition* (Asad, 2009) and the *technology of the self* (Foucault, 1984, 2001), which form the basic as well as complex structure of Islam's epistemology (Mekki-Berrada, 2019).

The White European (not a whiteness of skin, but rather one associated
with a domination-based relationship), heir to the Enlightenment, employs
Islamophobia as an ideological and organising principle to both lead the
Muslim world out of the obscurantism that supposedly characterises it, as well
as better assert its global power in the face of an equally global Muslim otherness that is to be subjugated (Bazian, 2019). Neo-Orientalism's Islamophobic
declination today serves as a form of racialised governmentality whose goal
is to better discipline and assimilate Muslims, while rendering them into
subjugated subjects (Easat-Daas, 2019; Sayyid, 2010). Among 19th-century
Orientalism's leading figures of authority, the scholar Ernest Renan asserted
in his inaugural speech to the prestigious Collège de France, on 21 February
1862, that:

> Islam represents the most comprehensive negation of Europe [of the West].
> Islam represents the disdain of science, the suppression of civil society, the
> dreadful simplicity of the Semitic mind, as well as the narrowing of the
> human brain, closing it to all delicate ideas, to all refined feelings, to all
> rational research. (Renan, 1862, p. 28, our translation)

What has become of Ibn Sina (Avicenna), Ibn Rushd (Averroes), Al Farabi,
Al Razi (Rhazes), Al Kindi, Al Idrissi, Ibn Khaldun, yet well known to Renan,
to mention only a few of the ancient Muslim scholars, and the plethora of
other physicians, physicists, chemists, astronomers, geographers, historians,
mathematicians, philosophers and artists who helped revolutionise universal
science and thought? In a similar vein to Renan's ideological forgetfulness,
the Islamologist, neo-orientalist and media star Gilles Kepel, perceives
Islamophobia as a 'foreclosure' (*forclusion*), a 'decoy' (*leurre*, 2016b), much
as it is for Michel Houellebecq, for whom:

> Islam emerged in the midst of a desert, among scorpions, camels and
> ferocious animals of all kinds. Do you know how I refer to Muslims? The
> wretched of the Sahara. It's the only title they deserve ... Islam could only
> be born in a stupid desert, among filthy Bedouins who had nothing else
> to do – forgive me – but fuck [*enculer*] their camels. (Houellebecq, 2001,
> p. 260, our translation)

Per Houellebecq, a novelist of undeniable literary talent, 'Donald Trump is one
of the best American presidents I've ever seen' (2019, p. 53). He refers here to
a president who sought to impose an exclusive identity card on Muslims, who
banned the entry of citizens from several Muslim countries into the United

States, who imprisoned children in forced migration situations (Jordan, 2019), who spent billions of dollars building an anti-immigration wall while discursively and politically portraying the Other as a threat to the Nation, who refused to condemn white supremacism despite its many fatal public manifestations (in Portland and Charlottesville in 2017, Pittsburgh in 2018, San Diego, El Paso, and Dayton in 2019, to name only some of the most recent supremacist and neo-Nazi killings) and who demonised democratically elected US females of Muslim and immigrant minority backgrounds. In his novel 'Submission', (*Soumission*, published in 2015), while radically rejecting the notion and the sociopolitical reality of Islamophobia, Houellebecq the fervent admirer of Donald Trump conceives of, or rather reduces Muslims to a horde of bearded men in heat raping Western teenage virgins following their forcible conversion to Islam. Elsewhere, in the course of a tense discussion with the Council of Europe (2015, n.p.), who denounced the 'trivialisation of Islamophobia', as well as 'the increase in racist, anti-Semitic and Islamophobic violence' and for whom 'Islamophobia is a violation of human rights and a threat to social cohesion', the essayist and polemist Pascal Bruckner (2017) perceived Islamophobia as being a form of 'imaginary racism' (*racisme imaginaire*) and 'a weapon of mass intimidation to silence criticisms of Islam'. The polemist added: 'Islamophobia is an invention to prohibit debate', as well as a 'creation worthy of totalitarian propaganda'. Thus, Islamophobia is reduced by these widely read authors to an ideological and liberticidal tool meant to prohibit any criticism of Islam, which, as we saw earlier in this chapter, as well as in the introduction to this volume (Mekki-Berrada & d'Haenens, chapter 1), represents a fallacious argument based on ideological opinions and very poor empirically grounded data.

Evidence-based Responses

Based on empirical data from both ethnographic fieldworks and media analyses, in Europe and Canada, this collective publication is the result of an inter-disciplinary, inter-sectoral and transnational collaboration, for which we have used two different dimensions of a single theme to examine, on the one hand, the dynamic interactions, or lack of interactions, between two forms of radicalisation (either violent or that leads to violence), namely Islamist radicalisation and Islamophobic radicalisation. On the other hand, we have also examined the interactions between academic or scholarly Islamophobia and Islamophobia as portrayed in the media. Does the scholarly Islamophobia inform, either consciously or subconsciously, the Islamophobia that is conveyed by the media?

This collective project brought together several academic disciplines, namely anthropology of religion, anthropology of mental health, transcultural psychiatry and psychology and media studies. On an inter-sectoral level, leaders in mental health, experts in media studies, social intervention, as well as activists and academics collaborated. Authors from Belgium, France, the Netherlands, Poland, Portugal, Québec, Newfoundland and Labrador and Spain provide the transnational voice of this project, reflecting many vantage points. With the conclusion of this polyphonic journey, we must note that in Canada and some European countries the interactions between Islamist radicalisation and Islamophobic radicalisation tend to be seen as binary. However, this is not necessarily the case in neither all European countries nor in all Canadian Provinces where violent or potentially violent radical movements are part of a plural network of interactions. These countries follow a model of coevolution that is defined by a plurality of actors and factors, all of which are specific to their own given contexts and own different kinds of extremisms existing within them (Toguslu & d'Haenens, Chapter 2).

As for possible interactions between 'intellectual' discourses and what is portrayed in the media, we observe that in Belgium, for example, debates about Muslim immigration and Islamophobia among intellectuals translate into a language accessible to all by way of the media. A similar phenomenon can be observed in Québec's French-language dailies, where essayists, mostly non-academics, are abundantly quoted and praised by columnists who present themselves as self-appointed saviours and publish refractory commentaries, ranging from banning Muslim immigration to calling on Muslim citizens to cut all ties with their ancestors, memories, traditions and convictions in order to be a *good* Muslim. It is as if the creolisation and inter-breeding of values and cultures were inherently a defect and served as an obstacle to a better living-together. Some of these essayists and columnists even go as far as to condemn French citizens, born in France, who name their sons Mohamed or their daughters Khadija in an attempt to preserve secularism. This secularism is here considered falsified (*laïcité falsifiée*, Baubérot, 2014), namely in France where the ideological affinities of these essayists and columnists are also those of a far-right presidential candidate in the 2022 French elections, himself essayist and columnist.

When it comes to the propagation of Islamophobic radicalisation, it is not just the general population that is influenced by the media. As we saw with the example of France, political decisions are not impervious to media influence, however indirect and subtle it may be (Areâs & Mekki-Berrada, Chapter 7). Incessant, intense, degrading and stigmatising media coverage of the wearing of the veil has contributed to the prohibition of its wearing in schools in particular and in public spaces in general. The media can thus serve as a pathway between visibility, spatiality and the law. Due to this three-pronged contextual reality (media, public space, legislation), Muslim citizens in France in general and Muslim women in particular see their bodies being transformed into ideological and political battlefields, thus contributing to upholding a climate of distrust and aversion towards French citizens solely based on their religious affiliation. This can be seen even more so on the Twitter account of the Spanish far-right party VOX, which lays out, in the most unabashed way possible, its vision of an imminent invasion of Spain by Muslim migrants described as blood-thirsty, bearded men who would pose a major threat to Spanish chastity, Christianity and identity (Coral et al., Chapter 10). It is as if a collective memory was reawakened in the 21st century to simultaneously condemn Muslim Andalusia of the 8th to 15th centuries and praise the genocidal and ethnocidal strength of Ferdinand of Aragon and Isabella of Castille who rid Spain of its Jewish and Muslim citizens in the 15th century. Regarding the potential influence of daily newspapers, which provide an important voice among their readers, as well as the convergence and divergence of the treatment of information by both left- and right-leaning daily newspapers, we must understand that this is not a static phenomenon. On the contrary, analytical nuance is paramount because media coverage of Islam and Islamophobia is so dependent on context, whereas the influence it has on readers and the editorial lines will vary according to whether it is a time of crisis (massive immigration, terrorist attacks) or a time of relative calm (Mertens et al., Chapter 8).

Deciphering the role that the media plays among young people requires looking at another dynamic. Essentially, this deciphering cannot be done without keeping in mind the need for nuance and not undertaking a causal analysis in search of binary results. While in Poland (Górak-Sosnowska & Sozańska, Chapter 3) it is social media that has a direct impact on the Islamophobic beliefs among youth, in Belgium (De Nolf et al., Chapter 11) it is the traditional media that seems to make the most impact while social media is used as a space of trust, providing a source of strength for youth in the face of racism, aversion, discrimination and other adversities. The idea that social media as a safe space is a conclusion that also rings true within the Belgian associative sector (community-based organisations), where young people, outreach workers and municipal representatives can negotiate the re-definition of central concepts (such as the example of radicalisation) that policymakers would gain a lot from if they considered them (Van Leuven & Trappers, Chapter 12). This bottom-up or emic approach is even more constructive with the havoc that the COVID-19 pandemic is creating (Al Majzoub & Rousseau, Chapter 14). With this, the involvement of imams, other Muslim leaders and citizens working in close collaboration with public health services in Canada has made it possible to create new solidarity in times of crisis by developing and implementing culturally sensitive prevention and intervention models, for the benefit of both the Muslim communities and Canadian society as a whole. Also, in two far-flung regions of the world, Germany (Aguilar, Chapter 5) and Canada (Shaikh & Selby, Chapter 13), we see how the media can contribute to upholding the status quo by ignoring Islamophobia, as it relates to conspiracy theories, and colonial violence that resurfaces in narrative strategies that still promote an aversion to indigenous peoples in the Americas and Oceania, to black citizens, and to immigrants who specifically come from Muslim countries. Political discourse is also not immune to this trend in Germany and Canada, even though these two countries symbolise social justice and democracy in the world.

In sum, the role of traditional and social media is much more complex and diverse than we initially thought. Only an inter-disciplinary and cross-sectoral understanding would allow us to better identify and understand this complexity, especially since this complexity is not static and is changing just as rapidly with time as the technologies and the increasing ease with which these medias are used. In the meantime, and to conclude this collective project, let us present, among the numerous recommendations formulated explicitly or implicitly by the various co-authors of this book, ten recommendations that we feel are urgent to consider by Muslim citizens of Canada and Europe, media professionals, community and academic stakeholders, policymakers at the municipal, provincial and federal levels, as well as academics:

1. *Semantics:* To provide a constant and evolving definitional effort during which the central concepts are regularly redefined, following the 'natural' transformation of all concepts and their permeability to the transformation of the local contexts of their emergence and their semantic evolution. This is a considerable challenge that multiple social agents are called to jointly and synergistically take on. Among the central concepts to be submitted to this semantic vigilance, a vigilance that we are all called to have but, above all, the legislative systems, notably that of radicalisation, Islamophobia, hate speech, discrimination, xenophobia and the nexus where the different forms of Islamist and Islamophobic radicalisations intersect and are articulated.

2. *Racism:* To officially consider, at the highest levels of State, Islamophobia as a symptom of a racism deeply anchored in the mentalities and political and media habits, which would allow for efforts to be more pertinently against racism and its Islamophobic component.

3. *Education:* To show an increased and continuous vigilance towards the educational contents that are used to teach young citizens and that maintain a demonisation of Islam and Muslims while continuing to make them into convenient enemies. It is presently urgent, according to the studies presented in this book, that these school programmes focus more on developing critical thinking and raising awareness of human rights, without tainting them with supremacist and Islamophobic ideologies.

4. *Social media:* Young citizens are in fact confronted with Islamophobia from two sources, namely the school curricula and social media, both of which youth value highly. It is, therefore, necessary to consider both of these sources in the prevention of and fight against Islamophobia.

5. *Plural perspectives:* To study, with different experts in the field, the cognitive substrates and the mechanisms of discursive and political construction of Muslims in terms of identity threats (Western and Christian values threatened), economic threats (the migrant as a job thief) and national threats (Muslims as terrorists by definition). These discourses, being tainted by colonial and orientalist preconceptions, will be a question of deconstructing them while simultaneously proposing alternative narratives that are inclusive and open to the plurality of perspectives that make the foundation a just and equitable society.

6. *Safe spaces:* To establish a more effective system for reporting complaints of hate, racism and Islamophobia; systems where citizens' voices are heard professionally and empathetically, in safe spaces and without the risk of stigmatising or berating plaintiffs.

7. *Critical thinking:* To invest in the human, intellectual and financial resources necessary to further develop the critical thinking skills of our decision-makers and the general population, who are both eager to be better informed and able to adopt attitudes and points of view that are based on a more critical and inclusive approach.

8. *Culture-sensitive action:* To welcome the many Muslim voices and perspectives, including religious leaders among those who are immune to Islamist extremism, and involve them in prevention and intervention programmes that fight against hate speech and hateful actions in general, and Islamophobia in particular.

9. *Best practices:* To identify and promote, through an unambiguous political will, the best practices that have already proven to be successful, to strengthen them and use them as a foundation for the creation of new interdisciplinary and intersectoral practices that are culturally sensitive and adapted to the groups that they are intended for.

10. *Academic responsibility:* Finally, to invite academic researchers and community workers to focus not only on social tensions and polarisations, but also on the emergence of new social solidarities between Muslim and non-Muslim citizens in times of crisis. This essentially allows them the ability to work on what separates us as much as what unites us. Although not perfect, let us note the example of the solidarity in Canada and New Zealand when Quebec City, in 2017, and Christchurch, in 2019, both experienced Islamophobic terrorist attacks against three mosques that led to the death of 57 people, several dozen injuries and the creation of hundreds of orphans who are still trying to learn how to live in the aftermath.

And it is with this word, as young as it is new, and whose content and definition will keep evolving, that we will end this collective project: *meta-solidarity*. Namely, a solidarity that, in the face of the unspeakable and unthinkable mass violence perpetrated against those whose only crime is being Muslim, a solidarity, therefore, called to transcend gender differences, differences related to where someone comes from, skin colour, religious affiliation from agnostic and atheist to devout, as well as to ideological and political differences. A solidarity that stands up against the pull of a violent modernity that offers so few examples or models necessary to uphold a collective maintenance of a certain psychological, social and political stability. A stability that depends upon the co-construction of safe societies, however utopian they may be, in the image of the safe spaces that youth seem to be much more able to create and inhabit than their elders. It seems as if we have not yet learned the importance of listening to the knowledge of our youth, without whom we will not be able to co-construct a world where inclusion would be a reality and no longer a mere academic and political fantasy.

In the hours following the Québec City, Christchurch and London (Ontario) killings in 2017, 2019 and 2021 respectively, tens of thousands of individuals, Muslim and non-Muslim, took to the streets of numerous Canadian and New Zealand cities to demonstrate their rejection of such violent Islamophobic radicalisation. Two ongoing research projects (2018–2023) in Belgium, Canada, France and Portugal are in the process of shedding new light on how these new social ties and forms of solidarity reflect transnational resistance strategies against violent radicalisation in general, and Islamophobic radicalisation in particular. Confronted with an Islamophobia that is growing as a symptom of broader societal malaise in the West, a resistance against it is also arising. It is now a question of better understanding this *meta-solidarity*'s and resistance's foundations and mechanisms.[5]

Notes

1.   The research for this chapter stems from a project mainly funded by the Social Sciences and Humanities Research Council (SSHRC): *Scholarly and mediatic Islamophobia: A transnational study of discourses and their impact* (Original French title: *Islamophobie savante et médiatique: Étude transnationale des discours et de leur impact*; SSHRC 2019-2023, #890-2018-0016).

2.   At best, Islamist and Islamophobic violent radicalisations tend to be 'co-reactive', in the sense that they cross-pollinate, one reacting to the contempt and alterophobia distilled by the other ('reactive co-radicalisation', Pratt 2019, p. 47; 'the reactionary extremism that is Islamophobia', Pratt, 2019, p. 37).

3.   Iner (2019) further reminds us that Islamophobic crimes committed by US far-right extremists are approximately double the number of attacks committed by Islamist radicals from 2008 to 2016 in the US.

4.   Might Islamophobia be an 'invention' of radical Islamism, given that the former considerably predates the latter? In fact, while Islamophobia dates to at least the 15th century of the very Catholic European kings and queens (Bibeau, 2017), and even to the Crusades, Islamism traces its origins to a radical backlash against both the European colonialism of the 19th and 20th centuries that fragmented Muslim cultural and geographical spaces, as well as local neo-colonial dictatorships that violently muzzled opposition.

5.   The two projects here mentioned are led by Mekki-Berrada, co-directed by several authors of this book, and funded by the Social Sciences and Humanities Research Council of Canada (SSHRC). The first project is entitled *An ethnographic study of the dynamic interactions between Islamophobia, emotional distress and problem-solving strategies in Quebec City* (Original French title: *Étude ethnographique des interactions dynamiques entre islamophobie, détresse émotionnelle et stratégies de résolution de problèmes à Québec*; SSHRC-2018-2022, #435-2018-1164), and the second is entitled *Scholarly and mediatic Islamophobia: A transnational study of discourses and their impact* (Original French title: *Islamophobie savante et médiatique: Étude transnationale des discours et de leur impact*; SSHRC 2019-2023, #890-2018-0016).

References

Abu-Lughod, L. (2013). *Do Muslim women need saving?* Harvard University Press.

Agamben, G. (2003). *État d'exception, Homo sacer* [State of exception, Homo sacer]. Éditions du Seuil.

Agamben, G. (2014, January). Une citoyenneté réduite à des données biométriques: Comment l'obsession sécuritaire fait muter la démocratie [Citizenship reduced to biometric data: How the security obsession is mutating democracy]. *Le Monde diplomatique*, 22–23.

Ameli, S.R., & Merali, A. (2019). A multidimensional model of understanding Islamophobia: A comparative practical analysis of the US, Canada, UK and France. In I. Zempi & I. Awan (Eds.), *The Routledge international handbook of Islamophobia* (pp. 42–58). Routledge.

American Psychiatric Association. (2013). *Diagnostic and statistical manual of mental disorders (DSM–5)*. APA.

Asad, T. (2009). The idea of an anthropology of Islam. *Qui Parle, 17*(2), 1–30. http://www.jstor.org/stable/20685738

Asal, H. (2014). Islamophobie: la fabrique d'un nouveau concept [No face, no social contract]. *Sociologie, 1*(51), 13–29.

Baubérot, J. (2012). *Islam et laïcité* [Islam and secularism]. YouTube. https://www.youtube.com/watch?v=9N_ehXIyYYk&feature=youtu.be

Baubérot, J. (2014). *La laïcité falsifiée* [Secularism falsified]. La Découverte.

Bazian, H. (2019). Islamophobia, Trump's racism and 2020 elections! *Islamophobia Studies Journal, 5*(1), 8–10.

Bibeau, G. (2017). *Andalucía, l'histoire à rebours* [Andalucía, history in reverse]. Mémoire d'encrier.

Bruckner, P. (2017). *Un racisme imaginaire. Islamophobie et culpabilité* [Imaginary racism. Islamophobia and guilt]. Grasset.

Bullock, K. (2017). *In brief: Policy backgrounder: Defining Islamophobia for a Canadian context.* Tessellate Institute.

Carr, J. (2016). *Experiences of Islamophobia: Living with racism in the neoliberal era.* Routledge.

Césari, J. (2011). Islamophobia in the West: A comparison between Europe and the United States. In J. Espositov & I. Kalin (Eds.), *Islamophobia: The challenge of pluralism in the 21st century* (pp. 21–43). Oxford University Press.

Cohen, S. (2002). *Folk devil and moral panics: The creation of the Mods and Rockers* (3rd ed.). Routledge.

Council of Europe. (2015). *Compilations of Council of Europe Standards Relating to the Principles of Freedom of Thought, Conscience and Religion and Links to Other Human Rights.* Adopted by the Steering Committee for Human Rights (CDDH) on 19 June 2015.

Derrida, J. (1972). *La dissémination* [Dissemination]. Du Seuil.

Easat-Daas A. (2019). The gendered dimension of Islamophobia in Belgium. In I. Zempi & I. Awan (Eds.), *The Routledge international handbook of Islamophobia* (pp. 123–135). Routledge.

Fanon, F. (1952). *Peau noire. Masques blancs* [Black skin. White masks]. Éditions du Seuil.

Fanon, F. (2001). *L'An V de la révolution algérienne* [Year V of the Algerian revolution]. La Découverte. (Original work published 1957)

Foucault, M. (1984). *Histoire de la sexualité III. Le souci de soi* [History of sexuality III. Care of the self]. Gallimard.

Foucault, M. (2001). *L'herméneutique du sujet. Cours au Collège de France, 1981-1982* [The hermeneutics of the subject. Course at the Collège de France, 1981–1982]. EHESS, Gallimard, Seuil.

Freud, S. (1981). *Essais de psychanalyse* [Essays in psychoanalysis]. Payot. (Original work published 1920)

Gauchet, M. (2017). *L'islamophobie ça n'existe pas* [Islamophobia doesn't exist]. Hors-Séries/Aux Sources. YouTube. https://www.youtube.com/watch?v=M4274RTVmmc

Geertz, C. (1992). *Observer l'Islam. Changements religieux au Maroc et en Indonésie* [Observing Islam. Religious changes in Morocco and Indonesia]. Éditions de la Découverte. (Original work published 1968)

Geisser, V. (2003). *La Nouvelle islamophobie* [The new Islamophobia]. La Découverte.

Girard, R. (1972). *La violence et le sacré* [Violence and the sacred]. Grasset.

Girard, R. (2005). La pierre rejetée par les bâtisseurs [The stone rejected by the builders]. *Théologiques, 132*, 165–179.

Hajjat, A., & Mohamed, M. (2016). *Islamophobie. Comment les élites françaises fabriquent le « problème musulman »* [Islamophobia. How the French elites manufacture the 'Muslim problem']. La Découverte.

Hentsch, T. (1988). *L'Orient imaginaire. La vision politique occidentale de l'Est méditerranéen* [The imaginary East. The Western political vision of the Eastern Mediterranean]. Les Éditions de Minuit.

Houellebecq, M. (2001). *Plateforme* [Platform]. Flammarion.

Houellebecq, M. (2015). *Soumission* [Submission]. Flammarion.

Houellebecq, M. (2019, January). Donald Trump is a good president. One foreigner's perspective. *Harper's Magazine*, 51–53.

Iner, D. (2019). Introduction: Relationships between Islamophobia and radicalization. In J. Esposito & D. Iner (Eds.), *Islamophobia and radicalization* (pp. 1–11). Palgrave Macmillan.

d'Iribarne, P. (2019). *Islamophobie: intoxication idéologique* [Islamophobia: Ideological intoxication]. Albin Michel.

Jordan, M. (2019, August 20). The Flores agreement protected migrant children for decades. New regulations aim to end It. *The New York Times*.

Kalin, I. (2011). Islamophobia and the limits of multiculturalism. In J. Esposito & I. Kalin (Eds.), *Islamophobia: The challenge of pluralism in the 21st century* (pp. 3-20). Oxford University Press.

Kaya, A. (2015a). Islamophobia. In J. Césari (Ed.), *The Oxford handbook of European Islam* (pp. 746–769). Oxford University Press.

Kaya, A. (2015b). Islamophobia in Western Europe: A comparative, multilevel study. *Journal of Muslim Minority Affairs, 35*(3), 450–465.

Kepel, G. (2016a, March 14). « Radicalisations » et « islamophobie »: le roi est nu. [Radicalisations and Islamophobia: The king is naked]. *Libération*.

Kepel, G. (2016b). *La fracture* [The divide]. Gallimard.

Kepel, G. (2017). *Le concept d'islamophobie joue un rôle essentiel dans le djihad. Chroniques des événements courants* [The concept of Islamophobia plays a key role in jihad. Chronicles of current events]. http://est-et-ouest.fr/chronique/2017/170109.html

Kumar, D. (2012). *Islamophobia and the politics of empire: The cultural logic of empire*. Haymarket Books

Mekki-Berrada, A. (2018). Femmes et subjectivations musulmanes: Prolégomènes [Women and Muslim subjectivations: Preliminaries]. *Anthropologie et sociétés, 42*(1), 9–33.

Mekki-Berrada, A. (2019). Prolégomènes à une réhabilitation de la notion d'islamophobie [Prolegomena to a rehabilitation of the notion of Islamophobia]. *Religiologiques, 39*, 5–49.

Office québécois de la langue française (2017). *Islamophobie* [Islamophobia]. http://www.grand-dictionnaire.com/ficheOqlf.aspx?Id_Fiche=8354162

Pratt, G. D. (2019). Reacting to Islam: Islamophobia as a form of extremism. In J. Esposito & D. Iner (Eds.), *Islamophobia and Radicalization* (pp. 35–53). Palgrave Macmillan.

Renan, E. (1862). *De la part des peuples sémitiques dans l'Histoire de la civilisation*. Discours d'ouverture au Collège de France [On the part of the Semitic peoples in the history of civilisation. Opening speech at the Collège de France]. Michel Lévy Frères.

Ricœur, P. (1969). *Le conflit des interprétations. Essais d'herméneutique.* [The conflict of interpretations. Essays in hermeneutics]. Éditions du Seuil.

Runnymede Trust. (1997). *Islamophobia: A challenge for us all. The Runnymede Trust: Commission on British Muslims and Islamophobia*. London School of Economics.

Runnymede Trust. (2017). *A 20th Anniversary Report: Islamophobia, still a challenge for us all*. London School of Economics.

Saïd, E. W. (2003). *L'orientalisme. L'orient créé par l'Occident*. [Orientalism: Western conceptions of the Orient]. Seuil.

Sakellariou A. (2019). «Islamophobia in Greece: The 'Muslim threat' and the panic about Islam» In I. Zempi I. & I. Awan (Eds.), *The Routledge international handbook of Islamophobia* (pp. 198–212). Routledge.

Sayyid, S. (2010). *Thinking through Islamophobia: Global perspectives*. Hurst.

Sayyid, S. (2014). A measure of Islamophobia. *Islamophobia Studies Journal, 2*(1), 10–25.

Sayyid, S. (2018). Topographies of hate: Islamophobia in cyberia. *Journal of Cyberspace Studies,* *2*(1), 55–73.

Semelin J. (2005). *Purifier et détruire. Usages politiques des massacres et violences* [Purify and destroy. Political uses of massacres and violence]. Éditions du Seuil.

van der Noll, J., & Dekker, H. (2016). Islamophobia and anti-Semitism: Etiological similarities and differences among Dutch youth. *Islamophobia Studies Journal, 3,* 56–70.

NOTES ON CONTRIBUTORS

Abdelwahed Mekki-Berrada is a full professor in Anthropology of Mental Health and Anthropology of Islam in the Department of Anthropology at Laval University in Québec City, Canada. His main research and teaching interests revolve around the dynamic interactions between culture, politics, mental health, forced migration and Islamophobia. He also explores Sufi systems of meaning, knowledge and action as 'self-technology' contributing to the complex emergence of an acting and inclusive spiritual subject. His ethnographic encounters take place in India, Morocco, Belgium, France, Portugal and Canada.
Email: amb@ant.ulaval.ca

Alexander Van Leuven is a PhD fellow in Media Anthropology at the Institute for Media Studies of the Faculty of Social Sciences at KU Leuven. He is also associated with the Hannah Arendt Institute, Mechelen, Belgium. His research focuses on the topic of institutional alienation, mostly of urban youth, and uses methods of ethnography, sociolinguistics and participatory valorisation.
Email: alexander.vanleuven@kuleuven.be

Alfonso Corral (PhD in Communication, San Jorge University, Zaragoza, Spain) is a lecturer at the Institute of Humanism and Society, San Jorge University. He holds a BA in Journalism, and an MSc in Marketing and Corporate Communication (San Jorge University). His broader research interests lie in the field of communication studies and the Arab-Islamic world, especially media Islamophobia and framing of Islam and Muslims. In addition, he explores media and political discourses on migration and minorities, focusing on newspapers, new media and social networks. He performs his research studies and projects at Migrations, Interculturality and Human Development (MIDH), San Jorge University. In 2019, he did a two-month research stay at the Institute for Media Studies, KU Leuven, Belgium.
Email: acorral@usj.es

Alfredo Brant worked as a freelance photographer after graduating in Journalism (Federal University of Minas Gerais (UFMG), Brazil), and obtaining a master's degree in Photography and Contemporary Art (University of Paris 8). He developed authorial projects in the field of documentary photography. In his PhD project in Cultural Studies at the Catholic University of Portugal, he aims to expand the concept of visual literacy as a discipline of social engagement through the development of the notion of "documentary poiesis". Within the field of Visual Studies, his research at the Catholic University of Portugal focuses on the production, circulation and perception of contemporary photography and its effects on culture.
Email: alfredobrant@gmail.com

Ana Flora Machado is a PhD student in Cultural Studies at the Catholic University of Portugal, where she also obtained her BA in Social Communication. After obtaining a MSc Degree in Marketing Management from Aston University in Birmingham, she worked for two years as a marketing and organisational communication assistant at Unilever and Energias de Portugal (EDP) Portugal. Her research focuses on social media and discourses of gender identity through visual culture.
Email: Anafbravo@gmail.com

Anabelle Vanier-Clément is coordinator of the CoVivre programme, supporting and collaborating with communities with regards to vaccination against COVID-19 and vaccine hesitancy. CoVivre is an emergency independent programme that aims to protect, inform and support marginalised communities during the pandemic. Anabelle holds a double master's degree in International Relations from Sciences Po in Paris (the Paris Institute of Political Studies) and the London School of Economics, as well as training in mediation from the Canadian Institute for Conflict Resolution, and she has professional experiences in journalism, human rights and coordination of intervention programmes in multi-cultural contexts.
Email: sherpa.dlm@ssss.gouv.qc.ca

Ann Trappers holds a PhD in Social and Cultural Anthropology (KU Leuven). In her current role of programme coordinator at Foyer vzw, she is responsible for the planning of and reporting on activities, and she has done research into current migration and integration phenomena.
Email: ann.trappers@foyer.be

Ans De Nolf holds an MSc in Communication Science. She has done research on young Flemish Muslims' experiences and coping mechanisms related to Islamophobia, as well as on causes and solutions. She is currently a PhD candidate at the Institute of Media Studies (KU Leuven, Belgium), where she continues to expand this research.
Email: ans.denolf@kuleuven.be

Antonio Prieto-Andrés is a teacher and researcher at the Faculty of Communication and Social Sciences at San Jorge University of Zaragoza (Spain). As a Doctor in Communication and a graduate in Law, his teaching focuses on Human Rights, Communication Law, Video Game Legislation, and Communication Deontology, especially journalism. He is a member of the Migrations, Interculturality and Human Development research group, his role in which relates to the legal and social aspects of immigration, and, particularly, its treatment in the press.
Email: aprieto@usj.es

Ashley S. Montgomery is a doctoral student at Concordia University in Montréal, Canada. Her research explores secondary and tertiary preventative frameworks of radical ideologies within education institutions, the evaluation of youth prevention programmes and pedagogical strategies for resilience in at-risk youth.
Email: Ashley.montgomery@concordia.ca

Camila Arêas is a lecturer in Information and Communication Sciences at the University of Reunion Island. She is affiliated with the Research Laboratory on Creole and Francophone Spaces (LCF-UR) and associated with the Research Centre for Communication and Culture of the Catholic University in Portugal (CECC-UCP). Her research is in the field of communication, journalism and semiotics, specifically media and religion.
Email: camila.cabral-areas@univ-reunion.fr

Cayetano Fernández holds a PhD in History and is a senior lecturer at San Jorge University (Zaragoza, Spain). He teaches History of Political European Thought and Sociology at the Faculty of Communication and Social Science and is the academic coordinator of the Institute of Humanism and Society. He has previously worked at Hassan II University (Rabat, Morocco), Cadi Ayyad University (Marrakech, Morocco) and the University of Sussex (UK), conducting projects and research focused on the analysis of migration processes, especially the configuration of social representations of migration

in the media, and their effects in social and political areas. Since 2017, he is the principal researcher at Migrations, Interculturality and Human Development, a research group funded by the Government of Aragon (Spain).
Email: cfernandez@usj.es

Cecile Rousseau is a professor at McGill University (Montréal, Canada) where she co-directs the Division of Social and Cultural Psychiatry. She holds a Canada Research Chair in the prevention of violent radicalisation. Since 9/11, as inter-community tensions were on the rise, Dr Rousseau began addressing social polarisation and violent radicalisation. As a practitioner, she has been both searching for ways to address the distress produced by violence and the despair that leads to it, and developing, through community programmes and advocacy coalitions, collective means to mitigate these expressions of social suffering.
Email: cecile.rousseau@mcgill.ca

Colin Robineau is a researcher associated with the Carism laboratory at the Paris-Panthéon-Assas University (Paris 2), teaching Social Sciences at the University of Reunion Island (Université de la Réunion). He is the author of *Devenir révolutionnaire. Sociologie de l'engagement autonome* (2022, Éditions La Découverte). At the crossroads of sociology, information and communication sciences, and political science, his research focuses on public spaces, socialisation processes, politicisation dynamics and militant commitment.
Email: colin.robineau@laposte.net

David De Coninck (PhD, Social Sciences, University of Leuven, Belgium) is a postdoctoral researcher at the Centre for Sociological Research – Faculty of Social Sciences, KU Leuven, Belgium. His current areas of research include multi-methodical approaches on media and migration attitudes (e.g., media consumption as a source for attitude formation on immigrants or refugees), threat perspectives, fear dynamics and policy analysis. He also investigates subjective well-being and family attitudes among Flemish youngsters.
Email: David.deconinck@kuleuven.be

Erkan Toguslu is a research fellow at the Institute for Media Studies at KU Leuven, Belgium. His research focuses on transnational Muslim networks in Europe, and the nexus of religion and radicalisation. He is co-editor of *Journal of Populism Studies*.
Email: erkan.toguslu@kuleuven.be

Helena Cruz Ventura graduated in Sociology at the University Institute of Lisbon (Instituto Universitário de Lisboa) (IUL), and in Communication Sciences/Journalism at the Catholic University of Portugal. She has worked as a media and communication manager and as a research assistant at the Research Centre for Communication and Culture of the Catholic University of Portugal. She recently coordinated two research projects in the field of media and religion, in partnership with the Fundación Blanquerna and financed by Porticus Iberia.
Email: Helena.Cruz.Ventura@gmail.com

Jennifer A. Selby is an associate professor of Religious Studies at Memorial University of Newfoundland and Labrador (MUNL) and is a white settler aiming for allyship. Among other qualitative research on Muslim life, she conducted a study in 2012–2013 on the everyday negotiation of Muslim life in St John's and Montréal. Significantly, despite contextual differences in culture and the presence of minoritised communities, the Islamophobic narratives heard in St John's did not differ in scope or significance from those gathered in Montréal.
Email: jsebly@mun.ca

Jihène Hichri is a PhD student in Education at Université du Québec à Montréal, Canada. Her research focuses on adult education and training, the design and evaluation of training and the transfer of learning. Her research also revolves around the perception of 'The Other', social exclusion, hate speech and the prevention of violent radicalisation.
Email: hichri.jihene@courrier.uqam.ca

Joanna Sozańska is a PhD Candidate at the SGH Warsaw School of Economics, Advisor and West Asia-North Africa (WANA) Expert at the Institute for Security and International Development under the auspices of the DEEP NATO programme. She has completed Erasmus+ scholarships in the Kingdom of Morocco and the Republic of Turkey and she is laureate of the second edition of the Top Minds Programme of the Polish-American Fulbright Commission. She has been a jury member of Innovation in Politics Awards since 2018 and a member of Women in Think Tanks Global Network. Her research interests focus on political systems and migration processes in the North African region, the role of non-governmental organisations (NGOs) in shaping migration policies, Arab feminism, human rights and diplomacy.
Email: js104087@doktorant.sgh.waw.pl

Katarzyna Górak-Sosnowska earned her PhD in Economics at the SGH Warsaw School of Economics, and her habilitation in Religious Studies at the Jagiellonian University in Kraków, Poland. She is an associate professor at the Middle East and Central Asia Unit at SGH Warsaw School of Economics. Her research interests focus on contemporary Middle Eastern and Muslim minorities in Europe. She published five monographs, including *Deconstructing Islamophobia in Poland* (2014), and edited a book on *Muslims in Poland and Eastern Europe* (2011). She is currently leading the research project Managing Spoiled Identity: the case of Polish female converts to Islam, funded by the Polish National Science Centre. She is also the head of the Association Forum Dziekanatów (Student Services Employees Association).
Email: kgorak@sgh.waw.pl

Leen d'Haenens is a full professor in Communication Science at the Institute for Media Studies of the Faculty of Social Sciences at KU Leuven. Her research interests touch upon young people and (social) media use, with a focus on vulnerable youth. She combines quantitative and qualitative methods, multi-site comparisons and, in recent years, 'small data' and 'big data' methods. She is co-editor of *Communications: The European Journal of Communication Research*, and associate editor of the *International Communication Gazette*. She is a member of the Euromedia Research Group.
Email: leen.dhaenens@kuleuven.be

Luis Manuel Hernández Aguilar is a Research Associate at the European University Viadrina Frankfurt Oder and a Guest Researcher at the University of Amsterdam. He holds a PhD in Sociology by the Goethe-University Frankfurt am Main. Among his publications: Hernández Aguilar, L. M. (2018) *Governing Muslims and Islam in contemporary Germany: Race, time, and the German Islam conference* (Brill); Hernández Aguilar, L. M. (2020) The interior frontiers of Germany: On recursive history and ritual male circumcision, *Journal of Muslims in Europe, 10*(1), 22–44; Bracke, S., & Hernández Aguilar, L. M. 2020) 'They love death as we love life': The 'Muslim Question' and the biopolitics of replacement, *British Journal of Sociology, 71*(4), 680–701.
Email: HernandezAguilar@europa-uni.de

Rawda Harb is a doctoral student at Concordia University in Montréal, Canada working on supporting at-risk youth in Montréal's adult education centres. She is the founder of Communité, an educator at the Lester B. Pearson School Board and researcher at Project SOMEONE.
Email: rawda.harb@concordia.ca

Salam El-Majzoub is a psychiatry resident at the McGill University Health Centre (MUHC). She obtained her medical degree at Université de Montréal in 2016. She has an interest in Social and Cultural Psychiatry and co-directed the 5th Canadian Muslim Mental Health Conference 2021. She led numerous advocacy workshops in the Muslim community of Montréal on mental health. Email: salam.el-majzoub@mail.mcgill.ca

Sobia Shaheen Shaikh is a professor at Memorial University of Newfoundland and Labrador (MUNL). Her scholarship focuses on supporting anti-racist and transformative justice community praxes. She self-identifies as Muslim and has a long history of anti-racist feminist activism and scholarship. Email: sshaikh@mun.ca

Stefan Mertens (PhD, Catholic University of Brussels) is a postdoctoral researcher at the Institute for Media Studies – Faculty of Social Sciences, KU Leuven, Belgium. He is also a partner for the Dutch-speaking part of Belgium in the international Worlds of Journalism Project (www.worldsofjournalism. org). His research interests include quantitative and qualitative content analysis, media and diversity, media policy analysis, survey research, research on cultural values and journalism cultures and audience reception studies. Email: stefan.mertens@kuleuven.be

Vivek Venkatesh, PhD, is UNESCO co-Chair in Prevention of Radicalisation and Violent Extremism and Professor of Inclusive Practices in Visual Arts in the Department of Art Education at the Faculty of Fine Arts at Concordia University, Montréal. He is director and co-founder of Project SOMEONE (Social Media Education Every Day), and an accomplished filmmaker, musician, research-creator and applied learning scientist. Email: vivek.venkatesh@concordia.be